# Calls Beyond Our Hearing

Also by Holly Menino

*Darwin's Fox & My Coyote*

*Forward Motion:*
*Horses, Humans, and the Competitive Enterprise*

*Pandora: A Raccoon's Journey*

# Calls Beyond Our Hearing

*Unlocking the Secrets of Animal Voices*

HOLLY MENINO

St. Martin's Press
New York

CALLS BEYOND OUR HEARING. Copyright © 2012 by Holly Menino. All rights reserved. Printed in the United States of America. For information, address St. Martin's Press, 175 Fifth Avenue, New York, N.Y. 10010.

www.stmartins.com

Design by Kathryn Parise

LIBRARY OF CONGRESS CATALOGING-IN-PUBLICATION DATA

Menino, H. M.
Calls beyond our hearing : unlocking the secrets of animal voices / Holly Menino. – 1st ed.
    p. cm.
ISBN 978-0-312-58757-4 (hardcover)
ISBN 978-1-4299-4236-2 (e-book)  1.  Animal sounds.  2.  Animal communication.  I.  Title.
QL765.M46 2012
591.59'4–dc23

2011045694

First Edition: April 2012

10  9  8  7  6  5  4  3  2  1

*For John and his song.*
*I still listen.*

# CONTENTS

# Calls Beyond Our Hearing

# I

# Sheila Jordan and the Mockingbird

⁓

This book begins with a concert and, three years later, a horseback-riding accident. The concert was a vivid experience of a woman's singing, and it impressed on me what a powerful and pliant tool the voice is. The riding accident left me with a grade 3 concussion and an uncomfortable awareness of how fragile perception is.

First, the concert. In the summer of 2002 I am sitting in the audience for a concert that caps off the Jazz in July workshops at the University of Massachusetts in Amherst. Outside the hall, the afternoon is hot and sunny. Inside, where the tall windows are open to catch what breeze there is, the stage is black. Black curtains, black piano, a drummer lurking over a black trap kit, and the man playing bass tipping back into the darkness with the long stem of his instrument. All of us in the audience are here to listen, and we are focused on this darkness when Sheila Jordan takes her place on the stage. She has been teaching at the university all week, and the morning found her in the audience, listening intently to students as she scribbled notes. Now it is her turn. She finds the mic and takes a tall stool near the bass player.

Jordan has attained a high perch in the jazz world and, now approaching eighty, seems entirely matter-of-fact about the task at hand. "I'd like to dedicate this song," she says quite innocently, "to President George Bush." With the mic in her hand, she marks off a bar's worth of tempo for the three other musicians. The song is a standard, one that is interpreted by everyone, and she begins it the way it is often begun, slow and sexy or, at least, sensual:

> *I'd like to get you on a slow boat to China,*
> *All to myself . . .*
> *Alone.*

There is something sinister in the way she isolates the last word and pressures the note with a tiny fluctuation of pitch. The note and the words it carries could have been tender, but they are somehow savage. Whatever she has in mind for the president isn't pleasant.

The slow boat to China is taking the president someplace dangerous. We can well imagine the tortures George W. Bush is enduring in Sheila Jordan's arms. Nervous titters run through the audience, and I am beginning to feel sorry for the president. But I am also laughing as openly as the people sitting around me. Her voice has such power that just a tiny wiggle in it can override language and stand meaning on its head. Her target is the president, but it could just as well be someone or something else. Inflection, the twisting of pitch and stress, is something we use to make a point or highlight a phrase in a joke on our way to the punch line. But song is a conspiracy of language and music, and not many of us have the vocal skills to bring inflection to song. Sheila has the chops to inflect melody and words at the same time and to elevate the result to art.

She pauses to let the piano player get in, and the keys speak so quietly that a sound from outdoors can be heard clearly. It is the backup beep of some kind of construction vehicle. The beep is loud, insistent. It cuts through the drums and bass, but the musicians ignore it. A big construction project has been going on in the center of campus, and I thought the digging was a half mile away in another group of campus buildings. But the backup beep sounds right outside the window, and for the musicians, there is no way to deal with the interference except to play through.

Jordan comes back in on the chorus, scat singing. No words, just syllables and notes. Leaving language behind, she responds to the piano, warbling in and out of the scale, sliding through half pitches, flying up through the octaves, then swooping down silently to snatch up the notes of the bass. Mimicking the songs of the other instruments, she repeats their phrases without actually replicating them, and she sneaks off with their rhythms and punches them up to make wilder, rougher phrases of her own. At some mysterious psychological and emotional level, her scatting says more about what might happen to George W. Bush than she had been able to imply with her dangerous melodic skewing of the lyric. Her song calls up violence, a bumbling victim, slow murder. It is a remarkable demonstration of the physical and expressive capabilities of the human voice.

The beep, the irritating beep, continues.

After the concert, we pause on the steps leading down from the hall, and the beep is still sounding, regular and mechanical. But I can't see any construction or any equipment. My first impression was correct. The excavation is going on in the midst of a neighboring cluster of buildings. The beep, however, is coming from a tree at the side entrance to the hall. I look up into the branches, and after a few moments, the beeper reveals itself with a flap of gaudy white wing bars. A mocking-bird. The bird is still for a moment, and I can hear a fainter beeping from the excavation site. The feathered master mimic is responding en-thusiastically to a backhoe. The call coming from the leafy inner spaces of the tree is not perfect in its imitation of the call of the backhoe, but it is convincing. The bird is good, as good at what he does with his voice as Sheila Jordan is with hers.

His is another forceful voice. The mockingbird is pouring all his energy into his singing, but his song doesn't affect me the way Jor-dan's did. I don't understand it the way I understood hers. In fact, I don't understand it at all. Of course not. I am not—none of us humans are—the right audience for a mockingbird. The bird has his own audi-ence in mind, other mockingbirds and other animals that inhabit his world, and you and I don't communicate in that world.

Sheila's song stays with me the way music can, returning to your mind in snippets, sometimes obsessively in the middle of the night when you wish it would go away and let you sleep. But I don't think much about her song until after the accident.

I have kept and ridden horses all my life. I like to be around them even when I'm not riding, like to take care of them, to watch them so-cialize and play in the pasture, touch muzzles and take in breath from each other. I enjoy trying to read them and also to read my dogs, trying to figure out what is going on in their heads. The day of the accident there is not enough going on in my own head. I am not thinking clearly, because only forty-eight hours earlier I was undergoing minor surgery. Maybe I'm hungover from the anesthesia. Whatever the cause, I don't feel right but manage to convince myself I am back to normal. I go to the pasture and bring the horse up to the barn. Stupidity is a major cause of accidents.

I have had the mare for several years. I was one of the first people on her back. I have brought her along through the basics and am beginning to work on more advanced moves. I know she has some life and a tendency to spook. As I say, stupidity creates accidents. When she spins, the legs I usually have on her are gone. Zero. I don't make any effort to stay with her, and I'm on the ground. If anywhere in your childhood reading you have learned that a horse will do anything to avoid stepping on a human, throw that bit of knowledge out the window. A horse is an animal of flight, and you do not want to be in the flight path. I am trampled and spun out from under the mare by her heels. Examining table, X-ray, MRI. Rest.

My ears and eyes don't seem to be working in synch. My perception and balance are out of phase. I am walking around on the funhouse floor, and I worry about my hearing. While the dizziness lingers a kind of reverse paranoia sets in: I am not hearing voices, and I am suspicious of silence. I become intensely aware of sounds that never reach me intact. There are plenty of these—fragments of conversations lost to din, the vocal undercurrents that precede a dog's growl, the louder breathing of a horse about to nicker, the slight grace notes that introduce a bird's call. I have always enjoyed sound and the way notes or words pass in and out of my awareness. But there hasn't been much of this awareness since my head banged down in the dirt.

Maybe I've stopped tuning in, maybe I'm no longer listening well. In college I was a music student, so I am aware I have a number of different modes and degrees of hearing, levels of intensity in paying attention. The same is true of the ways I attend to language. When someone speaks to me, sometimes what I hear is a stream of sound from which I extract information—opinions, gossip, instruction—other times what I hear are the qualities of the voice delivering the words. It's much the same with written language. Sometimes when I read or write I hear the words resounding in my head as if someone had actually spoken them. But sometimes when I read, the words are just icons on the page, waiting to deliver a fact or two. Now all the varieties of my awareness of sound have somehow moved into the background, as if the recording engineer has dialed down the knobs, and sound doesn't seem to register completely.

For months I walk through my routines in a woozy bubble and worry about the possibility of now-dimmer sound decaying into silence. It is during this period that I revisit the experience of Sheila Jordan and the mockingbird, and I begin to read about and reflect on their two voices.

Bird voice. Human voice. What's the difference? And why should this matter to you?

Your voice is the most powerful social tool that comes into the world with you. You use it to negotiate every transaction, from the simplest *I Want* to the most complicated *How Can I Possibly Explain This?* I have found that in even the meanest bouts of insomnia the best antidote is the sound of another person's voice, and I think it's probable that crisis center hotlines are a result of the same phenomenon. The voices of other people have great emotional power, and if you think about the most moving events and the most intimate moments in your life, you probably recall in these experiences the voices of certain people. The voices of our own kind accompany our births, our deaths, and all the growing and learning, the attachments and separations, the fights and reunions and successes and losses that stretch between our first and our last. The same is true for the mockingbird and for other animals.

A central fact about the vocal communication of any species is that voice stands in for touch, for physical contact. AT&T used to urge us all to "reach out and touch someone." And in fact, it is comforting to say, "I love you," to someone at the other end of the line when you can't physically hold that person. The substitution of voice for touch works just as well when aggression comes into play. It's so much easier and safer to say, "I ought to punch you out!" than to actually risk taking a poke at the offender. We say, "Keep in touch," when we really mean "Keep telling me things," and that's why slamming down the phone causes such unsettling emotions to the people on both ends of the line. That is why it is so difficult to be mute or deaf.

In reading during my dizzy uncertain period, I discover that this is also the way things work in the animals' worlds. But the contexts, the places they live and their perceptual environments, are quite different. Since the 1930s scientists have been eavesdropping on quite a number of animals to find out how, exactly, animals use their voices to negotiate their lives. Right now the scientific literature is flush with new findings and new theories about animal voices, and one assumption behind all this science is that the more you know about the mockingbird's song and its sources, the better you will understand Sheila Jordan's song and your own. So the real question about bird voice and human voice is not, What's the difference? but, What's the same?

On one level it isn't hard to pick out what Sheila has in common with the mockingbird. The mockingbird has a vast repertoire and an impressive range. Just like Sheila Jordan. It is also a fabulous mimic and shares this talent with Sheila, whose mimicry is most obvious when she scats, when she sings without words. She is copying, within her own vocal range, the tones and pitches and colors of "Slow Boat to China" and the sounds of the bass and the piano. When she reaches beyond the notes prescribed by the melody and the rhythm, she adds something very like the bubbly passages the mockingbird uses to connect the phrases it dutifully replicates. What she and the mockingbird share is mimicry, repetition of sounds in phrases, and rhythm, the spacing over time of sounds and the silences between them. These are fundamental elements of both birdsong and music, as a good deal of trite poetry points out. These are what you expect when you listen to music.

Audience expectation drives music and speech, and in fact, it is what empowers any use of the human voice. We sit down to listen to Sheila Jordan with a certain set of expectations about how her voice will fit with the melody, the rhythm, the lyric. Sometimes the musical passages that move us most strongly are the ones that thwart our expectations. We have other expectations when we speak with someone. There are rules of conversation like Keep Still While the Other Person Speaks and The Question Comes Before the Answer. Do animals have rules of expectation about repetition, patterns, and mimicry? And if they do, what does that imply about the biological and cognitive sources of our vocalizing and our expectations? Are these innate impulses or do we learn them?

Looking into these questions, I discover that animals as simple as insects communicate by audio. They have auditory organs, and insects such as crickets and cicadas have percussion sections, parts and pieces they can clap and scrape together. But what it takes for an animal to produce what we think of as "voice" is a backbone. What it takes to sing and to be part of an audience is real spine. Only vertebrates have a voice box add-on to their respiratory tracts—a larynx in mammals or, in the case of birds, a syrinx—that allows them to call and to sing. They all have some version of our eardrum and neural transmission. For the time being, let's just say we're using the same basic tools as other animals with backbones. When Sheila Jordan sings, her voice is created when the air she breathes out meets and pushes through her larynx, causing her constricted vocal cords—she has caused this construction because she intends to sing—to vibrate. The vibrations of her vocal cords emerge as sound. With some modifications adapted for the animal's habitats, this is essentially the way all mammals and birds produce vocal sound. Air from the respiratory system is pushed out through the folds of membrane we call the vocal cords, a resonating organ. In the case of a lion, this organ is the larynx, in the case of a red-winged blackbird, a syrinx, and in the case of a dolphin, a vomer and nasal air sac. The bat has a heavily muscled larynx that can squeeze tightly enough to produce ultrasound. The blackbird has dual membranes, one in the airway from each lung, and this doubling of pipes accounts for some of the fluidity and complexity of its song. A dolphin's blowhole substitutes for a pair of nostrils. It closes involuntarily, and the dolphin controls the flow of air from the nasal air sac by voluntarily opening the blowhole. The muscle that controls the opening of the blowhole allows a broad range of air pressures and variety of sounds, and it is thought that the dolphin uses the mound of fatty tissue on its forehead, called a melon, to bounce the sound of its voice in different directions.

We and the rest of the vertebrates have some common devices for collecting and transmitting sound to our brains. The essentials of this system are a tympanic membrane—a "drum"—and its reverberations transmit the sound vibrations through a tubular channel to sensory appendages, hair or papillae, where sound vibrations meet nerves that translate them into electrical signals that travel through the nervous system to the auditory brain. Quite often, as in the human and the bat, there is the fleshy structure on the outside of the head, a horn for gathering in sound. This is what we usually think of as the "ear." But this external ear is not necessarily standard equipment. In the frog it is absent, and the tympanic membrane is exposed on the side of the head. In dolphins and whales, fat tissues in their jawbones transmit sound to the inner ear. We're more adept at some aspects of hearing and vocalizing than animals, and they are more adept at others—in fact, some of their abilities are extreme.

Take, for instance, the bat, a member of our own family, the mammals, and so not that far removed from us. In an early investigation of what abilities separate the animals from us, the Italian abbé Lazaro Spallanzani came upon a mystery that would go unsolved for 140 years. Spallanzani served as a professor at the universities of Reggio, Modena, and Pavia, and he was an enthusiastic collector of natural phenomena. In 1793 while harboring an owl and a bat in his rooms, he began a series of nighttime experiments to determine how nocturnal animals make their way in the dark. First he released the owl in his darkened room and was surprised to find that the owl collided with objects in the room. Next he released a bat, which navigated handily among the books and candlesticks. Thinking that perhaps the bat had extremely acute night vision, Spallanzani then covered the heads of a number of bats with hoods. Some lost their ability to navigate in the dark, others did not, and this prompted Spallanzani to launch a round of experiments in which he covered different portions of the bats' heads.

At last, seeking to rule out the bats' use of their eyes for navigation, the abbé blinded the animals by rather gruesome means and waited for them to recover. After encouraging one of these subjects to fly again, he reported, "During such flight we observe furthermore that before arriving at the opposite wall, the bat turns and flies back dexterously avoiding such obstacles as walls, a pole set up across his path, the ceiling, the people in the room, and whatever other bodies may have been placed about in an effort to embarrass him."

Throughout his experiments, Spallanzani kept up an assiduous correspondence about his bat observations, and he urged colleagues at institutions throughout Italy and France to try to capture bats living near them and repeat his experiments. A French surgeon, Charles Jurine, heard Spallanzani's first letter read aloud at the Geneva Natural History Society and, taking up the challenge, repeated Spallanzani's experiments. Reporting immediately to the abbé, Jurine added an important observation: if the ears of the bat were plugged, it crashed helplessly into objects in its path.

Spallanzani was skeptical about the proposition that "the organ of hearing appears to supply that of sight in the discovery of bodies." "How, if God love me," he asked, "can we explain or even conceive in this hypothesis of hearing?" Nevertheless, he pursued its proof with some ingenious devices, including copper tubes that when installed in the bats' ears could be opened and closed, and he came reluctantly to the conclusion that "the ear of the bat serves more efficiently for seeing, or at least for measuring distance, than do its eyes. . . . Can it then be said that . . . their ears rather than their eyes serve to direct them in flight? I say only that deaf bats fly badly and hurt themselves against obstacles in the dark and in the light, that blinded bats avoid obstacles in either light or dark."

What became known as "Spallanzani's bat problem" resisted solution until 1938. In the meantime, scientific understanding of the physics of sound advanced enough to provide hints about how bats navigated, and after the sinking of the *Titanic* in 1912 Sir Hiram Maxim, inventor of a machine gun, began an effort to develop a shipboard warning system that would prevent nighttime collisions at sea. Recognizing the possibility that animals might perceive sounds that lay outside the limits of human hearing, Maxim's imagination settled on bat flight, and he proposed that bats navigated using low-frequency sound inaudible to humans. Because water is a remarkably efficient medium for sound, especially low-frequency sound, he envisioned a shipboard system that emitted low-frequency sound under the water's surface and received its echoes bouncing off solid objects. The returning echoes would cause bells to ring; the stronger the echo and, therefore, the closer the object, the larger the bell that would ring. A few years later an English physiologist named Hartridge suggested that, rather than using low-frequency sound, bats used high frequencies for nighttime navigation.

Finally, in 1938 an undergraduate biology student at Harvard, Donald R. Griffin, took a cage full of bats to the Harvard physics department, where new research on what was called supersonic sound was going on. Here G. W. Pierce had developed a device for generating and detecting sounds above the range of human hearing. Pierce's "sonic detector" could also transpose these high frequencies to frequencies within the human hearing range. Amplifying the transposed sounds from the caged bats, Griffin and Pierce were greeted with a sonic maelstrom, and once they separated the bats' audible chatter from this chaos, they were able to identify short bursts of high-frequency pulses.

Griffin's discovery of the ultrasound produced by bats established as scientific fact something that we have always intuited: that animal perceptual worlds do not necessarily lie within our own. The tree that falls in their forest might not fall in our forest, which might grow in another universe. Griffin would later famously declare that an animal's voice is a window on its mind and go on to propose and elaborate on contentious ideas about animal thinking and consciousness at a time when science in general denied the possibility of thought, consciousness, and intention to animals. While Griffin's progress from voice to thought seems natural, it is important that he started with voice and his account of his bat studies brings home quite clearly that voice is, first and foremost, sound. It is a physical phenomenon, and Griffin, like any other scientist interested in how animals communicate, had to master a highly technical understanding of sound.

After World War II he returned to Harvard as a graduate student to continue his pursuit of the bats' ultrasonic sound pulses, and he found he suddenly had access to what were state-of-the-art tools in that immediate postwar period. He had Professor Pierce's "sonic detector," a long parabolic horn focused on a crystal microphone fitted with vacuum tube amplifiers that caused the ultrasonic sound to be translated to lower frequencies audible to human ears. He had an oscilloscope with a cathode ray tube display, and he had a "very expensive" tape recorder. He used these as he resumed his studies of the bats' ultrasonic pulses and made detailed measurements of their frequencies and the bats' timing of them.[1]

For more than a century, physicists like Griffin's collaborator G. W. Pierce have been developing increasingly sophisticated techniques to visualize and measure the most fundamental physical attributes of sound, and the evolving technologies can help us understand such perceptual effects of sound as timbre, contour, and rhythm, as well as other physical characteristics of sound. Peacetime adaptation of World War II defense technology and the rapid acceleration of technological advance it spawned made animal voices much more accessible to scientists in all fields. But, not surprisingly, ornithologists got the jump on the others.

At Cornell University, the Laboratory of Ornithology began recording birdsong as soon as the technology became available. Until the early 1920s sound was captured for reproduction by mechanically transferring its vibrations into grooves on an impressionable material and then using a stylus over the grooved material to reproduce the vibrations. In 1929, less than a decade before Griffin recognized the ultrasound of bats, Arthur Allen, ornithologist and founder of the Lab of O, was approached by the Fox-Case Movietone Corporation for help using birds to demonstrate the company's new technology, the motion picture with synchronized sound. An electromagnetic microphone converted the sound vibrations into electrical signals that were captured on film, and the vibrations were reproduced by reversing that process. Using the company's equipment, Allen and his colleague Peter Paul Kellogg were able to record the voices of a song sparrow, a house wren, and a rose-breasted grosbeak. The equipment may have been new and for that time fantastically expensive, but it was also big and heavy and yielded a poor product. Even so, Allen and Kellogg were drawn by the potential of electrical sound recording and began to work with the university's electrical engineering department to develop their own equipment. By the early 1930s they were making expeditions across North America to record the voices and behavior of birds, including the soon-to-be-imperiled ivory-billed woodpecker and the California condor.

At that time the best available recording medium was the nitrocellulose film used for motion pictures. But the film was physically unstable, and when Allen, Kellogg, and Albert Brand undertook a military assignment to record birds in Panama during World War II, the corrosive heat and moisture of the tropics prompted them to adopt direct-to-shellac electrical recording. Vinyl was still a few years away.[2]

While the recording medium changed periodically—from shellac to vinyl to tape—the processes of electrical recording remained essentially the same until the introduction of digitization and the CD in 1982. In digital recording, the capture of the sound waves by microphone is still "analog," but the electrical signal from the microphone is stored in a series of binary numbers representing the characteristics of the sound wave. This technological shift has dramatically altered the working lives of scientists who work on animal communication. They can view and manipulate spectrographic images of animal voices on a computer screen, and they can produce digital imitations of these voices for experimental purposes. One interesting extension of digital sound in biological research is the application of digital signal processing to animal voices. This is the same technology that brings you those eerie and irritating automated telephone responses that devour your time as you try to eventually reach the person you intended to call, and a consortium of scientists called the Dr. Dolittle Project is using digital signal processing to automate detailed analysis and classification of animal voices. It can produce such specific analyses that it will allow researchers to identify not only the animal's species but the individual animal. It could become a valuable conservation tool for monitoring wildlife populations.[3]

In case you have arrived here without the essentials of sound—as I did—I am laying these out because sound recording and reproduction are the technological heart of the most essential experiment in vocal communication research: the playback study. This type of experiment was devised to solve a fundamental problem that vexes any investigation of animal behavior: animals can't talk. It has a simple scheme: play a recording of an animal voice to another animal, usually the same kind of animal, and watch what happens. There are more variations of this scheme than there are for "Twinkle, Twinkle, Little Star"—swap the sex of the caller or the listener, change some phrase in the call, alter some perceptual capacity of the listener—and some of them are ingenious work-arounds for this animal-human communications barrier. But the basic design and the need for sound reproduction remain the same. You'll find this is the case with every animal you hear from in this book, except Spallanzani's and Griffin's bats. This is because, as fascinating as the ultrasonic voice of a bat is, it isn't used for what we usually think of as communication; it is used for navigation. Echolocation is a form of self-communication: the caller and the listener are the same animal.

In spite of technological advances and the increased sophistication in the design of experiments that they allow, we are still, in a number of senses, listening in the dark. There are many voices to which we are

physically deaf, like the bat's ultrasound and the infrasound that elephants use to communicate over distances. When it comes to the
voices we can hear, we are in many cases too deafened by the din of our
own impossibly noisy world to be able to attend to them—and of course
we have polluted the sonic universes of other animals with our own
clatter and shriek.

As I begin to look beyond the technical aspects of the sounds of
animal voices, two big questions about the bird and the human singer
emerge: Why sing? and What does the song mean? The answers to
these questions should reveal similarities and differences between the
way we humans use our voices and the ways animals use theirs. Why
did Sheila Jordan want to sing and what did she want to do as she
opened her song? What effects was she aiming for? And what about
the mockingbird? I know that science, because of its current emphasis
on evolutionary fitness, will link the bird's singing to his survival or
the survival of his family. Is Sheila's art connected in even the most
remote way to her survival or ours? Did life-or-death desperation drive
the bird to open his mouth and sing in parody? Just what did the bird
think he was doing with that stupid beep? Did he, in fact, think anything
at all about the sound he produced or did he just receive and send, receive
and send? We don't yet know the purposes of millions of specific vocal
sounds. We don't know whether specific animal vocalizations are innate
or if the animals must learn to make these sounds—and if they learn,
how does their education take place?

⌁⌁⌁

Everything I am reading about animals and their voices declares that
humans are the sole proprietors of language and music, and nearly

everything I read about human vocalizing makes the same claim, often with the slightly defensive proposition that language and music *evolved* only in humans. The authors seem content to accept that assumption as an always-has-been-always-will-be and to look no further into it. I accept the fact that we humans are singletons blessed with singular capacities. But humans did evolve, and we recognize our biological relations to other animals, including the idea that our brains evolved as did the brains of other animals. I have trouble swallowing claims that we are biologically linked through evolution but features of our brains and thought processes came to us full blown by some other means. Apparently Darwin did too. He was interested in the similarities between the ways animals and humans communicated their emotions and expressed frustration with the prevailing attitudes of his time. In *The Expression of the Emotions in Man and Animals*, he declared, "No doubt as long as man and all other animals are viewed as independent creations, an effectual stop is put to our natural desire to investigate as far as possible the causes of Expression."[4]

When we talk about ourselves in relation to all other animals, we often resort to the word *higher*, and from a scientific perspective this refers to Darwin's metaphor for the scheme of evolution, the tree of life. He saw the process as branching upward from the very simplest forms of life into progressively more complex organisms. At the culmination of this process is the human, the conclusion of evolution. In the mid-nineteenth century it took both nerve and humility for Darwin to describe our place in the natural order this way, to place us among the animals. But even though we now have a much richer understanding of evolution, we still rely on Darwin's metaphor, and this assumption blinds us to the completeness of other animals on the branches beneath us, the self-designated tree-topping angels. It prevents us from seeing the elegance with which they solve the problems of survival and from understanding the parallels between the ways in which animals develop and the ways we do. Parallels, as well as direct links, are important not only because they are the way evolution expresses itself but because they are the sources of powerful insight about ourselves. If we can look at ourselves with Darwin's humility and accept human life as animal life, it will be apparent that the more we know about animals, the better we will understand our own lives.

It's a long evolutionary leap from the mockingbird to Sheila Jordan and you and me, and an even longer leap from a less developed vertebrate such as a frog to us. This leap flies over myriad animals that call and sing to find food, arrange for mates, defend themselves—just as my leaps between frogs and deer, and between birds and elephants, skip over hundreds of voices and thousands of sounds. Although many of these sounds are inaudible to us—they are too high or too low for us to hear—we know they occur because they cause changes in behavior. A bat zooms up to snatch an insect, a group of elephants sets out on a long march. The voices we can hear, like those of the mockingbird, the spring peeper frogs, the howl of a wolf, the roar of a lion, and even the sounds of the dog and cat we keep in our living quarters, are for the most part unintelligible to us. But we intuitively understand a central fact about these sounds: voices are social glue. They help animals locate and identify one another. They keep animal societies together in many of the same ways our voices integrate our social life—through flirting, bickering, mating, fighting, and making up.

Animals use their voices to establish their positions in their societies, and although many people don't seem to understand the connections between society and survival, these are vital to the persistence of
many species. For animals that live socially, family and social groups
are not just a happy add-on to the animal's circumstances. They are
part of the biological structure of the species. The more intensely social an animal is, the more complex its use of its voice. To advertise for
a mate, an isolated male túngara frog sings a whining glissando. In
competition with other males, the frog will embellish this vocal sweep
with a rudimentary chuck or two. At the other social extreme, the African elephant lives in a well-ordered matriarchy and uses two highly
developed systems of vocal communication, the familiar trumpeting
audible to humans, which it uses for close-range needs, and infrasound
utterances for long-range contact with other family groups.

Each animal, including humans like you and me, lives in its own
sound universe. It tunes into those sounds that are critical to its existence and essential to the social life that supports its survival. Each
voice, including our own, is perfectly adapted to a particular kind of
place in the world and to a society. Head injury or no head injury, hearing loss or no hearing loss, I would be missing many animal voices. So
would you, because we have a built-in deafness, the limitations of our
perceptual capacity. All of the other animals live with similar limitations, and each animal species occupies a unique world, its environment
as perceived and negotiated by that particular animal. A wild turkey and
a raccoon, for instance, may share the ground floor of the woodlot on my
farm, but they survive because they see the woodlot, smell it, and hear it
quite differently. Animal behaviorists call this package of physical and

sensory surroundings *umwelt,* and sound is a powerful, pervasive force in this sensory mix.

The mockingbird and its obsessive mimicry fit in quite comfortably in backyards and, yes, college campuses, where its voice has established a relatively secure livelihood for this bird. But what about Sheila Jordan? Where do she and her survival fit in? At the end of the evolutionary line? She has syllables. She has words and sentences that refer to things that exist only in our minds, which we call ideas. She has music. What Sheila Jordan has is a far cry, as it were, from what any other animal has. Or is it?

Many animals are often credited rather casually with having "language." But do they really? Are the chirps of a beluga whale mere primitive prototypes of the more complex series of more sophisticated syllables in Sheila's "I'd like to get you on a slow boat to China," or are they something more? A good deal of time and effort continue to be spent to identify what features separate our species from the other animals that have not been endowed with language and music. These are truly fascinating projects, but their goal is different from mine. I am interested in how animals' uses of voice have evolved to meet the challenges of survival and persistence, because any parallels between their vocalizing and ours will deepen our understanding of both. Certainly the speech skills that can be taught to chimpanzees or parrots yield a lot of valuable information about their physical and cognitive capacities, but these aren't skills that the animals call up when they live in the wild. They have been untapped or perhaps are left over from earlier evolutionary iterations. Somewhere in the gap between animals and humans, music and language evolved. I am interested in the traits that lead up to that gap and whether or not some fragments of those traits emerge on the other side of the gap, that is, in humans.

~~ ~~

These thoughts about animal voices are pressing as my bruised brain forces me to reevaluate my ability to hear and understand. I have been trying to dodge a medical appraisal because I don't want to admit to any losses, but eventually an incident in a restaurant calls the question about my hearing. I am at dinner with three friends from the horse world, all a little younger than me. Our table backs up on the bar, where the noises of the television and glassware and the conversations competing with them bounce between a long mirror and the opposite wall. I am saying something earnest about a horse, and my friends begin to laugh at me because they have long since left the topic of horses and are announcing their dinner decisions. I have just blundered into this conversation and spoken nonsense. I cringe, and the next day I make an appointment with a specialist.

The audiologist puts me through an intensive battery of hearing and balance tests. These are exhausting and take the better part of a day, and they don't reveal much. "You have some loss. High end, and it's not too bad now, nothing out of the ordinary for someone your age. But you'll probably lose more." I can expect to hear, but not everything. I can still take pleasure in music and in the rackety traffic of everyday conversation, but these perceptions are likely to fade.

Eventually, in the spring of 2008, after nearly three years of dizziness, I escape the fun house and move away from that woozy building. I have gradually recovered my balance, and I stop reading and put down my books to look outside to the natural world. It is time to go out there, while my hearing is still serviceable, to listen and to look into the questions that have been on my mind—Why sing? What does the song do? And what does the song mean? In order to be able to make sense of animal voices I need to hear them as they actually occur. It's time to get the show—compromised hearing and all—on the road.

It turns out that my timing is good. Not only are there some adventuresome field and lab studies under way, but also the role of evolution in human language and music—which was largely ignored and even explicitly denied until only about ten years ago—has become the subject of lively scientific speculation. Eventually this speculation may lead to some understanding of what actually happened in the gap between animals and humans.

I begin prospecting. The first person I call is Eugene S. Morton, an ornithologist recently retired from the Smithsonian Institution and whose book with Donald H. Owings on animal vocal communication gave me a good grounding.[5] Gene is an old Panama hand, and he has published on all kinds of birds, common and rare, and, just as important, on theories of vocal communication. He is very generous with his ideas and his contacts. As I begin to get in touch with scientists who work on vocal communication, I am aware that their current research, the projects in which they are most keenly interested, are works-in-progress. They may have only begun an investigation or they may be approaching some conclusions. In either case, I will be able to take away only a snapshot of the moment. I'll have to define the most compelling questions and figure things out from there.

Gene sends me to the young behavioral ecologist David Logue, among others. I have a lengthy discussion with David about his research on a bird that lives in the Neotropics, the black-bellied wren, and about what he sees as up-and-coming research trends. Of course, I want to see and hear this wren in real time and learn how David figured out what he knows. But I am aware that birds sing in complicated exchanges in a hard-to-reach realm, and what I want to do first is understand the most basic transactions set off by animal voices. So I tell David I would like to start with a simple, or relatively simple, animal, and he suggests that I contact Mike Ryan, who has been listening to the same frog and its communication system for decades.

When I phone Mike Ryan, I reach him in his lab at the University of Texas in Austin, and as is typical, he is very busy there, or writing something when he's not in the lab. But, as is also typical, he is willing to share his work with me. I go down to Austin to spend two days in Mike's lab. Happily, I am ignorant of his status in the field of animal behavior—he is a honcho, though too modest to make anyone aware of this—because otherwise I would have been uneasy about asking for so much of his time in Austin and I might not have invited myself down to his research site in the Panama Canal Zone. But I do, and two months later, I arrive in the dank hamlet of Gamboa, an outpost of the Smithsonian Tropical Research Institute.

# 2

# Don't the Girls Get Prettier
## at Closing Time?

⌐

On my first night in Gamboa, I ride out on the main road to
Panama City with Mike Ryan and his two summer research assistants, Jenny Saunders and Sasha Ozeroff. This is my second trip to
visit scientific research in Gamboa, and so I am not surprised by the
intense humidity that clings to you all day and persists after dark. Even
the Smithsonian's mini-truck moving through the night doesn't stir
much of a breeze. A couple of miles from Gamboa, Mike pulls the
mini-truck off the road. The rest of us strap on headlamps and follow
him into a thicket of edge-growth forest, down an embankment through
a fine mist of mosquitoes, and into a dark tunnel of leaves and roots.

The four of us emerge in a clearing, where there is a pond. Ocelot
Pond is a flat, glistening piece of water standing in the dark and the heat.
It is less than a foot deep and its total area isn't much larger than the
aboveground swimming pool that adorns many backyards. Sometimes

the pond isn't here. The area is just a low place in the clearing. But it is the wet season in Panama, when there seems little difference between water and the air we breathe. Enough rain has collected to draw a congregation of tropical frogs. They call intermittently, each with a distinctive voice. This is the chorus.

We don't pay any attention to most of the calls because we are listening for one in particular. The insects, especially the mosquitoes, are bad, but we don't have to stand around and wait for long. In fact, we have barely reached the edge of the pond before the call comes across the water more penetrating than the combined sounds of the insect noise and the calls of other frogs. The sound begins with the whine of a futuristic bullet through outer space, like something from a *Star Trek* sound track, and it ends with a light clunk as the bullet hits home. The túngara's name is Panamanian onomatopoeia for its down-sweeping bullet-whine call—you can approximate the call by sounding a tone about an octave higher than the note you want to land on and letting your voice slide in a downhill glissando to the syllable *chuck*. Science has a fairly flat-footed name for the frog, *Physalaemus pustulosus* or, more familiarly, *P. pustulosus*.

It is hard to believe an animal can make a sound so clear and technological, but this is the signature call of the tiny male túngara frog. It is also hard to believe that what this sound is all about is desire and attraction, but I learn from Mike that this is so. The space-age whine-chuck is the sexual solicitation, the advertisement call, of the male túngara. Although the male is only the size of a teaspoon, soft and slippery, and, no matter what your sex, wouldn't hold much appeal, he has irresistible sexual draw for túngara females, which are appreciably larger. The females do not call or respond. Both have brown warty skin.

"They look like toads," I observe. "Why aren't they túngara toads?"

"The Panamanians do call them toads—*sapo túngara*. But in fact, there is no scientific difference between frogs and toads," he says, "except in our own popular thinking about the animals." Apparently, this distinction is one made by people like me, who happen to believe that a frog is a smooth- and slippery-skinned water dweller and a toad has dry warty brown skin and lives on land.

Because it is so mouthy, the tiny túngara frog of Central America is one of the most intensely studied amphibians in the world. The frog's singing and sex life have made it a species of interest for herpetologists, animal behaviorists, and now neurobiologists—and the darling of three generations of scientists who have migrated to Gamboa to work under the auspices of the Smithsonian Tropical Research Institute. Mike is the current patriarch. He has been coming down to Gamboa to listen to the whine-chuck of the túngara for about thirty years. He is a good-humored, sharp-thinking mentor to an ever-rotating bevy of graduate students, and he resembles Charles Darwin. Mike is blockier, more muscular, and the hair around his pate and his beard haven't begun to turn white, but still, he would be believable cast in the role of the grand old man. The resemblance ends with physical attributes. Unlike Charles Darwin, Mike is gregarious, and he has a playful mind and a social network within behavioral ecology as robust as his person.

The path to Gamboa opened up when he was studying the calls of bullfrogs in New Jersey's Great Swamp for his master's degree. He was interested in the differences in their calls, and at that time there was no evidence of sexual selection by females. He began work on a doctoral dissertation, and when his adviser died, Mike moved to Cornell

University and a study of an animal called the red-eyed tree frog. This was the frog that took him to the Smithsonian Tropical Research Institute and its famous biological reserve, Barro Colorado Island.

The red-eyed tree frogs were hardly cooperative subjects. They live up in the canopy of the rain forest and emit rather weak calls. These calls were hard enough to detect even without interference, and on Barro Colorado there was plenty of din. The frog choruses on the ground threatened to drown out the red-eyed tree frog, and the keening whine-chuck of the túngara was a particularly insistent interruption. Since he couldn't lick the túngaras, Mike wondered about joining them. The noted herpetologist Austin Stanley Rand was a senior scientist at STRI in Panama City, and having done some preliminary investigations of the túngara in the 1960s, Stan Rand had the research rights to the species. Mike's question "Would you mind if I looked at the túngaras?" was the beginning of a long, productive collaboration and a close friendship. A few years after Mike had earned his doctorate, he resumed his túngara research with Rand in Gamboa. In the meantime, Mike published "Female Mate Choice in a Neotropical Frog" in *Science* in 1980. His finding that the females determined which matches were made went undisputed because the choreography of the nightly rituals at the pond edge was such clear proof. The males sit still and call. The females listen and then vote with their feet.

Simple enough, and I have come down to Panama because I want to start with the fundamentals of vocalizing, with a simple, short-lived animal and then go on to look at increasingly brainy animals, longer-lived animals, where the questions would undoubtedly be more complex. But when I first contacted Mike with the idea of starting with a simple animal, a simple call, a simple sound, I didn't consider the fact that I was inviting myself into a research agenda with a thirty-year history.

Mike returns to Gamboa for a month every summer to patrol the ponds and puddles and gutters. While some of his students remain in Texas, a few of the others come down to Panama and ensconce themselves for the entire summer. This year the Ryan team consists of Amanda Lea, a graduate student focusing on the male froggies, as she calls them, and managing Mike's lab; Ryan Taylor, a former postdoc under Mike who now teaches at Salisbury State University in Maryland; and the two undergraduates, Jenny from the University of Texas at Austin and Sasha from Simon Fraser University in Canada.

What Mike and his team are focusing on this summer is the brief chuck or series of chucks that round off the call. While the male's whine is blatantly audible, it is just the introduction to the most potent attractant in his call. What comes after it is what really gets the females going, what hits the sonic G-spot, the chuck. They know this. But how do these snippets of sound work?

∾ ⟩⧓

The night we spend at Ocelot Pond repeats itself. Just after dark every night, we drive out by twos and threes to catch frogs for the experiments in Mike's lab. We go to the same places we went before, because our containers are full of frogs we caught the night before and we need to take them home before we look for new subjects. These returnees are relocated in the very same place where they were caught in order to avoid disrupting the genetic makeup of the various populations around Gamboa—remember, this is a community where scientists keep close tabs on just about every aspect of rain-forest life. There are multitudes of túngara populations here and all over Panama—for that matter, multitudes of them from southern Mexico down through northern South America—in shallow ponds, puddles, and gutters. In spite of this abundance, we are hearing only a few sparse volleys of space-age bullets across Ocelot Pond on this particular night.

*Catch frogs* implies a good deal more sport than actually takes place after we arrive at the edge of Ocelot Pond and release the captives of the previous night. We cast our lights around the edge of the pond until the beam of Sasha's headlamp falls on what appears to be a very thick frog, and she reaches down to pick it up. This thick frog is actually two frogs, the smaller male riding on top of a female, his front legs clasping her around her abdomen. She has swum out to him because she is heavy with eggs, and he clings to her waiting for her to release those eggs. We do not pluck up any singletons unattached to a mate because their sex would have to be determined and, in the case of a female, her state of readiness to mate would be unknown. As I consider the coupled túngaras caught in the headlamp beam, it occurs to me that this mating is the only social incident either frog will likely experience. As Ryan Taylor—the Salisbury State University scientist, not to be confused with his mentor Mike Ryan—points out to me, all we know about the túngaras' life—or the lives of most frogs, for that matter—is what we have observed at the mating pond. We don't know what takes place in the leaf litter away from the pond. As far as we know, túngara society is the simplest kind. Each frog lives alone, striving on its own for food and safety until sex pulls a male frog and a female frog into physical contact. This sex-only social arrangement is a kind of primitive proto-society that, like the more complicated societies of mammals and birds, underwrites the animal's survival. Whine-chuck, the frog's voice, is what draws the two together to create this temporary society. The male's two-part call is one-way communication, like a bumper sticker. The female doesn't call back and, in fact, doesn't vocalize at all. She responds by silently taking action, and she follows the calls that she likes to locate the male.

Hunkered down in the shallow water at the edge of the pond, the male uses his trunk muscles to squeeze a pressurized stream of air over his larynx, at the same time filling the two vocal sacs aligned under each side of his jaw. In addition to the penetrating, outer-space zing this produces, the vocal sacs themselves are remarkable as themselves. They inflate until each one is larger than the frog's head and the frog appears to have huge water wings to keep him afloat. If there is any starlight or moonlight in the night sky, they reflect this, ballooning with luminosity. But the inflation of the vocal sacs does not directly cause the sound the túngara makes. The vocal sacs work the same way as the bag on a set of bagpipes. Like the bagpipe bellows under the piper's elbow, they are a reservoir for air that will be pushed out with the next squeeze of the frog's trunk muscles and the next whine.

The sound the male túngara produces with these athletics, like the ultrasonic pulse of one of Griffin's bats or Sheila's voice, is simple physical pressure. At the most elementary level, sound is a series of pressure waves, atmospheric pressure waves. Marine acoustics expert Peter Scheifele, whose work on beluga whales and dolphins I visit later, loves to point out that everything in the world, animate and inanimate, resonates with these waves: you, me, the plate on the kitchen counter, the kitchen counter. Each thing in the world has its own resonant frequency.

Frequency, one of the fundamental physical characteristics of sound, is the speed at which the atmospheric pressure waves are repeated, and this speed is conditioned by the medium through which the waves are transmitted. In a dense medium, sound travels five times as fast as it does in air. Frequency is what determines pitch, and it is measured in the number of wave cycles per second or hertz (Hz) or kilohertz (kHz), units named for the late nineteenth-century physicist Heinrich Hertz. The greater the frequency, the higher the pitch. Just to help you orient yourself, the note A given by the oboe, which is the pitch an orchestra tunes to, is 440 Hz. Because almost all objects vibrate in multiple frequencies at the same time, frequency or pitch rarely exists in isolation. It is accompanied by harmonics, which are oscillations in multiples of the frequency. This gives each sound a unique character, or timbre, especially the sounds of animal voices, our voices, and musical instruments.

A second defining characteristic of any sound is intensity, which we perceive as loudness. The amount of energy that carries the pressure waves along determines loudness. While frequency is calibrated in hertz, intensity is measured by watts. The intensity of my dog's alarm bark is far greater than the intensity of a spring peeper's call. In addition, there is the variable of attenuation—what happens to sound as it travels. The degradation of sound over distance affects its perception by not only intended listeners but also eavesdroppers, other animals that happen to be in the neighborhood. This is a factor not only in the vocalizing of birds, which communicate through the air, but also in the calls of whales and elephants, whose calls are transmitted through water and the earth.

If you are listening to any of these animals, the sound of its voice is a quantifiable physical event until it collides with your inner ear. Then it becomes a perceptual event. As soon as the tiny hairs in your cochlea begin to translate this sound into impulses of the auditory nerves and these travel the neural pathways of the central auditory system, you become aware of the sound. What begins as a simple pressure wave ends up as a cognitive construct.

Acoustics is the study of the interplay between these two kinds of events, physical and perceptual, and like acousticians, the behavioral ecologists and cognitive psychologists who have shared their investigations with me have to work both the physical and perceptual sides of the street. If you want to reveal what is going on between the túngaras when the male calls and why that is going on, you have to learn how the sound travels between the frogs, what happens when it collides with the female's ears, and how its impulses are translated into voltage that fires her auditory brain.

The frogs listening to the call near the pond, including those of their own kind, have ears located behind their eyes. It is a much-simplified version of our own ear—a flattened eardrum or tympanic membrane exposed at the skin surface and, instead of a cochlea with hair cells to transmit sound waves through nerve cells to the brain, two fleshy papillae, one for low frequencies and one for high frequencies. These papillae are the reason that frogs attend to calls from only their own species. They are "tuned" to a particular range of frequencies, making a túngara more acutely sensitive to the sounds of another túngara than to the sounds of other frequencies made by a different kind of frog.

The female túngara is built to be fussy about the frequencies and their duration within the male's advertisement. While the male's whine is enough to attract a female, the sonic sweep of the whine combined with the lower staccato chuck is five times more effective. Going even further, the female justly rewards additional repetitions of the chuck.

"One of my graduate students, Karin Akre, took a video," Mike tells me, "that shows that if the female has kind of settled on a particular male and she's swimming out toward him but doesn't get that second chuck, she makes him give it to her. She passes him, and as she passes him, she gives him a little shove." I have to watch the few seconds of video quite closely to be able to catch the brisk but barely perceptible bump. This little body slam usually works, and the male gives out with a second chuck. She must have more than one chuck, but so long as the male's whine is followed by at least two chucks coming after the whine with exactly the right timing in exactly the right rhythm, she requires no excitement beyond that.

This tuning to particular frequencies, intervals, and rhythms exists in many other animals. It is especially evident among birds, but it is also important to us in terms of how we hear conversation and music. We recognize a question by its rise in inflection, change in pitch, from the basic tone of conversation. When the question is repeated, we are alerted to its importance. If it is repeated again, it gains real urgency. Likewise, a musical note gains power with repetition—Antonio Carlos Jobim's "One Note Samba" is a telling example of this—and we take particular pleasure from melodic phrases that hover in certain intervals around the fundamental tone in the scale. Any departures from these anticipated tonal distances are often what we find most cogent and descriptive in a tune. Likewise also, as the female túngara waits for her eggs to ripen, she is listening for something telling. What it takes for her to hear something telling and then go to the male is readiness. The female won't tune into the space-age calls until her eggs are ripe enough, and to swim out to him she must be truly ready, urgently ready, because there is no teasing with courting frogs, no opportunity for foreplay.

For his part, the male needs to be stingy with the good stuff because he has to invest a lot in his calls. Each big sound he squeezes out of him costs a lot of energy—he can produce only so many whines and chucks during calling hours—and calling can cost him his life. Each successive call in a series has a higher probability of costing him his life. The same sounds that are so tempting for the female are equally alluring to predators, and, as Amanda points out about the diminutive túngaras, "everybody eats the froggies"—snakes and birds and, especially, fringe-lipped bats, the so-called frog-eating bats (this mundane-sounding name actually expresses the amazement of the noted bat authority Merlin Tuttle when he discovered on Barro Colorado a bat with a frog in its mouth). There is evidence that the bat targets the frog not by its usual echolocation but by the frog's calls. What all this means for the male túngara is that giving voice can wear you out, get you a mate, or get you dead.

There are thousands of the little frogs just in Gamboa and more than enough risk to go around. But as I walk around the hamlet I see evidence of the male's rewards for risk taking. In the gutters, drains, low spots where the leaf-cutter ants cross the lawns—any place where water collects—I notice the foamy white dollops of túngara egg masses. They look exactly like a couple of tablespoons of whipped egg white. These are what all the frog noise is about. When the whines and chucks finally draw the female close enough to him—or at least close enough to knock one more chuck out of him—he clambers aboard his bigger half and clasps her around her torso. She doesn't release her eggs right away, and it's not known exactly how this embrace eventually encourages the female to release her eggs. But later the same night they produce that frothy white mass that encapsulates the next generation of whines and chucks. This is the same kind of stuff that accumulates at the edges of the pond on our farm, and the locals have a euphemism for it, *frog spit*.

⊰⊱

When we take the evening's catch back to Mike Ryan's lab in Gamboa, the females are in a state of readiness. In most cases, they have already made their choices and the males cling to their backs. Readiness equals estrogen, Mike says, and his colleague Kathleen Lynch has established the rough outlines of the estrogen curve the female túngara rides every six weeks or so. Her hormonal peak demands an answer, and we watch the females in the lab to see how they respond to the answers they hear.

Mike has permanent quarters in the big central building everybody calls One-Eighty-Three, which serves as office space, dormitory, and communications headquarters for all the researchers in Gamboa. Here a couple generations of the Ryan team have spent thousands of nocturnal hours watching female frogs to determine the details of exactly what sounds will turn a female on and push her from readiness to decisive action.

His lab occupies two rooms, neither of them large. The smaller room is almost completely occupied by a sound chamber that looks like a giant white freezer box with a door in the side. This chamber is an exact replica of the one in Mike's lab at the University of Texas, where he tests captive-bred túngaras. Inside, nothing resembles the pond. The walls, ceiling, and floor are white plastic. When the door closes behind you there is near-total darkness and something that approaches true silence. I find the sensory deprivation a little dizzying and unnerving, but the female frog doesn't. According to Mike, frogs have very keen night vision but, interestingly enough, not particularly acute hearing.

As Amanda and the research assistants set up the sound chamber for the female túngara's first experiment, Mike describes the responses the experiment will elicit. "You know," he tells me, "there is a pretty good article on what's going on here–'Don't the Girls Get Prettier at Closing Time,' 1979." When I succeed in locating it, I find a country-western take on a topic in psychology: how time and urgency affect decision making. The article quotes songwriter David Allen Coe to assert that "there's more to country music than 'mama, or trains or trucks or prison or gettin' drunk,'" and it analyzes the responses of more than a hundred bar-goers, both male and female, in three different watering holes to prove Mickey Gilley's sung testimony that "the girls get prettier at closing time." Apparently it's not just the girls who get better looking. During three different time periods throughout a single evening, the researchers asked their respondents to rate the appearance of members of the opposite sex in the same establishment. When they crunched the responses through some statistical analyses, this revealed that, as closing time approached, people of the opposite sex did in fact look more appealing to the subjects. This was true for both the males and the females who responded. Although noting that the research design made no provision for accounting for the effects of booze on perceptions, the authors declared that Mickey Gilley's hypothesis was confirmed: narrowing the window of opportunity forces decisions that might not have been made without a time limit.[1] For the túngaras, closing time exists only for the females. For each of them, it comes about every six weeks, when she rides the crest of her estrogen wave. At this point she must choose a male or else the energy and physical resources she has invested in her eggs will go to waste. Mike's laboratory research is designed around this closing-time urgency.

The sound chamber is where the female frogs will listen to the jukebox until closing time. Mike is the only songwriter whose tunes are available on the jukebox, and although he is too modest to claim this, he has to know a lot about sound and a lot about physiology to write these tunes. The jukebox is a state-of-the-art software program on the computer outside the chamber, which drives the speakers inside the chamber. It is a highly sophisticated system with which Mike can tweak the frequency of the space-age whine or slice or add in a fraction of a second to a chuck, and although it has more bells and whistles than most of the systems I saw, these bells and whistles are designed with strict tolerances and fidelity equal to the best systems used for birdsong.

I stay outside the sound chamber with Jenny and Sasha and Amanda, who is Mike's straw boss in the lab. Amanda is a small, thin person with very long, very blond hair and very blue eyes. She is extremely well organized and in full command of the computers, custom software, and sound equipment. A brisk, efficient manager, she worked her way through a belated undergraduate degree at the University of Texas as a bartender in a "gentlemen's club" and tells me that dealing with drunks honed her management skills. While Sasha and Jenny defer to Amanda, all three of them have to be on their toes to keep the experiment running.

On the computer screen we can see video surveillance of the chamber floor. It looks like a basketball court under extremely dim light. At each end, located inside a rectangle resembling the free-throw area, there is a speaker, and in the center of the floor a circle like the one for tip-offs. The games here are always night games. They start around 10 P.M. and run until 3 A.M. or so.

Jenny separates a pair of frogs, disentangling the female from the male's embrace, sets her down in the center circle, and gently claps a plastic funnel over her. The cord attached to the funnel runs up through the chamber ceiling to allow Jenny to raise the funnel from outside the chamber.

With the female túngara hunkered down under the funnel in the center circle, the game inside the chamber begins with an interlude of frog song. First the female frog is treated to a single whine repeated from both speakers, then to a whine-chuck played by a single speaker at the opposite end of the chamber. Thirty seconds of silence. Then Jenny pulls the cord to lift the funnel and release the female. She is on her own and loaded with eggs. This is a test of preference and memory. Will she be able to keep the two calls in mind throughout the period of silence? And which speaker with which call will she choose?

Play commences. The female has five minutes to leave the center circle and a total of fifteen minutes to indicate her choice by hopping into the free-throw zone around the speaker with the most enticing sound. Because Mike has already established that the females prefer calls that include the chuck, this game is a test of memory. The female that can listen to the introduction of the chuck and retain that sound impression throughout the distractions of the less appealing unadorned whine calls, throughout the silence, and hop up to the speaker responsible for the more delicious whine-chuck scores one point for memory and cognition.

The three women outside the chamber work intently. The experiment requires concentration and coordination and quiet. We don't

talk much, and when we do, no one speaks at a normal volume because even this built-to-spec sound chamber can't preserve pristine
silence, which, although the frogs don't have particularly acute hearing,
is required to preserve the integrity of the experiment. Jenny manages
the frog contestants and the stopwatch, Sasha controls the sounds played
back and records results on a data sheet, and Amanda, who has a number of seasons' experience, spots the two of them and advises.

On the computer screen the image of the court is very large and the
player, the female, is tiny, the size of a bread crumb. The frog calls are
playing at either end of the court, but nothing happens. The female is
apparently unmoved. She remains hunched down in the center circle.
Jenny consults the stopwatch. We keep our eyes on the screen. No go.

Amanda shrugs and says in a whisper, "Well? This froggie may
foul out."

But she doesn't. Just moments before the stopwatch blinks up to
five minutes, the female makes a quick, slippery move out of the center
circle. She appears to be on her way to the speaker on the right-hand
side of the court. But maybe not. She pauses and turns back into a life-
less bread crumb. The digits flash by on the stopwatch. She now has
only about four minutes to make her choice.

Amanda is not sympathetic. "She is the kind you'd like to squish,"
she says under her breath.

In the end, this female túngara fouls out. She exceeds the fifteen-
minute time limit without making a choice. The bar closes, and she
goes home alone.

The next contestant is more decisive. After an initial minute or
two of deliberation in the center circle, she makes a long, smooth bound
out of the circle in the direction of the right-hand speaker but far to

one side of the court. After a pause she begins to approach the speaker in an arc. Her arc is punctuated by a series of delays—for deliberation, reconsideration, whatever.

"This is characteristic," Amanda says softly about the approach. "It's a kind of dance."

In her final hop, the female enters the free-throw rectangle and parks herself sideways in front of the speaker. She scores!

There is a general sigh of satisfaction, and Jenny enters the chamber, her back filling the video image on the screen, to scoop up the frog and place her back under the funnel.

Each female is presented with four variations of the same test and has fifteen minutes to complete each one. Taking into account occasional retests, it's not unusual for each frog to spend more than an hour as a contestant. Amanda tells me Mike's goal for the summer is two thousand frogs, and I wonder, What is it about two thousand female frogs, sounds from two speakers, and the decisions the frogs make that has anything to do with the sounds that Sheila Jordan makes—or, for that matter, the sounds that you and I hear and make? Is it just that the frog song buzzes into their frog ears and resonates through the auditory brain?

⤛⤜

In the nocturnal universes of the sound chamber and Ocelot Pond there are two evolutionary forces at work, both of which were recognized and defined by Darwin: natural selection and sexual selection. Although Darwin is more readily associated with his ideas about natural selection and survival, he was also the first to observe the systematic process that is the "struggle between individuals of one sex, generally the males, for possession of the other sex."[2] As he saw it, sexual selection was a secondary process that played out either through direct combat among males vying for a female or through mate choice, a prerogative usually exercised by females. "The males," he said, ". . . do not obtain possession of females, independently of choice on the part of the latter." But, probably because the idea of combat made the struggling males and the trophy female a more individually dramatic scenario, the notion of males vying for a female became the underlying assumption in research about mating by scientists who were, not coincidentally, predominantly male.

This stereotyped assumption about sexual selection prevailed, and Darwin's proposals about sexual selection in general and mate choice in particular went largely untended until the 1970s. Biologists, now including more women, began to turn their attention to the process of sexual selection, mating, and reproductive "success." In the 1980s this trend progressed, and behavioral ecologists, including Mike Ryan, began to focus more intently on the roles of the female and female biology in mate choice.

With the frogs, mating takes place in darkness and in pandemonium that involves not just a couple of male frogs and a female but multitudes of males and females of many species. The males of each species have a distinctive call, and their calls are a force for order. Consider frog courtship at Ocelot Pond without benefit of vocal communication. Nighttime mayhem: combat among males of all the frog species calling in the chorus, struggles between males and unwilling females, indiscriminate matings producing offspring that mock the protections of speciation. By enabling species recognition, standing in for combat, and separating the ready and willing from the unprepared, frog calls and their reception enforce social order. They constitute an evolved process supporting the evolution process itself. Short-lived animals like frogs and mice serve as models for human biology. We know a lot about how the mating process works in túngara frogs, about what hormonal and neurological transactions drive the call-and-response that pulls male and female túngaras together, and that should tell us something about the nature of our own vocalizing and sexual responses.

Female readiness and receptivity are critical elements of human matings, and Mike's investigations of túngara desire have brought him recognition as an authority on sexual attraction even outside the realm of ecology. He served on the dissertation committee of a psychology student who was studying receptivity and behavior of women. In order to look at how readiness influenced how women try to make themselves look during the various phases of their menstrual cycle, the psychologist handed out a play-money budget to each of her woman subjects and monitored their Internet purchasing decisions. Her rather unsurprising finding was that women become increasingly interested in revealing, come-hither clothing when their hormonal readiness begins to peak.

At one of his public lectures the year before, Mike met a film director who was working on a romantic comedy in which the plot was juiced by pheromones, and one of the characters was a biologist who was an expert on pheromones. A Cameron Diaz-like star would play the part of the woman attracted by the pheromones. Would Mike read the script and correct matters of scientific fact? His response was characteristic, open-minded, and imaginative, even about this commercial romance. He read the script, and afterward, acting on spritely inspiration, he went back to the story and suggested a telling change in the ending: The charismatic male lead pursuing Cameron Diaz didn't get her. The biologist did. The director liked the change and suggested that, if the film ever made it into production, perhaps Mike should play the biologist.

Without ever turning his attention away from his little frog, Mike Ryan has asked deeper and deeper questions about túngara voice and sexual attraction: What is it about the whine-chuck and its frequencies that draws the females down through the leaf litter to the edge of the pond? How does the female pick out the male túngara's call from the other noisy calls in the rest of the chorus? When she hears an irresistible call, does she remember where the sound came from? If the males sing in competition with one another, how do they know when to chime in and what sound will be winning? Is the sound of the whine-chuck the only cue that compels the female to the male or some combination of signals? Is there any cognition involved in the female's choice, or is it unconsidered, just a response to a stimulus? How do these female decisions affect the ways in which the males evolve?

～ ～

These questions have a legacy older than Mike's field, which is now known as behavioral ecology. Darwin recognized that behavior and evolution were inextricably interconnected. But like his ideas about sexual selection, his writings on the connections between behavior and evolution were largely ignored until the years just after World War II. In the meantime, there were any number of biologists who were becoming interested in animal behavior in and of itself and in ways of observing animal behavior without imposing ideas about human behavior on the animals. Like all scientists, they wrestled with subjectivity to reveal objective, factual information. This trend rolled out on two tracks: field studies undertaken in the United States and the United Kingdom and those launched in Continental Europe.

In the 1920s the German theoretical biologist Baron Jakob von Uexküll began to develop a set of ideas that put the animal and its perceptions front and center without prejudging them. He proposed the idea that every animal perceives the world through its own particular sensory apparatus, and he called this world *umwelt*. Your umwelt is composed of the sights, sounds, smells, and other sensations available to you through your physiology. The túngara umwelt is the leaf litter, the pond, and the puddle as experienced by the frog. Your *innenwelt*, and that of the frog, is the interior processing of those perceptions. Uexküll, who resisted Darwin's account of evolution, simply ignored the question of how the behaviors he was trying to systematize would affect a species in the long run or influence the emergence of new species. Yet the distinction he made between our perceptions and those of animals remains important today.[3]

In Austria in the early 1930s, the freshly minted PhD Konrad Lorenz was making detailed observations of home-raised jackdaws, which are members of the crow family, ducks, and geese on his family estate while he waited for a university appointment. Like von Uexküll, Lorenz was interested in scientifically separating our understanding of animals from our thinking about humans, but he subscribed wholeheartedly to the theory of evolution and understood there must be some connection between the process of evolution and behavior. Lorenz was very opinionated, confident that his years of firsthand observations of animals gave him superior insight, and he had a tendency to disparage much of the behavior research going on in Europe at the time. There were notable exceptions. The first was von Uexküll's work, whose attempts at systematization and ideas about umwelt and innenwelt Lorenz respected, and although von Uexküll was a generation older, he returned this respect and even drew on Lorenz's jackdaw experiments for his own writing.

Another exception was the work of Niko Tinbergen, a young professor at the University of Leiden. Tinbergen had been engaged in field studies of herring gulls in the Netherlands, and he and Lorenz began to correspond and then to visit to discuss their ideas about what made animals tick. One summer Tinbergen moved with his family to Lorenz's estate in Altenberg, and over the next few years the friends drew other scientists into the study of what was soon to be called ethology. This term was appropriated. Originally, it designated the study of human nature, but soon this definition was swamped by the term's new association with animal behavior. Eventually, in 1973, the two friends, along with Karl von Frisch, would jointly receive the Nobel Prize for Physiology or Medicine for their work in "ethology." Before this, however, World War II broke into their work on animal behavior and nearly devastated their friendship. Although Lorenz was struggling for academic recognition and found it financially difficult to maintain his estate, his upper-class origins made him sympathetic to Nazi ideas about racial purity and superiority. He published articles promoting the superiority of the "pure, wild" over the "domesticated," and like many other Austrians, he welcomed the Germans' bloodless takeover of Austria. He received a long-awaited appointment to a chair at the University of Königsberg.

As Lorenz jockeyed for standing in Germany, Tinbergen's work was thrown into disarray. The Nazis invaded the Netherlands in 1940, and two years later, Niko Tinbergen was imprisoned in an internment camp for two years. By pulling strings in Germany, Lorenz was able to secure an offer of release for his friend. Tinbergen refused.

Then in 1944, Lorenz, who had been called up by the Germans to serve as a physician, was captured by the Russians and imprisoned for almost four years. After the war, Tinbergen, discouraged by the difficulties of research and the morale in his own war-torn country, moved to England to take a position at Oxford, where he continued the efforts he had begun before the war to build an international community of ethologists.

For several years, relations between Tinbergen, who had trouble tolerating the fact that Lorenz had been "more or less nazi," and Lorenz were tetchy. But Tinbergen was keenly interested in reconstructing the group of ethologists that had begun to form before the war and tentatively began a reconciliation with Lorenz, who, worried that Tinbergen might harbor lingering resentments, responded cautiously. Documenting their interactions is a remarkable photograph, taken at a 1952 conference, of the two friends out hiking in the midst of their colleagues, as if Europe and their friendship hadn't been torn apart by the war. In later years there would be clashes between the two, but these were over scientific issues.

As the field of ethology was rebuilding from years of war and coalescing as an international endeavor, Lorenz and Tinbergen were much preoccupied with "releasers" of behavioral energy and the natural systems that expressed these. Lorenz envisioned that the forces that shaped animal behavior worked something like water in a hydraulic system, exerting pressure until they were released as animal activities. He continued to refine these ideas and to publish books for popular audiences that propagated the ideas emerging in ethology.

Lorenz, who is generally credited with being the father of ethology, considered himself a psychologist, and he held appointments in departments of psychology. While Tinbergen's early academic positions were in departments of psychology, he considered himself a biologist who happened to study psychology. Like von Uexküll and Lorenz, Tinbergen stressed that in order to understand how animals behave, you need to recognize that animals experience the world in ways that are different from the ways we do. But he went beyond this fundamental of ethology to bring significant advances in rigor and theoretical sophistication to the new branch of science. Focusing on enforcing systematic order on scientific notions about the reciprocal causes of behavior and evolutionary effects, he wanted to unravel the Gordian knot of biology, psychology, and inheritance that each animal represents. He spent years in a detailed consideration of instinct and sought to reduce scientific understanding of it to its essential, objective terms. He was trying to steer clear of soft, emotive terms and to replace these with statements of objective, observable fact. It is due in large part to his influence that animal behaviorists by and large no longer use verbs like *think, feel, intend* or nouns like *consciousness* or *mind*. Animals behave. That is what they do.

Eventually Tinbergen boiled down the process of understanding behavior to four essential but interrelated questions that when answered could explain any behavior: What is the physiological cause of the behavior? How does the behavior help the animal survive? How has the behavior evolved? And last, How does the behavior develop within the individual animal? These were the issues that set the research agenda for ethology, linked the study of animal behavior to ecology and evolutionary biology, and prepared the ground for the transformation of ethology to what is now known as behavioral ecology. This is a large and still-growing field in which biologists like Mike Ryan examine the things that animals do, the ways they act, under the lens whose primary designer was Niko Tinbergen. The concepts propounded today by Richard Dawkins and other biological theorists who see the gene as the primal force in and explanation for all biological life flow directly from Tinbergen's determination to reduce any account of animal behavior to irreducible fundamentals.[4]

Accordingly, if you are a behavioral ecologist, what is going on at Ocelot Pond is communication, which is the sending and receiving of signals, pure and simple. It is not frog language, and it does not *mean* anything. It is stimulus and response. While I am in Gamboa I am aware that this thinking is dominant, but because of my training as a music student and my work as a writer, I return often to Donald Griffin and his ideas about animal consciousness. Griffin, while keeping up his work on bat sound for quite a while, went on to explore the animal minds that perceive sound signals and to produce books that questioned the premise that only humans have consciousness and experience thinking. I love these books because, like Kipling's animal stories, they try to enter the minds of many different animals, from insects to apes. There is no way to read Griffin on animal cognition without becoming acutely aware of the processes of your own thought. This is probably why the signaler-signal-receiver model strikes me as being about as cold-blooded as the túngaras themselves. But Griffin is not in ascendancy in Gamboa, and the highly objective models spawned by Tinbergen are. Whatever communication takes place between two organisms takes place in *signals*, and eventually I will discover just how useful this idea is.

Mike takes this objectivity a step further, finding that even *signal* is burdened by too many assumptions. In behavioral ecology, you frequently come across the notion that *signals* convey *information*, but while I am in Gamboa Mike and two equally senior colleagues have in press a commentary that, after criticizing the use of *language* for animals on the basis of subjectivity, strips *signal* of even an association with information. In this article they point out that animal behaviorists have found *information* a convenient grip and use it quite loosely, and they call for tighter definition that drills down to what exactly information is.[5]

*~(>~*

Mike has parsed the sounds of the male túngara's signals in minute segments to specify the female's choosiness within precise tolerances, and now team member Ryan Taylor is trying to put the male call itself into perspective by asking if sound is the only thing at work in the female's decisions. Is it only the frog's voice that draws the female across the dark pond to the male?

In an apartment at One-Eighty-Three two floors up from Mike's lab, Ryan Taylor is at work trying to figure out what role, if any, the flash of luminosity from the fully blown-up vocal sacs plays in the female's decision. When I visit the apartment, Ryan is keeping it dark, and the heat and humidity up here are crushing. Occupying the combination living and dining room is a tent of black plastic in which play will take place without the benefit of soundproofing or video monitoring. To watch, Ryan will just poke his head under a flap in the plastic tent.

What he needs in order to test for the effects of the inflated vocal sacs on the female frog is not just a fresh batch of female frogs every night but also a male frog whose vocal sacs he can control. Enter Robo-Frog, who after morphing into successively more sophisticated versions is now officially Faux Frog. As the progression of his nomenclature suggests, Ryan, who was raised in Louisiana, has a twinkle in his eye, a little southern amusement about what is ridiculous or ironic. Good thing he has this, because he has had to go to some pretty funny lengths to get a facsimile of the male túngara that the females can believe in. Ryan began with a wire skeleton with a balloon attached on either side of the head, an air compressor, and rubber tubing to send air into the balloons. The only reliable thing about the balloons was that they would break. He moved on.

Using the same system for inflation, Ryan next tried faux vocal sacs made of condoms tied to the frog frame with dental floss. He braved the long looks at the checkout counter and bought condoms by the gross and skeins of tooth twine. The condoms performed only slightly better than the balloons. But after a while, there was a happy accident one night in which something else broke, the frog skeleton. In order not to lose results from the females still waiting to be tested that night, he replaced the broken frame with a clothespin to secure the faux vocal sacs in front of the speaker. This caused Taylor to discover an essential fact: so long as the imitation vocal sacs inflated credibly, the female túngaras were undeterred by the lack of a frog body.

In the meantime, however, to eliminate questions about the importance of the image of the male's body in the female's choices, an engineer working on other biology research projects in New York City and a graduate student in Mike's department who was a talented artist had set to work to build a more accurate representation of a túngara. Faux Frog is plastic, and he is perfect: his size, his hunkered-down ready-to-bound posture, his lifelike warts. His blue-green skin is only slightly bluer-green than túngaras recruited from the ponds and puddles around Gamboa. Along with this new and more beautiful body, Faux Frog has more reliable faux sacs—an inflation device that allows for calibration of the timing between the faux sacs' inflation and the faux calls. This is a urinary catheter with the bulb segmented into two "sacs."

"The female," Ryan says, "has to make the best of a bad job," and he explains that the female túngara has to make her decision amid the din of the chorus of as many as eleven different kinds of frogs, the distraction of many túngara males, and the physical urgencies of her estrogen ramping up and her eggs getting heavier. His description reminds me of a childbirth instructor who said that when the moment to push came, the urgency would be undefeatable. "It's like being in a line in Filene's Basement. You have found a pair of shoes that you really love, and you need to pay for them. You can't get out of line because there are fifteen people in line behind you, and suddenly you have an attack of diarrhea." When I tell him about this he nods, and then he says with a characteristic twinkle in his eye, "There's a pretty good article that might help you with all this—'Don't the Girls Get Prettier at Closing Time.' Did Mike mention that one to you?"

Turns out that in Panama the country-western bar metaphor is controlling. It is a fun, simple explanation of the pressures enforcing the túngaras' mating decisions. But it doesn't address the details of how many chucks of what duration it takes for the male to reel in a female or of the involvement of visual corroboration of the call, and it certainly doesn't begin to say anything about how the frogs develop their calls or the way túngara calls will influence the evolution of the frog or vice versa. I begin to ponder what these myriad details imply about the voices of larger, bigger-brained animals and about our own vocalizing.

"I thought this was going to be simple," I confess to Mike as we are driving back out to Ocelot Pond on my last night of frog catching. The túngara may be a simple little animal with a one-way communication system that is about as interactive as a bumper sticker, and its call may be a couple of simple sounds. But simplicity stops right there. Mike's research over the years has made it evident that the apparently simple scenario of the male's two-part call summoning a female for insemination and the female's approach is actually an elaborately wrought transaction involving the endocrine system, larynx and tympanic membrane, nerves, and brain.

"The frogs?" He smiles. "Not so much simple as scientifically accessible. That's what I usually say, *scientifically accessible*—and," he adds as if this will make everything clear, "you know about Tinbergen, right? The four questions?"

I do—Immediate cause of behavior? Survival effects? Evolution? Development in an individual?— and I can see how the experiments, the hormones, the perception, reflect Tinbergen's systematic views on behavior. "Still, it's pretty complicated."

"Yeah. But not so complicated if you consider some of the other animals," he says. "I mean, some of the mammals—and then there are the birds." He pauses, and after a little while he says, "Yeah, then there are the birds. . . ."

But it is too soon to go there just yet. Mike has set me on a path of hormones and signals and social life, and this will lead me to a park in England.

# 3

# Liars, Dupes, and Honesty

~

At first, the scene doesn't seem a likely one for hormonal highs and aggression. It seems quite peaceful. Nevertheless, I am in the midst of an experiment about lust and power and sound. The red deer rest in a grassy area edged by woods near the road. Even though it is autumn, most of the leaves in Richmond Park are still green. But the grasses where the deer sun themselves have turned a gray blond, an indisputable sign that summer is lost. The park, one of England's Royal Parks, is carved out of southwest London, and by any urban standards it is huge, three times the size of Central Park and almost four square miles. In addition to the now-repurposed former homes of royalty and their gardens, the park incorporates a number of meadow and woodland areas. There are about twenty deer, most of them hinds, the females. Posed upright and resting chest down with their legs tucked under them in the particular way that grazing animals lie in order to leap quickly to their feet to flee a predator, the hinds are gathered around a big stag with an astounding set of antlers. A little off from the edge of the group are a few other stags, clearly not important to the hinds and, because they are submissive, not worrying the big stag at the center of this diorama.

Although the stag's rack looks heavy enough to give him a perpetual headache, he surveys his harem, the people moving along the sidewalk not far away, the baby strollers, and the construction equipment a couple hundred yards away with lordly equanimity. The sounds of the city, the noise of traffic on the perimeter road and farther away on the A3 passing between the park and Wimbledon, the occasional siren, penetrate the bird and insect hum in the park. The stag takes all of this in complacently, unbothered by anything—until a barnyard bellow blasts through the background sounds. The stag immediately gets to his feet and, standing over his hinds, he stretches out his neck, tipping back the unwieldy rack, and issues a matching bellow. At the same time, he begins to stalk toward the source of the first bellow. The intruder bellows a second time, and the stag answers forcefully, at the same time moving beyond the group of hinds to put himself between his challenger and his harem. The silent pause that follows seems to enrage the stag. He paws the ground, then drops his head to drive his antlers across the ground. This is rutting, a demonstration of what he will do to any stag foolish enough to get close. The hinds, for their part, are largely unconcerned. Only one of them gets to her feet, and the rest of them remain on the grass chewing their cuds. They are already the property of the stag, but those he has not already inseminated potentially could still be lured away by another stag. The intruder issues one last raucous insult, and the big stag responds with even more impressive belligerence.

He has the last word, but he is a dupe. His challenger is a digital recorder and speaker hidden in brushy growth behind some tumble-down fence rails, and at a safe distance away, crouched behind another fence and more brush, a young woman named Megan Wyman is videotaping the stag's posturing. She has tricked him into strutting his stuff, but when the recording ends, the big stag, unaware that he has been duped and satisfied that he has fended off trouble, returns to his couch among the hinds. Megan, a tall, lithe young woman with notable poise, is a postdoctoral fellow at the Centre for Mammal Vocal Communication and Cognition Research at the University of Sussex. The bellowing duel that she has staged is the first of two experiments examining the acoustical properties of what biologists call the roaring of red deer and the perceptual psychology involved in this animal's communications.

⟞⟝

Not much time has gone by when Megan begins the second playback experiment. The autumn scene is almost unchanged, and peace has returned to the herd of red deer. The big lordly stag has returned to his bed and placidly surveys his harem chewing their cuds and, beyond them the few, meek, lesser stags. The angle of the sun is the same, the grasses the same shades of gray and blond, and the soundscape the same mix of insects, birds, traffic, and sirens. Then the animals' calm—or at least the hinds' calm—is interrupted by a high-pitched whinnying snigger. What has changed in the scene is the call coming from Megan's digital recorder. It is the voice of a sika deer stag in rut.

The sika deer, a native of eastern and southeastern Asia, was imported to England in the nineteenth century, at first as an ornamental animal for parks, and similarly made its way to many countries on other continents. It is very different from the red deer. A small spotted deer as fine-boned as an antelope, the sika is only about half the height of the red deer, and the antler rack of the stags is a whisper compared to the red deer's bold statement. The sika's voice is a good octave higher than the red deer's, and although its whinny—what biologists call a moan—descends, its larynx does not drop. In spite of their high voice and delicate appearance, the sika deer have had a robust experience in Britain. The park populations of sika have leaked into the wild, where numbers are burgeoning and the deer have begun to hybridize with the red deer. It is thought the mixing of these two races of deer begins when a lone sika stag wanders into an area where sika females are hard to find and red deer hinds are not well patrolled. This seems startling, not only because of their wildly different voices but because of the variation in their body sizes. Imagining the little sika trying to mount a much taller red deer female makes the whole enterprise seem preposterous. "How do they *do* it?" I ask Megan. She just smiles and shrugs. "We know it happens. From the DNA."

There are hybrid sika deer wandering England whose mating calls are a blend of the sika moan and the red deer roar. The numbers of these crossbreeds and of the offspring of further crossings are increasing, and Megan tells me that the British are not happy about the corrupting of pure red deer blood—for one thing, the smaller racks the sikas introduce make the stags less desirable as trophies. On another level, the hybrids disturb their British convictions about majesty and nobility, and they find it difficult to include the more delicate, spotted sika with its high little wavery call in their national identity. There is something hilarious about the sika's skinny whinny, and it's contagious. Whenever you hear it, you have to laugh.

But the red deer stag in Richmond Park doesn't laugh. He doesn't respond at all. He looks as if he has heard nothing. He keeps his regal position settled on the ground and continues to gaze beyond his harem at people strolling along a sidewalk some distance away. But the hinds do react. Several of the same hinds who didn't give the recording of the red deer roar any more than the flick of an ear get to their feet and begin to mill about, moving in the general direction of the playback speaker.

"Usually what happens first when they hear the sika call is that they kind of bunch up together," Megan comments.

After a second shrill nicker, two of the hinds actually walk out of the harem to investigate, and at this point the big stag labors reluctantly to his feet and intervenes, positioning himself between the infatuated strays and the source of the foreign voice.

It is all very puzzling. Why would the hinds be so moved by an animal voice they have never heard before? What quality of the voice draws them? The attraction seems as bizarre as the gaga appeal of Rudy Vallee's crooning through a megaphone for crowds in the 1930s—girls went nuts over his amplified falsetto—or, more recently, of Michael Jackson's vocal delivery.

The red deer is widely dispersed by nature throughout Eurasia and coastal northern Africa, and it has been introduced in New Zealand and South America. It is a very common species, but in spite of this, Megan tells me, the British take a proprietary national pride in their red deer. The stags, which are massive compared to the hinds, are icons of strength and nobility, of the wilderness of the British Isles before they were overrun with people. The quintessential expression of these associations comes into view for long moments in the movie *The Queen.* Stranded by the breakdown of her Land Rover on her estate in Scotland, Elizabeth II is privileged by the visit of a red deer stag with a huge rack who appears on a bleak windblown hillside opposite her. This stag doesn't make a sound. He just stands proudly, his steadfast gaze on the queen. She admires him, we admire him. When he is shot later in the film we are meant to associate his death with the royal family's loss of relevance.

The red deer in Megan's London study can hardly be considered to be living in the wild. But the fact that they are accustomed to the presence of humans makes them easy to observe without disturbing them. Their social life, like the túngara's, is temporary. But they form groups, and they stay together longer. In the wild, the red deer hinds live apart from the stags for most of the year. Then in midsummer the stags begin their annual antler growth, and soon after they're fully adorned—we allude to this annual shift in hormonal state as "horny"— they begin to move toward their traditional rutting grounds in areas where hinds graze most frequently. There the rut gradually becomes more intense, and each stag begins trying to gather a group of hinds. The goal is to monopolize as many of these mating opportunities as possible, and a large harem is an indication that the hinds have confidence in the breeding worthiness of the stag. Once he has taken possession of the hinds, the stag's next challenge is to defend them from the advances of other stags who are also intent on gathering harems. His roars serve him in competition with other stags and in drawing females.

The rutting season is the occasion for many dramatic rituals of mating and fighting. To gather the hinds, the stag herds a single hind with his head lifted and turned away from the direction the two are moving, which is usually toward the center of the hind group. His eyes are half-closed, and he drives the female with a characteristic stiff-legged trot. He uses a briefer, less aggressive version of this kind of driving, called *chivying*, to move the hinds about within the harem. Then, when all is quiet and the hinds are settled in the grass, a stag may walk over and begin licking a hind's face around her eyes and perhaps later around her tail. When he eventually mounts her, penetrates, and works toward ejaculation, the climax of this is a moment when his hind feet leave the ground. There is a photograph that catches this moment, which looks both amazing and ridiculous.

The many fights between stags during the rut are even more ritualized, and perhaps this ritualization, which allows the opponents to progressively assess their chances as the aggression escalates, is a way to limit the number and the seriousness of fights. In the beginning of the contest, the animals' voices take the place of actual physical combat. The two stags start off the proceedings with bouts of roaring, and when these vocal advertisements of their size and strength don't settle the matter, the stags move fairly close to each other and begin a measured walk in parallel. This is an opportunity for direct visual comparison of their respective bodies. At length, one of the stags lowers his head, his antlers inviting an opposing pair, and almost instantaneously, the two have locked horns. They drive against each other, each trying to dislodge his opponent and force him to move backward. It's a surefire recipe for goring and other injuries. But although the rutting season witnesses hundreds of altercations between stags, in the majority of the contests the song and dance of the roaring and parallel walk satisfy the requirement to prove superiority.

After they've held a harem throughout the period when the hinds are in estrus and they've likely impregnated most of them, the stags move off on their own to resume life in bachelor groups, and in the early spring their antlers drop off, making them look more like the females. Their only contribution to the raising of their young has been the insemination of the hinds. Even considering the substantial costs of holding a harem, the stags' return-on-investment is fairly high.

Probably because of the often-inverse relationship between an animal's commonness and the amount of scientific attention devoted to it, the red deer were studied very little until the late 1950s when ecologists began to look at grazing patterns and population fluctuations of red deer on the Isle of Rum, which lies west of mainland Scotland in the bay that separates it from the Hebrides. Then, beginning in the late 1960s, physiologists looked at the reproduction and antler growth of this island species. Until 1957 when the Nature Conservancy bought it, the Isle of Rum had been held in private ownership as an estate for hunting and raising sheep, and in an effort to restore the island to something of its natural state, the conservancy removed all the sheep. In 1972, the Cambridge biologist Timothy Clutton-Brock and several colleagues began the work that is usually associated with red deer, a more comprehensive investigation of their habits and reproduction. Clutton-Brock's interests began with questions around the evolution of sex differences: how and why the red deer stags and hinds have become so different in size and, to some degree, shape. Obviously, the stag's roaring was one of these evolutionary differences.

Here is where Karen McComb of the University of Sussex's Cen-

tre for Mammal Vocal Communication and Cognition Research enters the picture. In the late 1980s, as a graduate student of Timothy
Clutton-Brock, she began to investigate the reproductive function of
the red deer's roaring, and what she found was that while the roaring
was used by males in aggressive encounters with other stags, it also
pushed ahead the hinds' states of estrus. A number of other studies of
animals vocalizing during courtship have also found that the calls ac-
celerate the reproductive hormonal processes. In the case of the ring-
dove, it was discovered that the cooing of the female dove upped her
own hormonal readiness.

McComb has continued with this research, in partnership with
David Reby, a French scientist who has recently been delving into the
influence on the hinds of the pitch of the stags' roars and its surrounding resonant frequencies called *formants*. Megan Wyman is working with
Reby and, by legacy, Karen McComb to consider very closely the acoustic structure of the roars of the red deer stags. This line of research is
significant because it examines features of animal voices that were previously thought to be uniquely human.

With her soft voice and social grace, Megan is hardly the kind of
person you would imagine being concerned with rank, aggressive
males of any species. But before she joined the center at Sussex, Megan
studied the bellowing of the American bison. Like the red deer, the
bison is a grazing animal that lives in groups of males and females
and the males fight for the right to breed the females. "They have 'fighting storms,'" Megan reports. During these fighting bouts, the bulls,
like the red deer stags, work through a ritualistic sequence of loud
bawling and aggression before they actually put their heads down,
force them together, and try to push the opposing bull into submission.

This stirs up a lot of dust and pee and noise, and yet she was there and is directly factual about the science of sex.

Now she is in the midst of the red deer rut, parsing the stags' roars, and we are back to *signal, sender,* and the possibility that the signal conveys *information* to the *receiver.* The precise definition of *information* has never been settled on, as Mike Ryan has pointed out, and he would prefer that *signal* not carry any implication of meaning beyond a physical stimulus that passes from one animal to another.[1] Signals given by animals can be visual, chemical, olfactory, tactile, or the kind we're interested in, vocal. They stimulate electrical activity in the brain and often can stimulate the brain to formulate and instruct its owner to produce a response. When I phone you, you receive not only the signal of the telephone demanding to be answered but also a signal that is my voice coming from the other end of the line. According to this theoretical approach, you, as a receiver, then use the auditory-processing functions of your brain to analyze my signal and respond to it with action or a signal of your own. We're passing brain stimuli back and forth.

This is a primitive statement of the ideas behind animal signaling. This way of formulating how animals communicate with one another—visually and biochemically as well as vocally—is an attempt to understand the communication systems of other animals without having our consideration tainted by any perspectives that might view the animal systems in terms of our own. Overlapping the period in biological theory in which behavioral ecology came into its own was a parallel stream of theorizing in the field of semiotics, where the terms *sign* and *signal* took on abstract functions. A sign or signal is something that carries *information* from one entity to another, and this idea was used in everything from computation to literary criticism. *Sign, signal,* and *signaling* crept into hundreds of academic books and a number of popular books as well, notably Umberto Eco's *The Name of the Rose.* Due in no small measure to the work of Eco's friend and colleague Thomas Seboek, a linguist who enjoyed crisscrossing disciplinary boundaries, animal signals were folded into the purview of semiotics.

Although Sebeok was particularly interested in debates surrounding animal capacities for language and other linguists and anthropologists were also involved in considerations of animal calls and gestures, I do not know how much actual cross-fertilization of ideas occurred between the philosophers of *sign* and biologists. But I don't think it was an accident that a new line of speculation called signaling theory began to emerge within evolutionary biology. While signaling studies did sometimes include or refer to humans, they did successfully avoid assumptions about nonhuman animals being similar to us. They seemed for the most part to give credit where credit is due.

⁓ ⁊⁓

Scientific and linguistic ideas about signals and signaling came to the forefront not only about the same time as the transformation of ethology to behavioral ecology in response to Niko Tinbergen's theories but also about the same time as the rise and popularization of new ideas about genetics and the transactions among genes that control the fate of the individual organism, in this case, the individual animal. In its first real popular bloom since Darwin's publication of his theory of evolution and the place of humans in that scheme, theoretical biology and evolutionary theory began to pull away from the idea of groups or species as the controlling hereditary group and look to the individual as the site of evolutionary change and influence.

These theories about genetics under which Megan and other behavioral ecologists operate were derived and expressed through mathematics and logic, largely by biologists with previous training in a mathematical discipline. Although they have come to public notice only in the last few years, gene-centered arguments had been a strong undercurrent in scientific debate on evolution since the 1920s, when J. B. S. Haldane and biostatistician Ronald Fisher began publishing their mathematical analyses of genetic transactions and their effects. Mathematics became an accepted, then expected, mode of expressing ideas about the relationship between behavior and genetics. W. D. Hamilton, who took a degree in human demographics at the London School of Economics before shifting into an intense study of genetics and behavior, was concerned with explaining individual behavior that resulted in no direct benefit to the individual but only to members of its family. What was then called altruism is the organizing force in the lives of social insects such as bees and wasps and ants, and Hamilton used social life in their colonies to derive "Hamilton's Rule," the equation for which he is best known. His theory argues that investing in close relatives rather than oneself is a method for improving the fitness—the ability to survive and reproduce—of an individual's own genes.[2] In other words, self-interest prevails even in altruism.

Robert L. Trivers, a somewhat younger American working on evolutionary theory, also considered the social insects and took a similar line of approach to analyzing conflict and cooperation, and his ideas about genes and individual self-interest, along with Hamilton's, were

boiled down further by Richard Dawkins, who has become a dominant figure in evolutionary theory—although he is probably better
known by the general public for his atheism than the content of his
scientific work.[3] While every contemporary theoretical approach to
evolution features the gene as the primary player in creating nature's
productions, Dawkins, a student of Niko Tinbergen's, pursues every
other component that might play a role in evolution and tracks it
down to the blind, ruthless self-interest of the gene itself.

Having always thought of myself as an animal lover and encoun-
tering these ideas about signaling and self-interest for the first time, I
found that my first reaction was to be repelled. I was turned off by
what I thought was a bloodless reduction of animal life to the interplay of numbers, and I worried about the social implications of the
supremacy of the gene. After all, both Fisher and Haldane had participated enthusiastically in the eugenics movement, and England's
beloved medievalist and children's writer C. S. Lewis had labeled
Haldane "immoral." This was the kind of public reaction that Darwin
feared would result from the publication of his theory of evolution,
but he certainly couldn't have predicted the lasting conflict between
religion and science that his ideas ignited and continue to fuel.[4] His
writings simply represented his most objective analysis of how plants
and animals came into being. While he himself put scientific contribution above social convention, he knew the inflammatory potential
of his proposals, and this potential has been part of his legacy. A number of scientists have told me that reading Darwin sent them away
from their religious upbringing, and possibly Dawkins's atheism may
also be laid at Darwin's door. As I think about it now, I realize that
Dawkins has much in common with the grand old man, especially in

putting scientific concepts above all others—and that Darwin himself was something of a reductionist.

The catchall *signal* was adopted by Dawkins in his work in the 1970s. He had begun his scientific career under Tinbergen in behavioral ecology and was strongly influenced by both Hamilton and John Maynard Smith in his analyses of animal communication. Dawkins and his coauthor John R. Krebs saw signaling of any kind—vocal, visual, chemical—as essentially selfish behavior. The sender's purpose in signaling was to manipulate the receiver, to cause that animal to do something he or she might not otherwise do. The receiver's business was to divine the manipulator's intent and to respond with like selfishness.[5] The reduction of singer or roarer to sender or receiver was crystallized. This construct left me cold at first, but as I begin to visit research on more complex animals, its utility is becoming quite evident.

John Maynard Smith, whose last work, a book on animal signals, was published shortly before he died in 2004, had long been a key figure in theoretical biology. He worked as an aeronautical engineer during World War II but then apprenticed himself to graduate work in biology under Haldane. Maynard Smith's application of game theory to problems of evolution, particularly the evolution of sex and signaling theory, had a profound influence on theoretical biology.

Game theory? Didn't I know this stuff from research on such human concerns as international relations and social deviancy? Game theory is a logics practice that weighs the costs and benefits of behavior. One of the classic puzzles of game theory is the prisoners' dilemma, in which two prisoners are charged with the same crime and housed in different cells; each must decide whether or not to implicate his partner or to remain cooperatively silent. Animal behaviorists, like their fellows in political science and economics, often use game theory to address questions of cooperation, conflict, and strategy. "What's in it for me if . . . ?" is the central calculation of Maynard Smith's sender and receiver behaviors. His Hawk-Dove game, for instance, weighs the choices animals can make in intruding into territory held by another and in defending their own territory—What's in it for me if I announce my presence loudly? Or if I hang back? And what will I gain if I move in quietly and meekly? The parallels to political diplomacy are only too clear.

The Sir Philip Sydney game, another of Maynard Smith's logical puzzles, attempts to explain signaling in which the *receiver*'s response is costly. Maynard Smith named the scheme after the sixteenth-century English courtier and poet Sidney, who, having been fatally wounded in battle, is reported to have passed his water bottle to another wounded soldier, saying, "Thy need is yet greater than mine." The stereotypical scenario described by this game is a bird chick begging for food and the parent delivering the goods. Although most of us probably don't think of the feeding of young as giving up something, biologists view parental care as a cost to the parent in time, energy, and opportunity.[6]

In the thirty years since these ideas were proposed there have been hundreds of studies of the calls of insects, reptiles, birds, and mammals draped on the analytical skeleton they compose. Maybe you, like I, have come to lean on words like *think, want,* and *know* to describe animals. But to a behavioral ecologist, these words are no-nos, and as a result, that scientist's usual dispassionate prose has all the sparkle of flat Coke. Because I have come to lean on words that are not used in behavior ecology, words like *think* and *want, know* and *feel,* I find myself unsatisfied by such a deterministic and reduced vision of living things. But then I am also turned off by what I see as overly sentimental attitudes toward animals, particularly the one I call the person-in-a-fur-coat. So many people I know cling fondly to the notion that his dog or her horse is just like us only hiding out under a coat of hair—or feathers or fins. Can I have it both ways?

Science is always a battle between the objective and the subjective, and Mike Ryan made that clear to me when I was in Gamboa and Richard Dawkins had come into the conversation. I thought I knew what to expect when I asked Mike if the ideas that came down from Tinbergen through Dawkins didn't seem just a little too reductive. "I mean, it excludes the possibility that consciousness or will play into the way an animal behaves," I said. "Certainly Griffin thought these other factors were worth exploring."

"I'm kind of agnostic on this issue," Mike said, surprising me. Then he said, "You might want to take a look at an essay called 'What Is It Like to Be a Bat?' It's by a philosopher named Thomas Nagel. He knew Griffin when they were both at Rockefeller University. Maybe that was why he chose the bat."

When I dug out the article I found that Nagel, writing in 1974, just ahead of Dawkins's *Selfish Gene,* is concerned with subjectivity, objectivity, and reductionism. "Consciousness is what makes the mind-body problem really intractable. . . ." Nagel begins on the question of whether a human can understand what goes on in a bat's mind. "Every reductionist has his favorite analogy from modern science. It is most unlikely that any of these unrelated examples of successful reduction will shed light on the relation of mind to brain."[7] Mike had gently led me, like so many of his students, from sexual urgency and closing time at the bar to philosophy of mind, and then right back into the lab and objective fact.

I can see that I am doomed to change my mind about voice as signal and science's need to reduce animal behavior to the barest facts that can be objectively observed. During the same period I visit Gene Morton and his wife, the biologist Bridget Stutchbury, at their farm in northern Pennsylvania, and I make essentially the same complaint about signals and genes to them. Gene is passionate about birds, and his book on vocal communication and signaling launched me into my inquiry. We have been speaking about birdsong and evolution, and since he is good-humored and has been generous with me, I risk an opinion. "It seems so deterministic to think that all these songs and calls are hardwired and that all we have to do to understand them is figure out the math behind the circuitry."

Gene is ready for me. He says genially, "There's lots of beauty in hardwired creations—and in the hardwiring itself."

Bridget has been listening in and points out that the ability to adapt and change may be part of the hardwiring. "There may be genes for plasticity," she points out, "and there may be plasticity in the genes themselves."

That does it. I begin to see that examining the ways animals communicate through the lenses of genetic probability, game theory, and predictive statistics has allowed biologists an at least outwardly objective view of their subjects, and this is far less hampering to animals in the wild than the person-in-a-fur-coat perspective. Also, there is the fact that gene-centered approaches have brought us, scientists and public alike, to a happy point where each new animal that comes up for scientific study is viewed on its own terms, maybe only the terms of its genes but nevertheless terms that prevent it from being hopelessly disguised by too many other assumptions. So maybe calling a red deer stag a signaler and a red deer hind a receiver seems contrived, but these notions have carried us to our current understanding of the ways animals use their voices.

Megan's research continues this line of inquiry by focusing on a particularly troublesome but only partially answered question about signals and signaling. This question has cost a good many other students of animal signaling some heavy deliberation and equation writing, and perhaps her playback experiments with deer will shed light on it. Here is that question: When is a signal a reliable indicator of the sender's intentions? When is it honest? Does the roar of a red deer stag accurately represent his fitness? And how about the sika stag with his skinny whinny? Is he some kind of imposter?

～✕～

It doesn't take us long in life to realize that not everyone can be trusted, but even worldly adults can have trouble recognizing a liar, a con, or plain old cheap talk. Telltale indications of deceptive signals can be very subtle, sometimes imperceptible, but if we are fooled into being dupes, we usually pay. That is why the question of deceit becomes important not only to game theorists but to behaviorists studying vocal communication. Nature provides plenty of subject matter. Roosters are known to cackle happily when they come upon a nice food supply. But when researchers looked quite closely at this noise making, they figured out that the roosters made their announcements of food most often when the chickens nearby were hens. Otherwise, the roosters were silent. If the chickens around them were other roosters who could eavesdrop, they were likely to make a lie of omission.[8] Among lies of commission are those of the male California ground squirrels, whose use of alarm calls has been suspected to be sometimes motivated by the male squirrel's desire to send all the members of the colony rushing belowground so that he, the one who sounded the alarm, can follow, then sneak a copulation with one of the fleeing females.

Then there is the deception of disguise, mimicry. The burrowing owl in the western United States has a number of effective predators that it tries to dodge by excavating its nest underground. Some of its mammalian predators, such as the badger, can dig well enough to excavate a sequestered owl, but the owl has one more line of defense. When it is threatened by a predator at the mouth of its burrow, the owl emits a hiss that is remarkably similar in acoustic structure to the sound of a rattlesnake's vibrating tail. This is enough to discourage most prospectors. Donald Owings, the psychologist based at University of California, Davis, who studied this deception, believes that this mimic ability is a coincidental adaptation that has spun off from the food-begging hiss the owls make when they are nestlings.[9] The mockingbird that tried to upstage Sheila Jordan was probably not trying to defend itself with mimicry but more likely indulging in aggrandizement to keep his mate occupied– "I can sing anything, anything any of these other jokers can sing, anything you need to stay with me." Its routine is a lot like the shtick of the class clown in high school, who, surrounded by females of breeding age, tries to hold everybody's attention in order to keep the girls looking at him.

It takes some imagination on the part of a scientist to reveal deceptive signals. Looking at the question of why some songbirds develop big repetoires with many different songs and phrases, English ornithologist and signaling theorist John Krebs suspected this versatility had something to do with territory defense. He concentrated a good deal of his research on a British bird called the great tit. In playback experiments he tested male birds with both large and limited repertoires and proposed that a male bird with a larger repertoire was more daunting to a prospective intruder than a bird with a repertoire of, say, a single song. Why should this be? The ingenious explanation he devised was the Beau Geste hypothesis, which he named after a character in a popular novel. In that story Beau Geste, a hapless soldier in the French Foreign Legion, became the last man standing in a desert fort. His solution to defending the fort alone was to prop up the bodies of his fallen comrades and then, to make it appear that the fort was fully manned, run behind the corpses firing their rifles. The ruse worked for Beau Geste, and Krebs suggested that male birds use a similar strategy, only substituting different songs for different rifles. Krebs's version of the deception seemed to work as well. His playback of numerous different songs sent roving male great tits into the only corner of the woods that was silent.[10]

Although Krebs's research was not extensively replicated, his hypothesis crept into the scientific literature of that period. Deception has its purposes in survival and reproduction, but Maynard Smith has pointed out that the effectiveness of deception depends on limiting its use. A call or song must be honest most of the time. It must be a reliable enough signal to prompt the receiver to react. If the boy cries wolf too often, the villagers ignore his message. For scientists, the challenge of determining what is honest about an animal voice is even trickier than the villagers' assessment quandary, and this is the challenge facing Megan Wyman.

The red deer stag's roaring and the túngara's whine-chuck are mating signals, and as such these calls need to convey the desirability of the male as a breeding partner. They need to convey his evolutionary fitness, to get the message to the female that by choosing him she will secure the best genes in the bunch for her offspring. The largest animals on the planet have the lowest voices. A case in point is the infrasound of the blue whales. All animals, including ourselves, associate a low pitch with a large body, and apparently to a red deer hind a large body is most desirable. I was amused by a friend expressing her irritation about the relentless public rant of a local political hothead. She said, "He thinks he can get away with this stuff just because he's a big guy." I said, "*Big?* He's not much taller than I am. He just has a loud bass voice." She had been duped by his voice for the same reason other animals are taken in by a low voice—and you yourself have probably been surprised by a voice that doesn't seem to match up to the body it comes from, a low voice from a really small guy or a high, thin voice from a really tall one. The big, deep bellowing of the red deer stag is intended to both intimidate any roving harem seekers from approaching the harem he has established and to attract females who, theoretically, want to transmit the capability to hold a harem to their sons. Is it an honest signal? And if it's honest, what makes it honest?

A number of biologists who contributed to signaling theory have contended that in order for a sign to be honest—in order for something I tell you to be reliable—it must be costly. It might cause the animal to expend energy or expose itself to risk. Some of the risks might be posed by "eavesdroppers" like the frog-eating bat. The túngara's whine-chuck involves a significant investment of energy, and it sounds a loud alert to nearby bats and snakes that there is a túngara close at hand. If it costs me something to make a statement, would I lie to you? The most influential formulation of the notion of costliness was the Handicap Principle proposed by Amotz Zahavi. His observation was that a signal that handicaps an individual demonstrates via inverse logic that the animal is so fit it can prevail even with the burden of this handicap. Zahavi's well-known example of this, one of his simplest, is the male peacock. In order to be able to flash the glorious fan of feathers in his tail, the peacock has to be able to drag this big, heavy ornament around with him and still be able to avoid predators.[11]

The most obvious expenses that the red deer stag chalks up with his roaring, beyond the effort of forcefully projecting his voice, are the risks of the fights a call might instigate with an eavesdropper and the effort to draw together and defend a harem. The same sound that says "big, desirable body" to hinds challenges other stags by saying "big, scary body, scarier than yours." The roaring says "keep away from these hinds," and this assurance is what the hinds want to pass on in their offspring. But at the same time, the roaring risks a fight and the loss of the stag's harem. While many, many aggressive encounters during the rut end with the roaring match, they often progress to the parallel walk and the dropped antlers, and once the stags escalate to locking horns and pushing, injury is a strong possibility.

Rather surprisingly, given the general principal of low voice = large body, when McComb began investigating the stags' roars more than twenty years ago, she was not able at that point to demonstrate that the pitch of the stag's roars was important to the hinds. But her research did establish that the hinds were persuaded by how much and how often the stags roared and that the roaring–in whatever frequency– accelerated the hinds' shift into estrus. Later, in her work with Benjamin D. Charlton and David Reby, she had more sophisticated technology. Their joint investigations turned up the facts that other eavesdropping stags respected what they perceived as lower roars– what the experiments actually tested were low-formant frequencies and higher pitches. For their part, the hinds did indeed respond to lower frequencies in the makeup of the stag's roars, indicating that they did use the signals as indications of size and breeding fitness.[12] Here Dawkins might describe the genetic transactions as "genes for low voice = more females bred = more genes for low voice." But let's go on a bit further.

Red deer stags have an intriguing feature of their vocal tract that is shared by only a few other species, including our own. Our larynxes and red deers' are retractable. We can draw them down to lower the formants of our voices. When a stag roars, he draws his larynx down to the lowest possible point in the vocal tract. This signal conveys the most extreme impression of body size that the stag can produce. Is this signal a reliable one?

"All the stags in the area are using the same strategy," Megan points out. "They are all lowering their larynxes to the furthest possible point in their vocal tracts. But the largest stag among them has the longest vocal tract, so his bottom bass note is the lowest of any of the stags." While retracting the larynx might seem to be a ruse, all the stags are using the same ruse, and the largest animal still has the lowest voice. "The signal," she advises me, "still reliably represents the relative sizes of the stags."

The stags' roaring fits neatly into the research team's hypothesis about the role of pitch in red deer's vocal communications and breeding: the estrous hinds are turned on by lots of roaring, especially calls incorporating lower resonances. Of course, this brings us right back to the landscape of female choice and Mike Ryan's observations of the structure of male túngaras' calls and their effects on mating decisions of the female frogs—the big difference between the science on the frogs and the finding for the deer is the aggression factor, and this includes violence. Nevertheless, túngara frog or red deer, it seems that if you are a male seeking to enhance your mating prospects, it matters exactly how you shape your voice.

What is the hind, the female, listening for? What is it about the male voice, this signal buzzing through her auditory brain that prods her into obedience and receptivity? After Charlton, Reby, and McComb established that the deeper resonances of the stags' bellows caused significant responses from the hinds listening to these sounds, they began to look more specifically at the acoustic properties of the roars. They were able to identify the formants, the distinguishing frequency components of the deer's voice. These are key resonances in any voice, and they show up as peaks on a spectrogram. The term *formant* comes up most often in regard to singers' voices and pronunciation and in phonetics. It is roughly equivalent to instrumentalists' use of the term *harmonics*. You can get a good sense of the formants in your own voice if you whisper a phrase. Anyone listening to you hears all the harmonic frequencies surrounding your voice but not the tone, the core frequency. You are sending the envelope without the letter. The red deer stag is sending the envelope and its contents.

Megan has begun to try to ferret out the acoustic characteristics of the stag roars that convince the females to gather and exactly what kind of differences these characteristics make. This might have been a fairly straightforward investigation if it weren't for the fact that a ringer has come on the scene, the sika, an introduced exotic. Much as it complicates discovery, this ringer has the potential to tell Megan as much about sexual attraction in the red deer's voice itself as in the voice of the ringer.

⤛ ❧ ⤜

In England the red deer rut has tapered off, and by late November the harems are beginning to disband. The hinds and stags go their separate ways. Megan is also leaving. She is headed down to New Zealand to find out what it is about the sika stag's call that seems reliable to the red deer hinds or, stated a little differently, what they have in common with the sika hinds. Deer come into rut only once a year, in England from August through the rest of autumn. So, rather than wait for the next rut in England and lose almost a year of research time, Megan chases autumn to New Zealand, half a world away. Red deer and a few sika deer are farmed there to serve the trade in antlers for Asian medicine, for meat, and to stock exotic game farms. Antlers in velvet, the coat of tiny hairs that covers racks early in their annual regrowth, are the most desirable for traditional Chinese medicine; pieces of these are boiled up into a kind of tea that is ingested to improve vitality, forestall aging, and cure impotence. The hunters who patronize exotic game farms have learned that the sika's secretive habits and the natural camouflage of its spots make it elusive, and it is rumored that, once sighted, the sika is harder to kill with a bullet than most deer. The deer farms raise not only sikas but also red deer, wapiti, and various hybrids of these species. Their hybridization programs are aimed at improving the deer's meat and velvet production.

Megan tells me that one way for her to figure out what preferences the red deer and sika hinds have in common would be to stand her experiment with the two deer on its head and consider how a sika hind would react to the roar of a red deer stag. Would she prefer the call of a male of her own kind? Would she show any interest in the big, deep voice of the red deer?

In New Zealand Megan travels from deer farm to deer farm, hopping between the North and South Islands, and she is watching a large number of females, red deer and sika. Occasionally I hear from her. "Even watching this happen with so many deer, it is still not clear to me that the hinds are responding with sexual attraction," she reports. "I have definitely noticed here that the red hinds move towards sika calls"—as they did in Richmond Park. "In many trials, they literally run for the speaker. But I don't know why they are running for it. Are they attracted? Are they curious? Are they being aggressive?"

Most mammal voices are a rich blend of a fundamental pitch with a halo of formants, while birdcalls can approach a cleaner tone. In order to verify that the acoustics of the stags' roaring and moaning are what really bring a response in the hinds, Megan will need to try altogether different kinds of sounds on them, say, white noise, which is an equal mix of all frequencies. Or maybe she will test the hinds with female alarm calls or the voice of a predator. Then, to confirm that the calls of both kinds of stags actually produce a sexual response in the hinds, she says, she'll have to explore the internal physiology of the hinds. "One question I'll need to ask in order to get a look at what's really parallel between the species is whether the red deer calls can advance estrus in the sika hinds the way they do in the red deer hinds. And vice versa, can the sika calls advance estrus in the red deer hinds?"

To get at these questions, Megan will need to look beyond signals and game theory, frequency and response, into the physiological nitty-gritty of signal honesty and reliability. "For instance," she points out, "I'm *not* sure that when the red deer drops his larynx this movement is under his voluntary control. Maybe it's just a matter of how much force he uses, how much energy he puts into the roar. I'm going to be looking into the anatomy of the vocal tracts in both species and their hybrids. The red deer has these ligaments that attach the larynx to the hyoid bone near the tongue, and they're very stretchy. We think the sika does not actually lower his larynx. Although he has ligaments like these, they are shorter and not so stretchy—but maybe he has some other kind of elasticity in the vocal tract."

In the human animal, of course, the falling and rising of the larynx is, to one extent or another, under the control of the signaler. A really good signaler, like Renée Fleming, can transmit a seamless stream of signals up and down more than two octaves, and this makes those signalers attractive in many ways, including sexually.

In my conversations with scientists, the force of voice in sexual attraction, especially female decision making, and the force of sex hormones in that process have come up so often now that I have stopped thinking about it consciously. To me it is a given: the way a voice works in the reproduction and eventually in the survival of an animal is the reason to dwell on any call, song, signal, or whatever you want to call it. This is the fundamental assumption behind Mike Ryan's long, increasingly elaborate study of the túngara frogs: what is it, specifically, about the whine-chuck that makes the female come to the male? And what are the biological connections between the vibrations received through the eardrum and the activation of sex hormones?

In trying to sort out the mechanisms behind the hybridization of the sika and the red deer, however, Megan has begun to tackle a much broader, slippier set of questions. These have to do with the way Darwin's tree of life branches. The red deer's roar and the sika's moan sound the way they sound now because, for now, that's what works for them. But that can and will change, especially because of the mixing of the two species. This is what you would expect. Your voice may sound very much like your mother's or father's, so much so that friends may mistake you for one of them when you answer the phone. But you don't sound exactly like your parent. The generation that separates you has wrought changes. About ten years ago, a team led by A. M. Long from Ireland compared the acoustic structures of the red deer, sika, and hybrid red deer-sika roars and found that what our human ears detect is, in fact, true: the hybrid deer, the slighter red deer with spots, have a hybrid voice, a lower, less shimmying version of the sika whinny. How will this mixed sound function as an aphrodisiac to link stags and hinds, and will these matings result in offspring that reinforce the identity so that eventually the hybrid will emerge as a species of its own?

Ultimately, these questions lead to—and here is where the footing gets a little treacherous—questions about the process of evolution: How does the evolution of a vocal signal influence sexual selection and its evolution? And what is the relationship between the evolution of sexual selection and the emergence of new species?

"The need to create a mating call that helps prospective mates find fit partners is one factor that drives the evolution of signals," Megan tells me, "and the other driver of signal evolution is the need for mating calls that allow an animal to discriminate between its own kind and other species. This helps to prevent animals from wasting reproductive success by mating with animals that aren't likely to produce viable offspring. That's why I'm interested in exploring situations where reproductive calls may not be functioning as they are traditionally supposed to." In the simplest, most immediate terms, running between hemispheres to observe the red deer and sikas is Megan's attempt to reveal the boundary between choosing mates and choosing between their own kind and other kinds of animal. She has a big agenda. The answers to her challenging question about deer and their voices may shed light on the force of voice in the evolution of other animal families, but she is only getting a start.

What makes it feasible for Megan to even consider tackling this issue is the simplicity of the deer's vocal communications. A red deer roar and the sika moan are single calls that are used only during one season a year for just two primitive purposes, to compete with other males and to attract mates. Roaring is the kind of vocalizing that predominates during this period, and when a stag issues this simple, rude noise, there is no confusing its purpose or its results.

But when it comes to other animals with more highly developed communications and more complex societies, the complications of approaching questions about voice and evolution rise exponentially. The songbirds, for instance, provide abundant, often-conflicting evidence on this topic. They hybridize or at least split off in different races rather freely, and the sounds of their singing and calling, the frequencies, harmonics, and their durations, may both support the persistence of a species and drive the emergence of new ones.

There are too many species, too much evidence, for me to tackle it all here, but looking at even one bird and the way voice and mating and species work could give me a little bit of insight. As I leave Megan's deer and their roars and moans, the songbirds are much on my mind, and I am renewing a long conversation with David Logue, the young biologist whom Eugene Morton sent me to. I am hoping for one bird, and David comes up with three.

# 4

# Rules to Sing By

~

Since we last spoke David Logue has married and moved from his postdoc position at the University of Lethbridge in Alberta to an assistant professorship at the University of Puerto Rico in Mayagüez. Ornithology is a huge field densely populated with scientists. Because the redoubtable Gene Morton recommended David and because even at this early stage in his career he has the songbirds pretty well sorted out, he has become my bird guy. He's the one to show me how voice and mating work in the birds' aerial umwelt.

It's good to have his guidance because when we come to the birds, the complexity of their social lives ratchets up dramatically from those of the red deer and the sika. Furthermore, there are more calls and songs than there are species of birds and the structures of many of their calls and songs are complex and can vary over their lifetimes. There is so much birdsong to consider, and I think that along with scientists, we are drawn to these songs—this form of signaling, as Maynard Smith,

Krebs, and Dawkins would have it—because bird voices fall neatly within our own hearing ranges and because the analogies to cadence, tempo, and phrases in our own music have proved unavoidable.

You can get a pretty good notion of how much birdsong there is in the hour before the sun comes up on a spring or summer day when all the birds begin. Their voices make staggered entrances until the choir is complete. When you consider the number and variety of birds all giving voice in the same few minutes, the so-called dawn chorus is nothing short of amazing. It is a crowded acoustic space and an ancient mystery. In many cases the songs birds sing at dawn use different sounds than those the birds make during the day. Although each bird is competing in a very noisy atmosphere—the songs of other birds and the sounds made by insects, moving water, and human activity churn through the same airspace—the persistence of this ritual chorus indicates that none of the birds is wasting its energy. But what cues prompt the entry of the different voices and what purposes the dawn singing serves remain secrets about the great majority of songbirds.

These secrets are only a few of the many that have survived centuries of scientific investigation. As early as the eighteenth century, the English curate turned naturalist Gilbert White noted, "The language of birds is very ancient, and, like other ancient modes of speech, very elliptical: little is said, but much is meant and understood."[1] In the meantime, ornithologists and animal behaviorists like David pursue the mysteries of song bird by bird. Often using birds as common as the swamp sparrow and the red-winged blackbird, twentieth- and now twenty-first-century researchers have produced volumes of findings on the function of song in mating and defense, regional dialects in song sung by the same species, the role of mimicry, and any number of questions about whether and how birds learn to sing.

For scientists, one of the most baffling of song forms is the duet, the tightly synchronized sharing of song by male and female birds. David has been obsessed by bird duets since his first day in graduate school at Colorado State University. "There was something very appealing about duetting," David told me—ornithologists use the noun *duet* most often as a verb. "It was a very mysterious phenomenon that hadn't been studied very much. Nobody knew why birds coordinated their singing this way, and it was just so elegant and beautiful—I mean, it's *couples* singing together." He began to study the duets of a Neotropical bird called the black-bellied wren, and for six years he traveled back and forth from his North American bases to his field research in Gamboa, Panama. The result was his recognition of what he calls a duet *code,* a set of rules that govern the two phrases of the song and their timing.

Now, in his office on the campus in Mayagüez, his password to the university's computer network is a sly variation of "a bird in the hand is worth two in the bush." The adage perfectly describes his situation: the black-bellied wren, on which he has published a good deal, is his bird-in-the-hand, and he has just opened research projects on the duets of two birds-in-the-bush. He is at the beginning of both projects, doing the footwork and sound collection for playback experiments. But he will use his experience with the black-bellied wren to build his understanding of the duets of his new subjects.

David's birds-in-the-bush are very different types of birds with very different voices. Heard in quick succession, the voices and vocalizations of the elfin-woods warbler and the Puerto Rican parrot go a long way toward suggesting the prodigious variety of bird sound and birdsong that crowds acoustic channels around the world.

Both birds live only in Puerto Rico. Both are rare. One is listed as vulnerable, and one is hovering at the brink of extinction. The elfin-woods warbler is a tiny black-and-white bird that has been thought until quite recently to inhabit only the highest altitudes on the island, and the brilliant green Puerto Rican parrot is a larger, heavy bird that leads its loud, scrappy existence in the rain forests nestled low among the mountains. The primary threats to both birds' survival are the confinement of their populations to an island and their low numbers—once an animal becomes scarce, the odds against each individual are greater and the toll taken by predation, disease, or environmental change is proportionally much more damaging.

David's first bird-in-the-bush lives in the mountains not far from Mayagüez on the west end of the island. A decayed industrial town hesitantly making its way back to life, Mayagüez is poised on a narrow shelf of lowland that mediates between the big surf for which the Porta del Sol region is famous and the mountains that stand up suddenly a few miles from the beach. Narrow roads—narrower even than the stingy tracks of pavement that string the beaches together—make tortuous connections from the coast to mountain villages. At 5:30 one morning, an hour before it is light, David and his graduate student Daniel Pereira drive with me up one of these tricky passages to Maricao, a high village that is the center of Puerto Rican coffee production. Some of the curves where the land drops sharply away from the road are pretty scary, but they offer momentary glimpses in the near dark of scattered shaded coffee plantings, where the fronds of banana trees sometimes provide the shade. A couple of miles north of Maricao, just below the peak of a mountain, we pull the car off on the wrong side of the road, and David and Daniel off-load sound equipment from the trunk to their backpacks. We are looking for the elfin-woods warbler, and this is the first time I have gone looking for any bird with someone who knows how to do that. It is also the first time since I began to pursue animal voices that my hearing gets in the way.

David is lean with an angular face, close-cropped brown hair that runs down into equally close-cropped sideburns, and startlingly bright blue-gray eyes. They are the first sign of what I have learned is a restlessly active mind. The next one is the speed at which he snaps up any lead in the conversation. He is intense, interested in all things all the time, and he never seems to push the pause button. The very dark-haired Daniel is a good deal younger than David, just beginning a master's program, and, at least on the outside, more reflective. He is quieter and, as a Colombian in Puerto Rico, has a visitor's polite reserve. Even so, his keenness about the warbler is evident. They speak in Spanish about the strategy for the morning. Their goal is to use recorded song to call the warblers in close to them and then try to record the live birds' voices as they sing back.

The trailhead is not at all obvious, and the two men have to start walking toward its cryptic opening before I can even see it. The reason David knows how to find this trail is that when he went looking for the bird the first time his colleague at the university, Carlos Delannoy-Juliá, gave him its specific location. Delannoy is a conservation biologist who has developed most of the information we have thus far about the elfin-woods warbler, including the fact that it sings in duet. The warbler was first observed by Angela Kay Kepler and

Cameron Kepler on the east end of the island in 1968, and it was formally described as a species in 1972. During the 1980s Carlos Delannoy made intermittent observations of the elfin-woods warbler, and from 2003 to 2006 he carried out an island-wide survey of the bird. If anyone knew where to find the warbler, he did.

The sun is just beginning to show on the horizon, and I expect to hear the beginning of a dawn chorus. But the woods are surprisingly quiet, only a few weak titters.

"They're not singing much," David agrees about the birds.

The trail is a thread barely as wide as my foot, and it scrolls up and down the edge of the mountainside through the scrubby trees and vines that take over near the tops of the mountains. This scraggly growth is what the Puerto Ricans call the elfin woods, and although the warbler is quite diminutive, the *elf* in its name applies to the dwarf trees rather than to the bird. As we make our way through these woods, birdsong is picking up. Several voices begin to ring tentatively, and after a few minutes Daniel, who is ahead, stops and looks up suddenly, then points to some foliage high above us. I hear a sharp, thin note, and it apparently comes from one bird. When David listens, he says, "Yeah, give it a try."

Daniel brings out a long shotgun microphone, puts the two parts together, and waits for the song to start up again. When it does, I can't hear it—I'm beginning to find the new limits on my hearing—and after he turns off the microphone Daniel nods toward the mountaintop and says, "He went further up."

I drop back to get David's commentary. "Just one bird right now," he says, still listening and looking into the leaves, tracking something. "There. See him?"

I do. He is a small, dark shadow streaking against the early sun. He lands momentarily behind some high leaves and then speeds off again.

"Backlighting is a big problem," David says about the general problem of finding birds. There is also the fact that it all goes on over our heads, the singing, the flight, the sparring, the mating.

"Try calling them," David prompts, and when Daniel holds the digital recorder away from his body to broadcast, David listens and says, "That volume is going to be a problem." It is already a problem to me.

I have to catch up to Daniel to hear the song at all. I am really leaning on my ears and find this a little frustrating. The sound isn't the call I heard before. It is a thin, rhythmic rattle without a tonal center. It isn't at all what I have been listening for, certainly nothing like a melody. Even though we're not hearing as much birdsong as we would have expected and the airwaves in the woods are relatively uncluttered, I am struck by how difficult it must be for a bird to find a space in the soundscape where its song—the frequency, melodic motion, and rhythm—can cut through to reach the other birds for which it is intended. How does this happen? And how does the bird become tuned to the particular song that it's intended to hear? Does this work something like the way the red deer hind has come to be tuned to low roars? Or does its evolution involve a more intricate, tangled system of perception and response?

After a few moments I come back to attention when the thin, insectlike note I heard first sounds nearer and louder. Maybe this is part two of the duet.

But then David identifies the sound: "The tody." It is the song of another bird, and Daniel and I begin to search the foliage on the slope below us. I'm a little baffled, but the thin, sharp chirp repeats several times until I finally spot what the other two already hold in their binoculars. The Puerto Rican tody is a truly tiny bird, smaller than the elfin-woods warbler, and bright green with a white belly and a bright red patch under its beak. It is a lovely little thing but not the bird we are seeking.

If there are elfin-wood warblers here other than the one that passed us on its way up the mountain, they aren't paying any attention to the songs from Daniel's playback. Finding birds is a pastime for those who are patient. I consider how many hours must be invested in those fabulous bird photographs in the nature magazines. Maybe capturing the sound is a little easier. At about 10 A.M., we are working our way down the mountainside, and the few birds we have been hearing seem to tire of the singing effort.

"Ten more minutes," David decides about the playback. We make a slow trip back up the trail, still listening. We see a number of other birds, most often the bananaquit, a short black bird with a yellow belly, a strongly curved beak, and a voice like a noisy insect. Our limited sightings make me realize that I have always associated *tropical* with rich density and diversity of species, but Puerto Rico, although tropical, has nowhere near the ebullient abundance and diversity of animals as Panama. David tells me that this is because Puerto Rico is an island and that has constrained evolutionary processes.

The fact that it has been difficult to see and hear the birds impresses on me the diligence and effort that has been put into birdwatching and bird research over the centuries. The elfin-woods warbler may be a tough customer and there are undoubtedly easier birds to observe, but even so, birdwatching is a demanding pastime and a tricky art. I can see that it has taken many, many people as driven as David Logue—perhaps beginning with Gilbert White and his assiduous journal, which contains what are believed to be the first observations in English—to see, hear, and set down the records. I can only imagine the frustration along the way, but David doesn't betray any.

"We need to do something about that volume," he reminds himself, but he is philosophical about the low rate of return on the morning's hike. "It's just the beginning of the breeding season. It will probably pick up later, and some of the birds out here will sing like crazy."

Singing, he explains, is different from simple calls or utterances like squawks, and song includes a remarkable variety of sounds, from relatively brief, repeated sequences of notes like the robin's song to longer, intricately ornamented phrases drawn from huge repertoires, like the mockingbird's (this bird has earned its Latin name, *Mimus polyglottos*). While we may like to think of our own singing as personal expression, this is not a bird's purpose in singing. A bird can sing to stake out a territory, to attract and guard a mate, or to defend a nest. About mates, I should point out that for the many animals that form male-female pairs for the purposes of raising their offspring, this pairing is a social enterprise. But there are also matings that occur outside the institution of the pair. This is why mate guarding is as necessary for happy bird couples as it is for red deer stags trying to hold a harem.

If there is one dominant fact about birdsong it is that all birds in both hemispheres sing much more at the time of year when pairing and nesting begin, and the immediate trigger for this is a rise in the birds' testosterone levels. Testosterone is a steroid hormone that is commonly associated with maleness. In mammals, for instance, both male and female produce testosterone, but females produce much less of it than males—the adult human female makes only a tenth as much of the stuff as the adult male—and the male and female brains take up testosterone differently. Nevertheless, it is at play in both sexes. Studies on a wide range of animals implicate testosterone in signaling. While this hormonal vocal prompt is the same for the red deer stags as it is for birds, the social bonds between the male and female birds last longer, birdcall forms are much more complex, and the relation of vocalizing to evolutionary fitness is much less direct. With birds, what reproductive hormones trigger is something along the lines of art and culture—but this is hardly an original observation.

Across most of North America and in other temperate climates, birdsong is performed almost exclusively by male birds. The male is the one who has the time and the assignment. His mate of the season is busy laying eggs, brooding, and stuffing the oversize maws of their chicks. Although the male may help with the feeding, his main job is to stand guard over the pair's summer territory, and he sings to ward off any intruders, birds of any kind and predators. Their territory, their pairing, and their family are temporary. The birds initiate all this when they fly north and arrive in their nesting grounds, and they end it when the birds scatter back south.

"But here in the Neotropics," David tells me, "bird families are more stable." They aren't nomadic, and for many species, the pairs are more or less permanent. Because tropical birds aren't working under time pressure to produce chicks that can travel before their impending migration, the breeding and brooding schedules are more relaxed. The male and female share the work of raising the young, and both the male and female birds sing. On the whole, however, tropical birds don't spend as much time singing as birds that migrate and have to be efficient about making themselves known to potential mates and rivals. Fortunately for David, the black-bellied wren he studied previously is an exception to this last rule, and "they sing quite a lot, in fact," he reports.

"Will the elfin-woods warbler sing that much?"

"We'll have to see," David says as we climb the steps in the university's new biology building to listen to recordings of the elfin-woods warbler and the black-bellied wren. When he types in his bird-in-the-hand password and his computer comes on, the first sounds he plays for me are elfin-woods warblers in a duet. The thin rattle we heard on the mountain is there, and it is linked to a brief series of sharp *chits*.

"It may take some time before we get this in the field." He isn't discouraged, just aligning his expectations with what is happening on the trail. "In fact, we may not be able to get much data. But it wouldn't be the first time somebody had to let go of a project for that reason—any scientist who's honest will tell you that. And the research I did on the black-bellied wren started out worse, much worse. But it turned out to be really productive.

"Gene Morton"—Smithsonian ornithologist Eugene Morton—"told me about the bird. He'd seen it, knew where it liked to hang out, and he'd heard the duets. But the first year I was down in Panama I'd get up every day and go out to the places he told me about, spend the whole day, and not see a single bird. I knew I was screwing up, and so I felt lousy about the whole project. It was a low point. I wasn't sure I even knew how to find the bird I was staking my degree on."

A photo he took of the black-bellied wren is posted in a prominent place on the wall in David's small office. The bird is very shy and elusive, and compared to the truly flamboyant birds in the Canal Zone—the toucans, the flashy parrots, and the bright green but stolid motmot—the black-bellied wren's coloring is rather dull. It is the size of a large sparrow, and for a little decoration, it does have a striped black pattern below its white bib. But it is not any more eye-catching than a large sparrow with a splash of white on its breast. Although a whole family of these wrens will often move about together, their secretive habits enable even a group of four or five of them to stay out of sight.

What the bird lacks in flash it more than makes up for in song. Both males and females are prodigious singers. They sing in slow phrases and repeat them. And repeat them. And repeat them. Like the mockingbird on the University of Massachusetts campus, they seem to find it hard to stop. It was this fact that David exploited when he finally succeeded in catching a few elusive birds to band them. He played recordings of their songs, eventually luring dupe wrens into mist nets, and once they were banded, he could identify which bird was singing what to whom. This is the same general procedure he plans to use with the elfin-woods warbler, but the fact that the little bird is vulnerable, or endangered, as Carlos Delannoy would like it to be listed, will make it necessary to use very painstaking safeguards to control the amount of stress David's research might subject the population to.

On his computer, the black-bellied wren's singing takes up a sizable chunk of memory. David has myriad files to demonstrate the wrens' duets. While he scans through them, he imitates the typical phrases, making a low little scat song and tying it up at the end with a rising phrase. "*Whee-pheew, foh-loddle-loddle-lay.* The guidebooks say it sounds like *Cream of Wheat.* That's not what I get out of it. But all you have to do is hear it and you'll know it."

At first I have trouble hearing two voices. I can't tell where one leaves off and the other begins. But by the time we tour a good number of the files on his computer I have the hang of it. The male and female wrens are committed not only to their partnership to hatch and raise their young, but also to their continual enterprise of song. The male bird sings, the female responds; the female bird sings, the male responds. Over and over, without an audible pause between each bird's part. There is no slice of silence as there is between the soprano and the tenor on the opera stage.

With the wrens, it happens even faster, maybe faster in tighter sequence than you and I can hear and process sound and then produce voice to respond. It's a testament to the processing power of the wren's or any bird's brain. If you have been clinging fondly to the notion that a bird's brain is a tiny, inadequate organ of intelligence, you can hit the delete key and erase that from your mental screen. In relation to the size of their heads, most birds have fairly large brains. Birds in the parrot and crow family have a brain-size-to-body-size ratio comparable to the higher primates, and at least one group of neuroscientists, led by Harvey J. Karten, has established similarities between the lower-brain architecture of birds and mammals (thus, by extension, humans).[2] But one feature that distinguishes the lower brains of songbirds is the so-called high vocal center. Not much is known about how this area of the songbird brain works, but it seems to serve as a dedicated song processor and may help account for songbirds' capacity for almost instantaneous call and response.

∼⤳∼

"So why do two birds do this duetting thing?" David asks rhetorically after a couple of song bouts played on his computer. He loves to pose rhetorical questions and stack them up quickly before you can spit out an answer to the first one. "How does it help them succeed?"

Fortunately, I don't try to answer these questions, because there could be numerous correct solutions to the puzzle he poses. The first observations of the precisely coordinated vocal exchanges between a pair of birds that we call duets were those made in 1897 of an Australian bird, the magpie lark, and published by N. A. Cobb in an agricultural journal. In the early 1970s the Cambridge biologist William H. Thorpe, a colleague of Tinbergen who championed the idea of bringing him to England, published a digest of what was then known about duetting and the species that duet. Now, a hundred years after Cobb's work, David's colleague Michelle Hall, a researcher at the Max Planck Institute for Ornithology, has published a comprehensive review updating Thorpe's work and summarizing the ecological and evolutionary functions of the duet. In her discussion of function, Hall pointed out that pairs of birds in wildly different species with amazingly different voices coordinate their songs as a statement of a joint theme, and among the various functions that have been proposed for duetting she singled out cooperative defense, mate guarding, maintaining a bird's place in the pair, and signaling commitment to a mate. But she is quick to point out that for each of the species, the function of locking the song of the male and female together is usually some unique combination of those outlined in the hypotheses.[3]

Singing, I know, is costly. It consumes a bird's energy and time and it alerts predators to the bird's presence. But it doesn't cost the bird as much as actual combat with competitors, and because sound is a very rapid, very effective means of communication, singing is a good substitute for physical contact. Singing or calling can divert an approaching bird intruder or competitor or ward off a predator before an attack becomes necessary. It can mediate disputes and spares the birds the danger and energy of physical assault. The way these sounds work as a defense is not well understood. One intriguing theory involves a phenomenon called ranging, which Gene Morton proposed. Because sound atrophies as it travels through air or water, birds and other animals can judge quite accurately the distance between themselves and the singer they are listening to by the degree of decay in the sound.

In addition to song's function as territory defense, it is possible that the strength of singing also helps attract the female and to guard this mate the way a stag guards his harem. It has been proposed that a female bird equates the amount of energy a male bird puts into singing with the amount of energy he will put into helping her raise their young. This prediction effect of energetic vocalizing would not be possible, of course, for the red deer hinds, whose mates are elsewhere when their calves are born. But for birds, strong singing may signal a good mate.

❧

For a single singer like the túngara or red deer stag, the communications rationale is straightforward: sender, signal, receiver. When birds duet–I've given in to using this as a verb–there are two senders, two signals, and, along with any nearby birds that might be eavesdropping, two receivers.

"I think I'm the first person to look at behavior and the structure of duets," David tells me. "What I am asking is, What are the individual birds doing? And how does that produce these song structures?"

In the black-bellied wren duet that David is playing for me on his computer, each sender is continually altering its part.

"Each male bird has probably forty different songs he knows how to sing." In the bird world, this is a good-sized repertoire but not so prodigious as the number of tunes learned by some of the song sparrows. "But listen to this," David instructs. "The low-pitched parts are from the male and the high ones are from the female."

The computer speakers let loose a rollicking whistled song, and as David indicates the switches from male song to female song, I begin to hear how the duet works. The male's rich phrases alternate strictly with the female's soprano warble to make a seamless six-phrase duet.

It is possible that the wrens' duet serves as territory defense. One explanation of this is similar to John Krebs's Beau Geste hypothesis that large song repertoires simulated the voices of multiple birds, and proposed that duets may also create the impression of what rock producer Phil Spector called the wall of sound to let any stranger know the pair will mount a unified defense. In a subtle variation of this explanation, David has proposed that, by trading phrases, the black-bellied wrens are assuring *each other* that they will back each other up.

"If I play it song-by-song, you can hear that the male switches songs like 'A-B-A.' " Sure enough, the male's first and third songs are identical, but the second one is completely different.

David reclicks the same sound file, and as I try to hear what he is getting at, he says, "A pattern, right? It's a little different, but there's still a pattern."

Sure, it repeats and repeats. Sequences are the basis of music, the building blocks of music. Music moves through your brain in sequences and in bits of sequences, and I am so accustomed to hearing music that nothing about patterns in the wrens' songs strikes me as remarkable. Logue is a sometime musician like me—"I've got some talent, but I'm not gifted." First, though, he is a biologist, and for him, the repeated sequences were a revelation.

"Now check this out: the female switches along with him. See? She answers his A with one song type, but she answers his B with a different one."

These switches were the key to David's understanding how this particular bird's duets work.

"I had been slogging along, moving ahead one step at a time. Then suddenly I began to hear that the male would switch songs and the female would immediately switch her song. It was a code."

To test this idea in the field he ran playback experiments where he would play male songs in random order and see how she answered. "The remarkable thing was, she was so consistent with her answers—for every male song she had a particular response. And she also showed me she has some flexibility—if she hears a new male song that is similar to a song she's heard before, she can apply the code right away."

The wrens have a set of very real rules that they follow consistently. They have expectations for phrases and the pitch contours they should be hearing, as if these had been written into a score, and in fact, W. H. Thorpe recorded the bird duets he identified with musical notation. If one bird didn't hear what it expected, it gave up on the exchange.

"I thought revealing this code was something major, really big, you know, an article in *Nature*," David says wryly. "In a limited way, though, it was a kind of breakthrough."

It is all about timing, about tempo and rhythm. Each bird abides by its own internal tempo but also listens to its partner and adjusts as the partner speeds up and slows down. The calling is sustained. It's endurance singing, and the birds' stamina reminds me of a remarkable duet in Puccini's *Madama Butterfly*. Lieutenant Pinkerton, an American naval officer posted to Japan, makes a "Japanese" marriage to young Cio-Cio–Butterfly. Assured that such a marriage can be canceled at any time, Pinkerton doesn't take the arrangement seriously, but Butterfly does and is devastated when her husband ships out with the Navy and leaves her with child. When Pinkerton returns, "legitimate" wife in the background, Butterfly is overjoyed to see him because she has not yet figured out that he intends to take away their child. She leaves no room for silence in singing her impassioned responses to him, no room for explanation or qualification. The duet flows from her, and Pinkerton's song carries on between the overpowering phrases of her own. In the duet between the black-bellied wrens there is, even to my ear, an anxious, obsessive quality to the female's timing of her entries.

"Why is it so important that she get it right?" David asks, another one of his rhetorical questions.

He waits, and when I don't come back right away, he turns the question around. "What happens if she *doesn't* get it right?"

Thinking about David's code and its rules, I realize that his analogy to code and language might just as well be an analogy to music.

Although birdsong is often casually called music and a number of composers like Messiaen refer back to nature with their imitations of birdsong, the analogies I see between the duet code and music are structural. Birdsong is a set of tones, a set of frequencies, strung together in a rhythm. Similarly, music, other than the randomly distributed sounds of so-called aleatory music, is based on sets of frequencies in a rhythmic string of sounds, repetitions of these sequences, and, like the duet code, on the *expectation* of repetition. Enough repetition of these strings of sound and the musical spaces between the sounds and you begin to anticipate the sounds you will hear next. Is that the way the birds process their song, through repetition and expectation?

"So it's like jazz guys trading fours?" I offer. The piano player takes the first four measures of a tune and makes it personal with improvisation, then the guitarist moves on to the next four-bar phrase, acknowledging the piano player's innovations and adding a few more.

"No," David says quickly, "because when you're trading fours, everybody is working with the same set of chord changes. These birds each have their own set of tones—so what happens if she *doesn't* get it right?"

I don't come back with an answer, so he gives it to me. "He *attacks*," David winds up his monologue, "because he isn't convinced she's the female who is his mate. If she isn't, he might not want her anywhere near the eggs or juveniles he is responsible for—remember, we're in the Tropics, so he is sharing the work of raising the family."

It's a dangerous game. The male calls *foh-loddle-loddle,* and while his last note is still sounding, the female's warbling response has to come at exactly the right split second, on the right part of the beat, and continue in exactly the right yodel, the right sequence of melodic intervals. Otherwise, she could be beaten up.

The stakes are high, and I wonder how she calculates exactly when to come in. And because young birds are believed to go through a phase of trial and error in developing their songs, I wonder how the wrens learn their parts without failing in that process to create the duet bond in the first place. Maybe it's something like the way we learn to play music with other musicians. You learn how to blow and finger the notes of a scale. After that you have to learn the rules about how to connect those notes to form a musical phrase and how to link that phrase to others to make a musical statement. Then, once you have all that down pat, you have to figure out just when it will be appropriate to make your statement for the other musicians. Fortunately, your personal or reproductive survival doesn't depend on your learning those rules. But if music isn't related to survival in some way, why has human capacity for sophisticated music evolved with us? Even as I frame this question, I am aware that any number of theories in language, music, and evolution propose that our musicality is a lovely by-product of evolution that confers no fitness on the music maker. But don't the brief, whistled melodies repeated so obsessively by the pair of black-bellied wrens contribute to the wrens' evolutionary survival?

"It may be something like a password," David says about the strictness of the code, but I don't understand why the two wrens need a password. While birds have sound perception that pretty much aligns with our own, their visual capabilities are far sharper than ours. "Can't they just recognize the other wren on sight?"

All the birds look pretty much alike, he explains, although the males are larger than the females, and in the Tropics they are often seeing one another the way we see them, against backlighting or dark foliage. "Remember how hard it was for you to see that warbler this morning?"

"But *you* had to be able to tell them apart," I point out about David's research subjects.

He gives me a long look. On his computer, the wrens are still singing their parts. "It's not that easy, you know."

I'm finding it hard to give up on visual recognition. "Then how come I can order chicks and specify how many pullets, how many roosters?"

"Those chicken sexers"—he smiles a little at this term—"those guys are very, very highly trained. For my work, I had to get a little blood." He caught the wrens in a mist net, took a blood sample from each for genetic sexing, and banded them with color-coded bands he can read with binoculars.

Now it seems to make sense. If birds of the same species and sex look so similar we have to band them in order to identify them, the situation must be nearly the same for the birds themselves. They probably have to deal with the same difficulties I experienced in the elfin woods beyond Maricao: fast birds about the size of a leaf flying into foliage and backlighting that obscured coloration and only showed a silhouette. It must be hard for the birds, even with their very acute eyesight, to get a good look at each other until they are standing on the same branch. But it is critical to the survival of an animal to be able to recognize its family members. If you can't identify your mate, how can you ensure the persistence of your genes? The wrens are engaged in a game of blindman's bluff, and the outcome determines their success.

In a universe where any bird of the same sex could be an identical twin to all the other birds of that species and sex, the coded duet could be a means of positive identification, a continuing reassurance that the female bird is the wren's mate and not some look-alike intruder. Here, the notion that the voice stands in for physical contact to mediate aggression seems to work in a situation that doesn't involve sexual competition. The nonstop singing is an energy-saving alternative to constant scrapping.

This is roughly the evolutionary rationale for the wren's duets, the mechanism that helps the bird breed successfully. This rationale flows directly from Richard Dawkins's perception that an individual animal, say, a black-bellied wren, is simply a temporary vessel for its genes: the black-bellied wren exists solely to replicate itself, and any adaptation that helps it do this will likely be carried forward to the next generation. Any change in an individual wren that works against duplication will likely not be transmitted through many generations. Genes directly control physical traits like feather color and beak shape, and behavior, which may be tied to physical characteristics, can also be directly inherited. It can be innate.

Like most animal behaviorists, David is preoccupied with the notion of adaptation, and now that he has identified the wren's adaptation of song, he needs to find out *how* it is perpetuated.

"I would really like to know how she gets the code. Learning must be involved, but when does she learn and who does she learn from?"

David's questions about the black-bellied wren's song learning and questions about vocal learning in general are part of a broad stream of inquiry that began with Tinbergen's work on instinct and that runs parallel to current research on how we acquire music and language. These questions are difficult to get at because, although some animals, like dolphins and some species of birds, continue to learn new songs and calls throughout life, more often vocal learning is concentrated in the early phases of the animal's life. This is the reason often cited to explain why adults are slower to pick up new languages than children. It's also likely that song learning, which in songbirds seems to be one of the functions of the high vocal center, is related to other activities that require intricate mental and physical coordination. Quite recent research in musical perception finds that moving to music, dancing, is a talent that only vocal-learning animals have. The boogying of the cockatoo Snowball has brought him stardom on YouTube and considerable attention from perceptual psychologists.

The early phases of life, prime time for vocal learning, are unsteady states of neurobiology and cognitive development, as Peter Marler, at the University of California, Davis, has pointed out. He is the person best known for research on vocal learning, and although his long career was devoted primarily to birdsong, he also ventured beyond ornithology to make fundamental observations of primate vocalizations. As a graduate student at Cambridge University working under W. H. Thorpe, Marler began a long-term study of the songs of a common European bird with a big song repertoire that Thorpe himself had studied, the chaffinch. Thorpe had acquired one of the new sound spectrograph machines, and Marler began to collect chaffinch songs in various locations throughout Europe and to analyze the sounds on the spectrograph. Like Thorpe, Marler was heavily influenced by Tinbergen and Lorenz, and although he was aware that Lorenz believed that the acoustic structure of the signals birds made was more or less arbitrary, he thought this assumption deserved questioning. He wanted to see if changes in the chaffinch's circumstances changed the acoustic properties of its song, and one way to do that was to compare songs taken from birds in different geographical locations. He found significant differences among the songs of the different populations, which led him to the conclusions that the structure of their song had evolved with its function and that regional dialects' differences in these signals, were, to one extent or another, learned. These insights opened the door to a lifelong study of acoustic learning and the social, hormonal, neurological, and genetic factors that shape the learning process. Having established that birds' learning takes place early, both in the nest and throughout the young birds' first year, Marler continued to explore exactly which aspects of song are innate and which are learned—what part is nature, what part nurture. While these questions remain open for many species, Marler's work has attracted the attention of linguists, psychologists, and evolutionary biologists concerned with human language acquisition.

The fact of song learning helps account for the phenomenal number and range of birdsongs, song types, dialects, and rhythmic patterns, and that is why birdsong is such a rich demonstration that vocalizing is an obvious sign of culture. Birds sing a song or a set of songs, and when they mate—often with the help of their song—and their eggs hatch, their chicks learn, using to one extent or another a combination of inborn sound production capabilities and inborn imitative tendencies, to sing that song. The song they learn is part of their culture. Although in many scientific circles the word *culture* is a forbidden term, like *consciousness* or *intention,* Princeton biologist John Tyler Bonner uses it without flinching. Bonner has been working on signaling, communications, and other fundamental questions about animal complexity since the early 1950s. He studies cellular slime molds, and whether this specialization came about from good advice, happy chance, or brilliant insight, it has provided Bonner a privileged window on animal form and society. The slime molds, often referred to as the "social amoebae," are his muse, and their life course was the inspiration for Bonner's understanding of animal communication. Slime molds are common organisms that live in the soil, and while it might be difficult for you and me to bridge the developmental differences between social amoebae in the lab and a crèche of emperor penguins in Antarctica, it's an easy reach for Bonner.

Slime molds begin their intriguing life cycle as single cells feeding individually. At this point they are mobile, which allows them to eventually clump together as a multicellular body. This confederation of organisms sends a "fruit" containing encapsulated spores up into the air to disperse the spores. The cells that play the role of stem to the fruit full of spores then die. As Bonner says, again without apologizing for his term, "they are altruistic." From his perspective, it is the transition from single cell to an organism of many cells that ignites the first form of communication, the chemical interactions involved in cell division. This takes place in plants as well as animals, of course, but animals develop to become, at least at some point in their lives, mobile and also more elaborate in body form. As they do this, the signaling that began as chemical transactions within a cell and among cells evolves to become gestures and sounds. Bonner defines an animal society as simply a group of animals, each of which is composed of more than one cell. It stands to reason that a more complicated society would require more complicated signaling. It is at the point where animals use their signals to convey information and to learn from and teach the information that, Bonner tells us, they have culture. He sees culture as the transmission of information, not only among individuals but from parent to offspring, as well as, in many cases, the accumulation by the animals of a "tradition," such as migration routes. While Mike Ryan has recently asked the important question of what, exactly, is the *information* he and his colleagues are so fond of using as a handle in discussions about cognition, Bonner is content to assume the most commonly accepted meanings of the word.[4]

The transmission of culture from one generation to the next has also been taken up by Richard Dawkins, who links the idea to the transmission of genetic material. His ideas on this phenomenon are more loosely speculative than Bonner's, and while Dawkins also cites examples from song learning in birds, he does not attempt to delineate a process through which song and song variation pass down the generations. He designates the mechanism for this transmission as a cultural "replicator," analogous to the gene, the physical replicator, and he calls this transmitter a *meme* (partly, he has said, because *meme* sounds a lot like *gene*). He makes it clear that the meme is a stand-in for something more elaborate that we haven't been able to identify yet, the way that Darwin's *gemmule* stood in until the gene was discovered to be the mechanism for physical inheritance. Dawkins believes the meme works in tandem with the gene, and this allows him to account for transmission of everything from regional dialects in birdsong to ideas about God.[5]

~

Whether the wren duets David is playing for me are evidence of a tradition transmitted from one generation to the next or simply a set of innate vocal responses, what David has established about these duets is the existence of a stable code and its uses for locating their mates and cooperative defense.

"Do you think it's the same for the elfin-woods warbler?" I ask. "That there's something like a code at work?"

"We don't know enough about *that* bird yet."

This is the way that scientists looking at birdlife have to proceed. Bird by bird. When they have looked in great detail at one bird species, they can use what they established about that particular bird to make inferences to other species. What will verify David's theory of a duet code is the finding of a duet code in another species.

The song and culture of David's bird-in-the-hand, the black-bellied wren, are quite different from those of his bird-in-the-bush number one, the elfin-woods warbler. The black-bellied wren sings a good deal in a strong, penetrating melody, and the elfin-woods warbler, so far as David knows, is a reluctant whisperer whose song slips through a narrow swatch in the forest's soundscape. As striking as this contrast is, the contrast between these two songbirds and David's bird-in-the-bush number two is far more dramatic.

To have a look at the Puerto Rican parrot, we drive around the western edge of the island to avoid the mountain roads in its center and turn south for thirty miles or so to come to a place and a bird completely unlike the high elfin woods and their warbler. This bird-in-the-bush is much closer to hand for David than the elfin-woods warbler because the largest populations are captive. He knows exactly where to find them at any time.

When we turn up a tiny road that follows the channel carved by the Rio Abajo we are in the heart of what is called karst country, where the shoulders of lumpy limestone mountains hunch up through rain forest. The mountains are cut by narrow ravines and pocked with big holes that David explains were created by water eating away the limestone.

We follow the twisting path of the river through dense growth in the low, moist valley, and we pass through two gates, the second one locked to anyone who does not have a key card and the right PIN, before we come to the home—one of only two homes—of the Puerto Rican parrot. Native to Puerto Rico and confined to the island, the parrot is a loud-colored, aggressive bird with a typically raucous parrot voice. In spite of these pugnacious characteristics, the parrot is nearly extinct. It numbers fewer than four hundred, including both captive and wild birds, and this figure is up from its low of thirteen captive birds in 1975. The government is involved in a concerted captive breeding in one site on the eastern end of the island, El Yunque National Forest, and a second site here in Rio Abajo State Forest. Because of the bird's extremely fragile hold on existence, the site, the José L. Vivaldi Memorial Aviary, is closed to outsiders.

A Puerto Rican man about David's age meets us at the locked gate and swipes his card through the security lock. Brian Ramos Güivas has worked at the compound into which he leads us for more than ten years, and from these years of personal observation and his contacts with colleagues in the captive breeding program he knows the Puerto Rican parrot as well as anyone in the world. He has signed up to take a master's degree under David, and David is looking forward to having someone with such long experience as a research collaborator. Another factor that will smooth the path of their research together is that, with captive research subjects, it won't take much to make good observations of the birds.

Brian shows us two parrots in a large stand-alone cage, where he begins what must be his customary presentation about the birds and their progress away from extinction. He is a calm, solid person who is confident in his knowledge of the parrots and his duty as a host. The two birds are a brilliant green and roughly the size of a crow if you don't consider the crow's tail. The only thing to say about the color of this bird's feathers is *parrot green,* because the rich, shimmering color is the quintessential shade defined by this family of birds. Brian points out a brief bold band of bright red where the heavy, curved beak meets the head and notes that this stripe is more pronounced on male birds than on females. "Also, the eye–inside this white eye ring"–he indicates the iris–"is yellower in males, and it gets yellower as the parrots get older.

"Yes, the parrots are aggressive–," he agrees about the pair eyeing us and sidling a little toward us. "Very aggressive. But these two have been hand-raised, maybe because they were sick or needed some kind of extra care, and they don't show aggressiveness because we don't bother them much. They're not afraid, which is not good for the birds that will be reintroduced to the wild."

The two birds sit side by side on one of their perches, ogling us. Parrots have a penetrating stare that somehow radiates curiosity and bold intelligence, and I suspect that, in addition to the ability to mimic human speech, this stare that seems to single you out for the bird's personal interest is one reason that over the centuries people have coveted them as pets and will still break the laws about trafficking in birds to bring one home. Also not good for the birds.

The pair who sidestep carefully on their perch haven't made a peep, but we can hear plenty of squawking from a wooded area behind the largest building in the compound. Brian acknowledges the squawking and says proudly, "Since 2006 we have been releasing twenty-nine to thirty birds a year."

The circumstances that conspired to nearly erase the bird were, in addition to the pet trade, hunting, habitat loss, and infertility related to inbreeding of birds in an island population with a limited gene pool. Once the population dropped below a critical level, as it did for the passenger pigeon, the parrot's doom was nearly accomplished. The factors limiting the rebound in the parrot's numbers are their aggression toward prospective mates and the fact that, once a peaceful match has been made and eggs laid, the birds seem capable of taking care of only two chicks.

The program in which Brian works supports an intensive operation to replicate the bird's natural reproductive pattern. It begins with collecting eggs from nesting pairs, incubating them, raising the chicks without providing evidence of the fact that their caretakers are human beings, moving them to a special evacuation building when hurricanes blow over the island, and then, before release, training them to recognize and avoid their predators. This last task is accomplished by putting on a demonstration for the young birds. They are gathered like spectators at a little gladiator show to watch while a hawk swoops down on a decoy parrot. This decoy is a parrot of a nonendangered parrot species and is protected by a hawk-proof padding. These moments of theater, David points out, bring on the alarm calls of the captive adult birds, and the combination of the attacks and the alarm calls is enough to bring home the lesson. There are, of course, other threats to newly released parrots, mainly their inefficient foraging and homemaking skills, but Brian reports that losses of newly released parrots are diminishing every year. Sometimes the birds released from the aviary fly back into the neighborhood to roost for a while, and this gives Brian some indication of how they are adapting in the wild. Progress has been slow, but progress nonetheless.

We do not venture beyond the main building in the aviary until Brian has finished most of what he wants to say, and once we approach the huge flight cages where the breeding and young birds are kept, I can understand why. If one parrot's squawk is loud, ten parrots in full voice are overwhelming. In Panama I was awakened by roving flocks of parrots but buffered from the true intensity of the volume by the distance to the backyard fence. Brian tells me that the first time he helped move the parrots to their evacuation center in advance of an oncoming hurricane he failed to wear earplugs, and he felt the raucous calls as real pain.

Our arrival causes similar noise, but because the parrots are somewhat accustomed to seeing humans, it soon drops off. David comes over to explain that very little is known about how parrots live in the wild. Given that they are so brightly colored and blatant with their voices, this surprises me. But he says that, like the elfin-woods warbler, they are difficult to see. They live in very dense foliage and are almost always observed with backlighting. Most of what we know about parrots is what we have learned from captive birds, and the reasons we can observe captive parrots in such numbers are nest robbing for the pet trade and the commercial breeding of those poached birds.

Parrots are best known for their abilities as mimics, and we know a great deal about these abilities and the learning capacities of captive birds. Thanks in large measure to Irene Pepperberg and her fabulous Alex, we know that parrots, African grays at least, can not only mimic the sounds of human speech but also be trained to adopt some human cognitive constructs. In spite of how much we know about the use of voice by captive parrots, we know very little about the vocalizing of parrots living in the wild.[6]

Most parrots live what is called a fission-fusion lifestyle. Every morning, the flock leaves a common roost where the birds have spent the night, and they fly off to forage, separating into smaller groups until late in the day, when they gather closer together to settle on a new common roost for the night. Their continual changes of night roost are thought to be a defense against predators that might stake out a particular group of trees after spotting the flock. As they try to decide on the roost for the night, groups of parrots call back and forth, imitating one another's calls. It has been proposed that this mimicking is to mediate the reuniting of the two groups separated during the day before they settle on a roosting place in the evening. "That isn't duetting," David explains about the exchanges between groups of birds. "That's *call convergence*—if they sang, it would be called *song matching*." The parrot groups test the similarities of their voices to find out if it's safe to roost together for the night.

"Then what is duetting?"

"You'll hear that," he said. "It's a lot different than the black-bellied wrens' duet. It's a loud, long exchange, and they do a sort of dance."

In a top corner of one of the big flight cages hangs a metal cylinder with an opening at the bottom and an enclosed compartment at the top. This, Brian tells me, simulates the nesting situation of the Puerto Rican parrot. The birds move into tree holes, preferably vertical cavities because they are less accessible to predators. Housing considerations for the parrots' breeding are relatively straightforward. The rest—aggression and song exchange between prospective mates—is not.

There are other flight cages beyond the two we are touring. But breeding season has begun, and Brian can't impose our presence on those birds. With only thirty birds being released every year and only some of those surviving to make a pair, it is important not to miss a single opportunity to create a single egg.

"The pairs," Brian tells me after we are out of the blast of parrot calls, "are permanent," meaning that like Panama's black-bellied wren, the birds are monogamous until one of them disappears for some reason or there is what David calls a "divorce," when for some reason the couple can't keep it together to raise another clutch of chicks. The male parrots don't incubate the eggs, but they do feed the chicks.

"What I want to see," Brian says about the vocal communication research project he has proposed to David, "is if the duets affect how often the males feed the females." His research scheme is relatively simple, and it's based on situations he has already imposed on the parrots in the breeding program. He is testing the hypothesis that the parrots' duetting may communicate something about commitment to the partnership—in other words, he is asking if duetting behavior has anything to do with breeding success.

In a row of three contiguous cages, Brian will house a female parrot in the middle cage with a male in the cage on either side of her. When he figures out which male she prefers, he will house those two together. When the parrot matches have been made, he will monitor how often they duet and what form the duets take, and he will try to relate these aspects of their calls to their mate feeding and the pair's ability to raise young parrots.

"When the pair starts duetting," I raise my voice against the ratcheting background of clamoring parrots, "how can you tell the two parts from each other?"

Brian says he has learned a little from females that were released and then returned to roosts near the breeding facility. "They make a slightly different sound, more like crying than squawking," Brian characterizes it. I wonder how he will ever be able to hear it well enough to distinguish this in this pandemonium.

We drive out of the compound with parrot calls still reverberating in our ears. None of it sounded like singing, and I wonder how a bird could duet without making some attempt at melody or harmony or counterpoint. Or at least some audible indication of compatibility. When we stop for lunch I say, "I wonder what those *voices* will sound like when they get into a duet."

David gives me a bright, wary glance. "That was a lot of what you were hearing this morning." Evidently, during all the clamor he hadn't thought it necessary to point out the exchanges of raucous sequences between the males and females.

"That was a *duet*?" All those raucous squawks and brays? But what about all those comparisons to happy monogamy? All those musical analogies and Butterfly and Pinkerton's impassioned musical exchange?

"That's what you were listening to."

Apparently, those sounds haven't changed his ideas about pair bonds and biological parallels to the bonds between human couples.

# 5

# A Verb, Perhaps

If duetting is the vocal glue that binds a pair of birds together, how does vocal glue work within a family of more than two? How does vocalizing keep them together? And if duetting is code transmitted between two animals, is that code extended and made more complex when it is transmitted within a family?

To take this next step in thinking about animal calls, I get in touch with Swiss researcher Marta Manser to ask to visit her work on the meerkat, a small African mongoose whose life in the Kalahari Desert has been abundantly documented by the television series *Meerkat Manor*. But its real life, its scientific life without theatrical embellishment, is what Marta is interested in. Like other members of the mongoose family, the meerkat, *Suricata suricatta*, is a long-bodied carnivore that has primitive teeth and, oddly enough, a fairly advanced inner ear. Its slender gray body weighs only about a pound and a half, and it carries this body in a stiff-legged gait with an arched back. Many photographs show it posing upright on two legs as if it were bipedal, its sharp face at a vigilant angle and its dark-ringed eyes intent. Meerkats live and forage in tightly coordinated family groups, and they have an extensive repertoire of calls and cries.

Over the past couple of decades, Marta has looked with increasing specification at how the meerkats' vocalizing brings coherence to their family group. Among all the sounds of meerkat vocalizations, Marta has identified a system of calls that meerkats use to warn their group of specific types of predators: those that swoop down from the sky, mammals that come over land, and snakes. The year before I contacted Marta, I attended a scientific meeting where she talked about these findings and showed a video of a playback experiment that demonstrated the power of the meerkat's alarm system. It began with a family of meerkats rummaging for food through the sand. When Marta played back the call warning of a threat from the air—a hawk or an eagle—the meerkats dashed immediately, without looking around, to a deserted burrow in the sand; in response to an alarm call for a predator coming by land—a jackal, maybe, or a dog—the meerkats gathered together and looked around. When Marta played the recruitment call, indicating the presence of a snake, the meerkats' heads came up attentively, and then moving away with their hip-hop canter, rolling obediently toward the calls, the family crowded around Marta's playback speaker, standing upright and peering up inquiringly into her videocam. They were looking for the meerkat that had called for them. And then, in contrast to the first three episodes, she played a less disturbing call, the "animal moving" call, which indicates there are other animals moving in the vicinity of the meerkats. This only caused the meerkats to briefly stop their foraging, stand on their hind legs, and look around before they went back to the business of food.

It was Marta's remark as she closed out the video that caught my attention.

"There—for any of you interested in the evolution of language—," she declared carefully about the first three episodes, "is what some people interested in psycholinguistics have suggested *may* be a verb-like vocalization." I think she was actually referring to the evolution of speech, one of the modes in which we use language. But never mind, it was the first time I had heard a scientist refer to an animal's voice as carrying anything like what we would construe as meaning, and this made me wonder about meerkat capacities that might be precursors to the capacity for language.

*Language* is one of the terms forbidden to behavioral ecologists, who deal with communication in terms of signals, and even the word *meaning* will make most of them uncomfortable. Partly this is due to the discipline's taboos against imposing human presumptions on animals, and partly it is due to the very strict limitations imposed on the definition of language by philosophers, linguists, and psychologists, who have been squabbling for generations over what these limitations should be. Generally, these restrictions have to do with syntax, sound as symbol, signals and meaning, and the capacity of a communication to be transposed to other forms of signals. In its recent history, this debate was dominated by the MIT linguist Noam Chomsky, his theories of generative grammar, and his assertion that language and the brain structures associated with it occurred only in humans.[1] Then the anthropologist and linguist Charles F. Hockett came forward with his Thirteen Design Features of Language. He believed that some of these features were shared with animals, and I can pick out five. The first and most notable of these features, in terms of animal voices, was the simultaneous engagement of voice and hearing, which, he observed, allowed animals to communicate while performing other life-supporting tasks, such as foraging. In addition, his observations about transitoriness, the matching of specific signals with specific meanings, patterns of sound combinations, and transmission from generation to generation could well apply to what I have been learning about animals and voices. The remaining eight of Hockett's design features attempt to identify what distinguishes human language from other signaling systems.[2]

For the moment, the debates seem to rest. But no matter how *language* is defined, there is one point on which most behavior ecologists and theorists of language agree: only humans have language. This follows a long tradition in Western thought, which early on linked language and speech to reason. Because animals have no speech, Aristotle denied them the capacity to reason. Following on this, the Stoics honed the reason-language connection to syntax: in effect, "they don't have syntax, so we can eat them." Descartes then developed this idea with more elaborate specification.[3] Until quite recently, the origins of our communication talent went relatively unexamined. Maybe this was because investigating them would have put science and the humanities on a collision course. Now the evolution of languages has begun to attract scientific attention.

Marta said the words *language* and *verb* without hesitation, probably because she hadn't been the one to suggest the parallels between the meerkats' calls and our language, and she didn't dwell on them.

Although she was confident about the functions of the meerkats' calls, I wasn't sure how interested she actually was in the evolution of language. Nevertheless, the fact that she had said those two words was one of the reasons I wanted see the gregarious little animals in their desert homes. A body of research suggests that although only animals like you and me can talk and write, some features of our capabilities have developed in other animals. Who would not try for an opportunity to meet one of these species in its living room? So to encounter the meerkats and their calls for myself, I go out to South Africa, to the Kalahari.

*Out* is the operative term here, because the research station, Rus en Vrede, is roughly four hundred sparsely populated miles west of Johannesburg and a hundred fifty miles from Upington on the Orange River, the nearest town with modern services. A couple of hours after my plane lands in Upington, another plane from Johannesburg lands, and I am joined at the airport by Simon Townsend, a British postdoc working with Marta Manser at the University of Zurich. In Marta's absence, Simon has been assigned to be my guide. We take one of the two roads leading north from Upington and drive four hours, passing only two cars, to reach Rus en Vrede.

In the Kalahari, the sky fits over the thornveldt like a shallow lid, and that first night there is a sky-splitting electrical storm that comes up slowly and leaves quickly. In the predawn of the next day, the thornveldt seems limitless. The sun, still lurking under the horizon, casts a pink light over the sand, thorn bushes, widely spaced clumps of tawny grass, and, at long intervals, acacia trees.

*Humh-humh HMMM.* Simon hums the most fundamental musical interval, the fifth to the tonic. In music the fifth is often called the *dominant*, but in the context of meerkats, whose lives spin around another kind of dominance, I shouldn't mix my signals.

*Humh-humh HMMM.* Everybody who works with the meerkats hums it the same way, not because the fifth has any special resonance for the meerkats. Although our tonal perception is locked into it, their ears aren't tuned to that interval. The sound is to let the meerkats know that it is only humans again—inconsequential, completely innocuous humans making their rounds again.

In a hole near a thorn bush, a sharp, big-eyed face appears. The fuzzy head swivels, warily scanning for something dangerous on the expanse of sand between the burrow and the surrounding bushes. A couple of tentative steps, a couple of quick glances from side to side, and the first meerkat of the day stands up. Using his long, stiff tail for support, he poses straight and precise and vigilant, like a human soldier, except that his arms drape loosely over his belly.

There is not much to the meerkat. On all fours, this mongoose stands less than the height of a cat, and he weighs less than two pounds. In his upright position, with his nearly hairless gray belly and darker gray nipples exposed, his slender body is vaguely pear shaped, like an old man's. His fur is a close match for the color of the sand, and the darker bands over the top of his body are perfect camouflage against the dark stems and branches of the thorn bushes. His head is mouse-like, pointed and chinless, with eyes as round as mouse eyes and very black. Although his ears lie flush against the sides of his head like a human's, the overall impression is of a stretched-out edition of a mouse. Give him a jacket and trousers, and he could pass for an elderly Stuart Little.

Before the others in his family take courage and follow him up into the early light, the first meerkat checks out the situation above-ground. He pays no attention to Simon or me but remains at attention, staring. His vigilance is intense. But there is nothing worrisome near the burrow, and after a couple of minutes another sharp face pokes up in the hole. A grain of sand decorates the corner of one eye.

"*Humh-humh HMMM*–the habituation sound," Simon explains. "It reassures them that there's nothing to be afraid of." "Nothing to be afraid of" is a relative statement, because meerkats are always afraid, afraid of everything, and with good reason. A number of animals–hawks and snakes and jackals–hunt them quite successfully, and their primary means of protection is living in a group, a vigilant family. To be separated from your family is to venture into the Valley of Death. The fact that the habituation call actually works to soothe the meer-kats is a good indication of how much they depend on their hearing.

Another face pushes up over the second meerkat's back. When the two newcomers stand upright to look around, the first sentinel makes a soft sound, drops back to all fours, and goes off a little ways from the burrow to look for food. Other meerkats creep out of the den, and mov-ing away from it in the odd toddling walk they use to get around, they begin to forage, patting the sand tentatively and then digging in. In a minute, sand is flying.

The sun slides up suddenly, and the heat begins to escalate even as day breaks. The meerkat voices begin. These are not loud. But then no sound out here is actually loud. Until a herd of wildebeest crosses the path or a truck clatters up the gravel road that runs past the farm on its way south a hundred miles to Route 14N, there is only the hush of the wind, accompanied at low levels by the insistent rasping of the col-lared doves and the occasional cries of other birds or blats of sheep on the neighbor's big tract of scrubland. I have to concentrate on listen-ing to become aware first of the regular exchange of the adults' chirring—"Contact calls," Simon advises me—and then, when the pups emerge, of their more raucous demands for food—"Begging." Simon seems to register all of the voices at once. He is here to decipher what is going on among the meerkats and what is indicated by the sounds. His par-ticular interest is the relation between social and vocal complexity and the role of cognition. The meerkats are the first animals I have visited for which research on their vocalizing has a bit of a psychological com-ponent.

The animals in this particular family, the Friskies, are some of the stars of *Meerkat Manor*, which ran for four seasons on Animal Planet. There is something quite endearing about these oddly humanoid ani-mals, and they draw affectionate responses from the people who see them on television or, if you are as lucky as I have been, living in the wild. They seem like earnest children, droll miniatures of ourselves, and this immediate association is only reinforced when viewers learn that the little fellow is helpful to the other meerkats in his family, and they to him. He stands guard for his family while they forage over the desert floor. His older sister babysits newly arrived pups, and when they are old enough to toddle out of the burrow to begin foraging on their own, she brings them food, serving them just as she did him.

The series portrays the lives of these intensely social little animals as a soap opera, a continuously unfolding drama that pits family mem-bers and the families themselves against one another in the struggle to gain power and survive. The meerkats of the manor have names, and they have personalities. They are caring and helpful, but at the same time they betray one another with abrupt acts of savagery; they keep up determined feuds with other meerkat families; they make war. The soap-opera approach has been very successful with viewers, who get to know the meerkats, become attached to the characters they play, and remain interested in their fates—maybe they like to believe that a meerkat, like their own pet dog or cat, is just a tiny human covered in hair. It's pretty sentimental, but in spite of this and the absence of biological detail, the television portrayal of the meerkats is not far off the mark. The meerkat story is about vulnerable individuals grappling for power within their families. It is about feudal dynasties at war, and it is about a society struggling against the outside forces that could bring it down.

Most people who watch the meerkats on television are not concerned about what makes this all happen, the biology that churns out the plot. To get at the facts that drive the meerkat story, it takes a biologist, or rather it takes a group of biologists, a couple of decades. The fact that the meerkat can accommodate human observers has made this member of the mongoose family one of the most systematically studied animals on earth. Most of what we know about it was learned during the past twenty years in the Kalahari Desert, at the Kgalagadi Transfrontier Park (*Kgalagadi* is the most recent transcription of our more familiar *Kalahari*) and here at the Kuruman River Reserve, on the southern edge of the desert. Initially launched by the research of Cambridge biologist Timothy Clutton-Brock, whose ongoing study of red deer on the Isle of Rum set the stage for Karen McComb, David Reby, and now Megan Wyman to investigate the acoustic structure and drawing power of the stag's roar, the Kalahari Meerkat Project is as vigilant as the animal itself. Its work goes on mornings and evenings every day of the year.

When Clutton-Brock first began investigating the meerkats in the 1990s, it was because, like a number of other theoretically inclined biologists at the time, he had become interested in the social arrangements of mammals that share reproductive roles. Initially, these animals were referred to as "altruists," but now, with the gathering influence of the gene-centered ideas about behavior of Dawkins and others, they are called "cooperative breeders." This refers to the fact that only certain individuals in each family group reproduce and the other members of the family devote their energies to helping the offspring survive. In the 1960s and 1970s W. D. Hamilton and Robert Trivers had made observations of cooperative breeding in social insects such as ants and paper wasps. They were trying to answer questions like, Why do the drones give up their own reproductive agendas to wait on the queen? and, What's in it for them? Clutton-Brock was interested in applying these questions to mammals.

When he saw the film *Meerkats United*, about the work of Oxford carnivore specialist David Macdonald, it occurred to Clutton-Brock that because this amazingly social mongoose was active in the daytime and not elusive, it would be relatively easy to observe. He made a preliminary trip to South Africa to find out how feasible such a study would be, and when he began working in South Africa's Kgalagadi Transfrontier Park he found he had been right. Meerkat society was, in fact, accessible to science.

With a little patience on his part, a little humming, a little calling, a little hard-boiled egg, a family of meerkats became accustomed to the presence of Clutton-Brock and his assistants. Humans accompanied by food were the same ingredients that habituated the deer on the New Zealand farms where Megan Wyman worked. For the ever-wary meerkats, however, the sound of the human voice was added to reinforce the food offering and reassure the meerkats about their safety. Clutton-Brock could easily witness their comings and goings, their sex life, and the development of their families, and he began to publish extensively on the ways meerkats did meerkat business. But after ten years in the park, the meerkat research and the vehicles it required were beginning to outstay their welcome, and eventually Clutton-Brock arranged the purchase of a farm about two hundred kilometers southeast of the park, next to the border with Botswana. The farm has become the permanent home of the Kalahari Meerkat Project.

Although everyone calls Rus en Vrede a farm, the place is more like what people in the United States think of as a ranch, a vast expanse of flat, dry scrubland—giving me driving directions to another house on the farm, Simon warns me, "Stay left. Otherwise you'll find yourself in Botswana." There is always a small crowd of meerkat researchers in residence at the farm—volunteers, research assistants, master's candidates, doctoral candidates, and fully fledged scientists. When I visit, Marta is on duty at the University of Zurich, Tim Clutton-Brock is in England, and a crew of twenty or so circulates through the low cinder-block farmhouse that serves as project headquarters. The crew is young, most of them under thirty—and although he is only twenty-six, Simon, as a postdoc, is a senior member. He has come up the rungs of the academic ladder fast. He is slight, with short, dark gold hair that curls when it comes near his face, and he's given to wearing cargo shorts that stop below the knees and running shoes tied absentmindedly. On the surface, adolescence doesn't seem far behind him, so at first I found his sharp command of scientific ideas and the research at hand a little startling.

The crew carries out the research in a strict, uninterrupted proto-
col. They are monitoring between eight and ten meerkat families, and
the crew members rotate duty from family to family according to the
assignments scribbled on a big whiteboard in the central hall. Every
day, Sundays and holidays included, the crew vehicles leave the farmhouse in time to reach the meerkats before the sun comes up and the
first meerkat can emerge. *Humh-humh-HMMM.*

When all the meerkats have come out of the burrow, it's time to
take their weights, and the food comes out. *Yum-yum, yum-yum!* This
high-pitched call repeating the same tone is another standard usage. It
draws the meerkat family to a kitchen scale, where a crew member rewards them with tidbits of hard-boiled egg, and the meerkats take
turns hopping on and off the scale with a kind of competitive enthusi-
asm. Sometimes more than one meerkat claims the scale, and then the
researcher has to give a gentle nudge to dislodge the meerkat that has
overstayed its turn. After they spend the morning feeding, the meerkats will be weighed a second time. A loss or gain of weight is a measure
of how a meerkat is faring at a particular location. The crew returns to
the farmhouse at midday, waits out the heat with computer work, reading, and naps, and then, a couple of hours before dark, they set off again
so they can weigh the meerkats again before the tail of the last meerkat
in each family disappears into the burrow. Every fact about each meerkat family is recorded. The researchers take attendance and try to account for absentees and newcomers. In addition to taking the weights
of the individual meerkats, they note changes in general health and
reproductive states.

For more than seventeen years, a succession of crews has documented the day-to-day facts of a gradually increasing number of meer-

kat families, unraveling a plot that is roughly equivalent to the drama that plays out episode by episode on *Meerkat Manor*. The plot goes something like this: Vulnerable animals gather in protective families. In these families they are committed to rituals that ruthlessly perpetuate the internal power structure and maintain the territorial boundaries between families. These families, like those of wolves, which also breed cooperatively, are matriarchies organized by a female and a male hierarchy. The details of the dynamics of meerkat family life have appeared in what is now a good-sized body of scientific papers, but for our purposes I will briefly outline how this two-regime family life takes place.

The females call the shots, and the dominant female rules the family. She is a breeding machine and gives birth two to four times a year, usually to two but up to six pups. Her daughters live with her throughout the breeding cycle until just before she gives birth to a new litter. Because the daughter most likely to succeed her as top female will kill her infants, the dominant female evicts this daughter, chasing her out of the group into meerkat hell, solitary living. It is meerkat hell because living in groups, especially large groups, protects many animals of prey. Remember, these little mongooses are fraidy cats, and being ostracized from the family exposes them to all dangers, leaves them without protection. It is a dangerous, stressful existence, but for evicted females it usually doesn't last long. After the new litter arrives, an evicted daughter usually returns to the family, and she may be one of the daughters who take on the role of babysitter.

Why should a daughter put off having young and instead spend her energy on raising her mother's pups? Why should she cooperate? What does cooperation cost her? And how will she benefit? Considering the "unselfish" behavior of paper wasps, W. D. Hamilton deduced that the more closely animals are related, the more likely they are to breed cooperatively. He reasoned that female wasps are more closely related to their sisters, with whom they share both the same mother and the same father, than they are to their mother. The mother carries only her genetic material, not that of her mate. Hamilton saw that reproducing shared genes was the goal of "indirect selection." By helping the sister who will later become a queen, the daughters are promoting the future of their own set of genes. Hamilton's Rule predicts cooperation when the degree of relatedness and the benefits of cooperation exceed the costs of the behavior.[4]

The wasps are an extreme example of indirect selection, but the female meerkats' struggle for genetic influence works in a similar way. The dominant female, who is only 50 percent related to her daughters, seeks to retain the genetic preeminence of *her* genes by gaining the help of her entire family to raise a generation of pups that can be as much as 100 percent related to the daughters whose help she elicits. Although this help is called *cooperation*, Clutton-Brock and his colleagues have recently speculated that the meerkat's version of cooperation may not be strictly voluntary. It may be enforced by punishment from the dominant female.

A similar genetic logic underlies another brutal aspect of meerkat family life: infanticide. It is not unusual for a female, dominant or subordinate, to slay new pups when tensions between family members tip out of balance. The dominant female tries to suppress breeding in her daughters, and if one of them should become pregnant, the dominant female, pregnant herself, may kill the pups to ensure the best conditions for the success of her own pups. Likewise, tit for tat, a still-pregnant subordinate female may kill the dominant's pups so that they will not compete for adult care with her own offspring. It is important for the pregnant subordinate to time the delivery of her pups in relation to any delivery of pups from other potentially pregnant females, so that she is the last to give birth.

While the females are sorting out their roles, the males are also undergoing continuous upheaval in their ranks. The dominant male, who is not related to the dominant female, is father to the younger males in the family. In order to find an unrelated female with whom to mate the young males must leave the family, and they do. They "rove," wandering alone to the fringes of other meerkat families. This solitary phase is another version of meerkat hell. Relying mainly on stealth and trying to avoid fights with members of these other families, the rovers lurk at the edges of a family group and wait for a female in estrus to be unguarded and available. Of course, they are often spotted and chased off by both males and females of the family, and when they can't run fast enough, they get beaten up. Less frequently, a rover will make an alliance with an evicted female and start a new family group or be fortunate enough to wander into an opportunity to take over as dominant male.

There is danger and stress in all these family events, and they are repeated on an almost daily basis.

⁓⋋⋋⋌⋌⁓

Every week the crew of the Kalahari Meerkat Project, all ranks, crowds into the sitting room of the farmhouse for the Life History Meeting. The person who has most recently visited each family gives an update on the individual meerkats in that family. Although, like animals in most long-term studies, the meerkats have identification numbers, they are also known by familiar names, and reports that rely on these names go around the room: "Diana? No, no pups yet. Maybe in the next few days"; "Frida's been evicted, and we saw her with the rover from Drie Doring"; "And also, could you please remember to pick up feces?"; "Her pups are about a week, so I expect she's in estrus–." It's a roll call of research housekeeping and meerkat family happenings, births, shifting alliances, evictions, reunions, missing meerkats, and of health issues and reproductive status–"Yup, I thought we were going to see meerkat sex. And we almost saw it."

In the mornings and evenings I go out with a crew member to visit one of the meerkat families. It might be Simon or Stephan Reber, a serious, thoughtful graduate student from the University of Zurich, or Luci Kirkpatrick, an exuberant volunteer from England with a curly aura of bright red hair. Whoever is my guide, whichever family we are following, the meerkats' routine hardly varies. The family emerges and begins to forage, moving as a constellation that slowly circulates over the thornveldt, with their voices providing a muted sound track. As they nose around and dig energetically for a juicy scorpion or centipede or skink, the adults intermittently exchange soft chirring sounds, and the pups, who are going through some of the motions of looking for food, keep up a louder rasping complaint. Sooner or later an adult will unearth a succulent prize and deliver it to one of the pups. The pup's complaints usually cease only long enough for him or her to chew and swallow the gift. On the periphery of their group at least one meerkat, sometimes two or three, stands guard, watching intensely for the things meerkats fear. There are a lot of these. In the air, eagles and hawks–the meerkat has an amazing ability to look up, straight up so that the tip of its nose is plumb with the base of its spine. Things they fear might come over the ground—invaders from other meerkat clans, snakes, and jackals—and, within their family, they fear a beating from the dominant female or male. At the slightest hint of danger, a speck in the sky, the flicker of a thorny branch, a whiff of a strange meerkat, the sentinel gives a small cry, and the family veers as one, the way a flock of birds turns in the sky, and speeds toward the nearest bolt-hole. They remain underground for a calculated interval before they reemerge cautiously and feed until they are interrupted by the next danger.

Looking at their life from the point of view of someone like Princeton biologist John Bonner, who has devoted his career to animal social complexity and the communication and culture that result from it, the meerkats are as highly cultured as the emperor penguins half a world away. The meerkats are a group of organisms operating and communicating under a shared set of rules. In fact, as Simon points out, their behavior is "kind of robotic"—fifteen bodies, one aim. Within the group there is some teaching and a great deal of social learning going on. The babysitters demonstrate for the pups the great foraging traditions of the Kalahari—how to immediately pin down a scorpion to detach its tail with the punishing stinger in it, how to drag a millipede through the sand to erase the toxins that form on its carapace when it is exposed to sunlight. There is also their shared fear and the vocal communication system that helps them steer clear of danger. Tension radiates from every animal in the family. This tension is built of conflicting pressures that threaten at any given moment to go wildly out of whack—hunger, fear of being eaten, worry about the pups, antagonism toward outsiders, apprehension about status within the family. While the meerkat soap opera may make for entertaining television, the meerkats themselves have to experience the actual physical struggles that drive their television plots. They are tense animals in a tense society, and somehow in this culture of fear there is also powerful cohesion. If voice stands in for brutal antlers-locked-in-antlers shoving with red deer stags, it also stands in for the comfort and protection of another meerkat pressing close.

One evening as Simon and I turn away from a burrow into which the last meerkat tail has vanished, I mention this tension and how fraught the families seem.

"So, Simon, it's the vocalizing that keeps the family together, keeps everything straight?"

"Not only that, but visual cues and scent, of course." He nods at a male meerkat crawling lasciviously over a clump of grass. The meerkat toddles purposefully over to Simon's backpack and begins to apply the same treatment to it. When Simon lifts the pack out of reach, the meerkat proceeds to Simon's running shoe. He sighs. "You *animal*."

In their use of scent and scent marking, the meerkats don't differ much from most carnivores. They mark out territory and other belongings by rubbing their anal glands against roots, stones, sand, and the openings in the sand, and they are guided in their wanderings by the markings of members of their family and, particularly, by members of other families. Although crew members often exclaim about the strong smell of the fluid the meerkats wipe on their surroundings, I am blessed with a sense of smell too dull to pick up more than an occasional hint of musk. By conveying information on the whereabouts and sexual status of individuals and the boundary claims of other families, scent is a medium for communication. Carnivore biologists have long understood this, and maybe because of this general understanding, the role of scent in the meerkat's life has only recently come on the agenda of the team at Rus en Vrede.

The team's interest in the meerkat's vocalizing, however, has been a big agenda item for the past twenty years. In 1994 Marta, a graduate student at the time, joined Clutton-Brock's Cambridge group to begin looking closely at the meerkat's calls, and in 1998 she produced a dissertation on the evolution of their communication system. Since then, as a co-director of the Meerkat Project, she has guided an extensive study of the types, functions, and acoustic structures of the calls. Simon and Stephan are the latest researchers to sign on with Marta to help extend this work.

Initially Marta investigated those calls that received the most obvious reactions from other meerkats, the cries of the guards that sent the family speeding for a bolt-hole. Many mammals and birds give alarm calls when a predator approaches, and scientists have speculated that having a variety of different-sounding alarms is an effective defense for a social animal, especially a small one that lives in the open and is vulnerable to predators using different hunting techniques. Using a charateristic sound for one kind of danger may indicate the family's best choice of escape route. Analyzing the acoustics of the sentinels' calls and linking them to what was happening to the meerkats at the moment the sentinels gave voice, Manser recognized that a vigilant meerkat gave a specific sound to warn the family of a predator in the air—the most feared martial eagle or a goshawk—and another sound that warned specifically of a terrestrial predator, and yet another for a snake.

When Manser began her experiments on the alarm calls, the idea that animals could use their voices to refer to something in their environment rather than to their emotional state was not new. In the late 1960s and early 1970s, Peter Marler, on a busman's holiday from birdsong, began recording and analyzing the acoustical structure of the alarm calls of forest monkeys.[5] These projects paralleled his studies of birds, as did his findings: calls that had similar functions had similar acoustical features. This initial observation laid the groundwork for more intensive attempts to link the structure of vocal sound to behavior. Working with chimpanzees in the 1970s, David Premack observed that a call could carry specific information to a listener even when the animal that produced the sound had no intention to refer to something specific. I think what Premack was trying to describe was the kind of reaction you and I have when we hear "Watch out!" or "Oh, my god!" As Premack saw it, reference occurred only in the ear and brain of the listener.[6] But, following up on an earlier report that vervet monkeys appeared to apply specific sounds to specific predators, Robert M. Seyfarth and Dorothy L. Cheney gave authority to the proposition that animals could intentionally use their voices to denote specific events. Seyfarth and Cheney recorded vervet calls and classified them according to the predators the sounds appeared to indicate. To verify these sound references, they played them back to the vervets and documented the monkeys' responses. This revealed that the vervet alarms were coded, and the monkeys' vocalizing became a prime example of what are now termed "functionally referential" calls.[7] These calls, which point to something in the world around the vervets rather than simply mediate social interactions, have sparked the recent wave of scientific interest in how human language evolved. While much of the conversation you and I have regulates how things go between us, just as much has to do with external happenings in our human umwelt.

Working with Seyfarth and Cheney at the University of Pennsylvania, Marta began to apply their methods to the meerkats, leading to the revelation that the meerkats also use specific call types to alert their families to specific kinds of predators. Their call indicating an approaching jackal turned a relatively widespread group of foraging meerkats into streaks of gray-yellow animals that ran, looking around at the same time, converged near the sentinel, and then fled to a system of bolt-holes. Another call indicated an eagle in the sky overhead, and depending on how immediate the threat was, the meerkats froze in place, flattening themselves in a crouch, or they scuttled to the nearest single bolt-hole. The alarm denoting a snake was featured in Marta's video that ended with the meerkats clustering near her speaker. It was a call to arms that caused the meerkats to approach the caller at a deliberate pace—in Marta's video the meerkats were duped into mistaking her speaker for a meerkat—and, once gathered together, to turn as one, tails arcing stiffly over their backs, and mob the snake. This produced a lot of meerkat mass for one snake to deal with, and their harassment usually discouraged an attack.

It's a relatively sophisticated system of security codes, and Marta's team has gained some insight about how the guard's vocabulary is perpetuated from one generation to the next. The immediate questions are, Is it learned by exposure and experience? Is it an innate development that matures with the meerkat? Or is it some combination of these factors? The youngest meerkats, the pups, rarely attempt an alarm call, but the subadults, now less dependent on the adults in their family, do try out the calls. They frequently make a mistake. They name the wrong predator or they call when there is no predator—but occasionally adult meerkats do the same. Young vervet monkeys, who remain dependent on their parents for a long time, go through a much more prolonged period of babbling before they find words. Eventually, either experience or maturity makes the meerkat a reliable signaler, and in the meantime, given the many perils in a young meerkat's life, the only serious error would be silence.

⚬ ⚬ ⚬

Watching the Friskies family in the white heat of the late desert morning, I can't decide whether the alarm calls are verblike orders to escape—*Run!, Duck!, Go like hell!*—or whether they are nounlike references to external phenomena to which the only response is an action—*Dog!, Eagle!, Snake!* But whatever part of speech these calls are, their mode is imperative. Since identifying the functions of the meerkats' alarm calls, Manser has further parsed the acoustic structure of the calls to discover that alarm calls not only command a reaction to a particular kind of threat but also indicate how urgent the need for action is. Simon tells me this was an important revelation because it implies that meerkats can do something only humans were thought capable of: using a vocal utterance both to refer to something and to convey emotion.

Are these calls some kind of proto-words? Has the evolutionary path that led to today's meerkat endowed it with a primitive capacity that evolved more elaborately in the human as a spoken word? The definition of *word* is almost as elusive as the definition of *language,* but one generally accepted definition in terms of speech is that a *word* is a sound to which a meaning has been arbitrarily applied. While *meaning* may be too deep a word to use for *reference,* there is another aspect of speech that may apply more directly to the meerkat calls. Something linguists, such as Philip Lieberman, have pointed out about human speech is that it is fast. It is a very efficient way of signaling, of putting across a lot of information quickly. This speed, Lieberman believes, is a way to lighten up the load that communication puts on short-term memory. Although Lieberman doesn't consider meerkat calls in his work, his observations about speed and memory capacity may also apply to meerkats and to the development of the meerkats' alarm calls, as well as to other species that use alarm calls.[8] All the meerkats need to be speedy to dodge their predators, and meerkat guards, who have to alert the many other members of their family as well as escape, need a vocal shorthand to pinpoint which danger is approaching.

Marta has not speculated on this possibility thus far. She, like Mike Ryan in his work on the túngaras, has focused on exploring deeper and deeper in the biological details of the meerkats' lives, even as those entail cognition, and she leaves her evidence on vocalizing for language researchers who might want to trace the development of this kind of capacity through a number of different species.

What Marta is speculating on now are the connections between the intricately balanced dynamics of meerkat families and the apparent number of functions their vocalizing serves. In a study that contrasted simplicity and complexity, she compared meerkats and their alarm calls with those of a similar but much less social animal, the Cape ground squirrel, which lives in strong numbers all around Rus en Vrede. A slighter, yellower version of the groundhog that lives here in the States, the Cape ground squirrel is the original excavator of most of the burrows the meerkats eventually take over. The ground squirrel has alarm calls, but these don't refer to the cause for alarm. The calls just convey the need for immediate escape. The ground squirrels live in family groups like the meerkats, although in the ground squirrels' case the groups are segregated by sex. But they do not forage in groups, and they do not venture far from their burrow holes to look for food. They go without much companionship, making their social life simple. The intensely organized meerkat groups, however, range widely from one burrow system to the next and communicate via a much more elaborate system of calls.

⁓ ⁓

After a few days in the desert, I am beginning to recognize some of the meerkats' organizational methods. At first their wanderings struck me as rudderless, but it is becoming apparent that the family always knows exactly what neighborhood it's entering and exactly where the nearest bolt-holes are. When an alarm call comes, the meerkats use the kind of predator it names to choose which escape route to take.

Although none of their calls is loud, once I tune into the meerkat channel, the undercurrent of sound eddying and pooling as they forage seems to have been scored as a sound track for their daily activities. The alarm calls and the interruptions they bring are punctuation points in the scattered mix of meerkat voices that accompanies the animals' daytime travels. All the time they are circulating through the scrubby thorn bushes, they are in touch vocally. Against the insistent background *gimme-gimme-gimme* of the pups' raspy begging, the adults interject soft, chirring contact calls—*I am here; here I am.*

Occasionally, when the family has been mining a patch of thornveldt for a while, something will cause one of the meerkats to stand up and issue a command. Often it's the dominant female: *Move.* All the other meerkats will leave off their digging, gather up, and, without pausing to look for food, head out for a new location. A slightly less imperative version of this is *Let's go,* and Manser and her PhD student Christophe Bousquet have found that at least three meerkats must take up this call before any of them begin to move out to different territory.[9] It's a form of group decision making.

Animals living in groups often maintain social contact through grooming, and primatologist Robin Dunbar speculates that when groups become too large for animals to keep up with manual grooming they resort to "vocal grooming." As they move from one-on-one physical contact to vocal contact with many, their voices stand in for touch.[10]

What to make of the various sounds the meerkats put out? Do the begging calls say anything about the youngster who is squawking? Can the grown-ups recognize one another by their particular contact calls? What authorizes a meerkat to call out the *move* order? Drilling down further into Marta's general hypothesis relating social and vocal complexity, Simon and Stephan are each running a set of experiments that take place alongside the Meerkat Project's daily monitoring of the families. Both of them focus on the contact calls.

Simon and I wait by a burrow in dwindling light for the Friskies to gather for the night, and we talk about how his experiments and the rather different experiments that Stephan has begun will feed into this hypothesis. "For me," Simon decides, "the general question is, What part of vocal communication is tied to social complexity and what part to cognition?" Like Marta, Simon has worked with a primate researcher, in his case, psychologist Klaus Zuberbühler at University of St Andrews in Scotland, who supervised Simon's dissertation research on the vocalizations of wild-living chimpanzees (wild versus captive is an important distinction for primates, because, according to Simon, they behave quite differently when confined).

In the dwindling light, the Friskies are beginning to show up singly and in pairs at the burrow.

"Chimp society and vocalizing are quite complex, and these guys," he says about the meerkats toddling up to us, "also show some complexity in the way they coordinate their activities. But the chimps have big bodies, big brains, and more highly developed cognitive capabilities. These guys don't have any of that. You know, small bodies, small brains. *But*"—it turns out that the meerkats are among some striking exceptions to the well-worn generalization about body size and brain size—"they have impressively complex vocal communication." The magpie, another exception, has used its bird brain to demonstrate that it recognizes itself in a mirror, which is considered one benchmark of intelligence.[11] In my travels to listen to animals, this is the first mention I have heard of psychology. Until now, cognition has been a player standing offstage, but from here its role grows more important.

At the moment, the immediate piece of the social-vocal complexity equation he is attacking at Rus en Vrede is, What happens to female communications—their contact calls—during an eviction? In other words, What happens to your body, and what does your voice sound like on your way down to meerkat hell? Simon tells me that the acoustic features of the chirring noises they exchange to remain in contact with one another are not all the same and that the sounds of these calls appear to change according to how things stand in the family at a given time. Although I am getting habituated enough to hear a meerkat and identify the type of call, I can't tune into distinctions finer than that. "The dominant females give out lower-frequency calls that have a kind of growly entropy"–the sound as it fades. He is talking about formants now, the envelope of frequencies that shrouds the core tone. "The contact calls made by the submissives are higher frequency and they're more tonal. They don't have noise in the sound." All of this accords with the general rule of low-frequency voice denoting big-body dominance.

In the families Simon has designated for his experiments to link call sounds to hormonal activity, he records the contact calls before an eviction takes place, then begins to collect feces, which, when he analyzes them back in Zurich, will yield information about hormones that confirms the results of earlier experiments. "We've seen an increase in testosterone in the dominant female, the one who's doing the evicting. And, even more obvious, we saw higher cortisol levels in the females who have been evicted. These go way up."

Cortisol is the universal indicator of stress in mammals–distress, the negative experience, rather than eustress, the pleasurable experience of exploring gains. As the evictions occur, Simon is recording the meerkat contact calls. Eventually he should be able to link before-and-after sound patterns to before-and-after hormonal analyses.

As we talk, he is following a particular female meerkat, and when she deposits poop in the sand, he dives for it with a small plastic bag. This is one of the indignities of trying to correlate biochemistry, cognitive activity, and behavior in animals.

"You know, don't you, that all mammals have steroid receptors in their vocal tracts?"

This intriguing fact could be big news. Watching and listening to the frogs, the deer, and the birds have made it clear that hormonal activity is the back-end system for vocal activity. Now these specialized vocal tract tissues seem evidence of a direct physical channel for this, although Simon points out that no one is sure how the receptors work.

"We're just getting into these experiments, so we don't know if we'll see what we expect to see. But one thing we have noticed already is that during an eviction the dominant female doesn't call as often."

When I mention this at dinner this evening, Luci Kirkpatrick crows, "Right! I've seen her change! She gets kind of quiet, and the daughters start groveling, licking and grooming. But she doesn't seem to pay any attention to them. She gets this sad look, and then she fixes on the daughter who has got to go. You can tell that this daughter knows she'll be the one. She knows what's going to happen. The next minute, the dominant and her sisters gang up and pound on her."

Meerkat hell. Her cortisol levels will soon go through the roof.

These biochemical explanations for aggression and voice quality may eventually prove to be satisfying descriptions of typical meerkat behavior, but they don't get directly at what is going on in a meerkat's mind as the animal rides out waves of hormonal activity. Although it is not actually discussed at Rus en Vrede, the issue of perception has gradually crept more and more into my thoughts as I follow the meerkat families until now, on my last morning at the farm, the question pops into my mind as plain as day in the desert. What happens in the meerkat's mind in that instantaneous interval between the moment when a call from a family member strikes the meerkat's ear and the meerkat reacts? The gap between signal and response is a wide playing field for cognitive psychology.

Stephan Reber's experiments at the Meerkat Project begin to approach this gap. He is trying to learn if the meerkats use their calls to identify one another. Obviously, if they are found to discriminate among individuals, that will enrich our understanding of the role of vocal communication both in the meerkats' social behavior and in their cognitive psychology. "This might tell us something," Simon suggests as he sends me out one evening with Stephan to record contact calls of the Drie Doring family, "about whether the meerkats have some image or mental impression of other individuals." In other words, does the stimulation of the meerkat's auditory cortex toggle the processing of a stored mental concept?

This sounds like a tricky question to puzzle out, but there is nothing tricky about Stephan's operation. He chooses a female babysitter who has finally emerged very late from the burrow to finally get a bite to eat just as dark is coming on, and he follows her closely with a microphone on a boom. Then he spends a long night in the farmhouse's sound studio prepping and organizing the sounds of her voice.

Before dawn the next morning, he is back at the Drie Doring burrow with Simon and me in tow. Stephan, whose stint in the Swiss army is not far behind him, is a contrast in personal style to Simon's rather hip one. His dark hair is clipped in a crew cut, his fair skin precisely shaven, and his short-sleeved shirts crisp. All of this, together with his brisk, Swiss-accented English, somehow makes him seem younger than he is. Simon, in fact, is only slightly older than Stephan, just more senior in academic rank. The difference in their rank is not something anyone could spot right away, because they are relaxed in their work together, but it's there. Simon has come along not only to help Stephan with the sound equipment but to advise.

As we follow the meerkats Stephan carries a large backpack, and in midmorning he brings out a digital recorder and a small wireless speaker. He straps the speaker to his bare leg. The speaker is an ordinary store-bought model, but the back of it is designed in a curve that conveniently cups Stephan's calf. While Simon operates the recording playing back the calls, Stephan walks slowly after the dominant female with the sounds of meerkat voices gently broadcasting from his leg. An episode of a meerkat's contact call will be followed by a specified period of silence, and then the voice of a different meerkat will call.

Among the contact calls is that of the babysitter, who is the ringer here. Stephan is testing whether her call indicates her identity to the dominant. The babysitter's call rotates in random order with the calls of the other meerkats. This provides a fairly normal backdrop of contact calls, except that the babysitter's isn't supposed to be heard out here aboveground. She is supposed to be down in the burrow tending the dominant's pups. Will the dominant female recognize the voice of the daughter who should have remained in the burrow with her pups? And will this alert her to potential danger for her pups?

Both men watch the dominant female intently, even for a long interval after the speaker becomes silent. Without talking, they repeat the playback routine twice more.

Then Stephan begins to assess the results. "She looked up."

Simon cocks his head, looking doubtful.

"She looked up. The first time, she looked up like she was concerned about the call," Stephan contends hopefully.

Simon isn't convinced but doesn't argue. After a few moments he says, "You'll get more."

It is not yet eleven o'clock. But the heat is white, and the meerkats are less interested in digging around for food. They leave off calling and begin to dawdle where there are small patches of shade. Stephan and Simon leave it at that and begin to pack up.

The morning's test has been just the initial foray in what will eventually be an entire season's worth of forays. But it demonstrates the elaborate stratagems we have to use to try to understand the mental perceptions and processes of another kind of animal. It shouldn't surprise us if, with their one-fact-at-a-time methods, Marta's team does eventually reveal a series of links between the levels of animal social and vocal complexity. In the course of my travels I have been listening in on animals with progressively more complex social lives—from the solitude of the túngara that is broken only by mating to the Puerto Rican parrot's comings and goings in fission and fusion—that are accompanied by more elaborate vocalizing. We humans, of course, max out both kinds of complexity, social and vocal. Meerkats, which survive because of the protection of the family, have evolved with an intercom system that allows them to coordinate the movements of the individual animals in the group. No matter how these communications are related to language, the social glue they provide is essential to the animal's survival.

By looking into the question about the links between social complexity and vocal communication—never mind the questions about referents and language—Marta has opened the door to a room filled with intertwined Gordian knots. Simon Townsend has located a string leading into one of the knots in this room, and Stephan Reber holds a thread leading into another. Marta's team will have to unravel many of these knots before other researchers can advance to the next door and the next roomful of knots, where the questions about biological precursors of speech and language wait.

The meerkats' retreat into the shade is a clear sign that they are done with foraging for the morning and that it is time to take their weights.

*Yum-yum! Yum-yum!*

They hop obligingly up on the scale and then move back into the shade. A few of them flop down flat to rest, and we return the scale to the backpack. The meerkats give no indication that they see us leave, but then, because of our habituation calls, they had barely noticed our arrival. They may have needed the reassurance of the *humb-humb-HMMM* greeting, but they don't need to hear any good-byes.

# 6

# A Phrase by Any Other Name

It is Peter Scheifele who impresses on me that a call, a song, a signal, is just a sound until it reaches an ear that can receive it and send it on through the brain. He knows a lot about ears and hearing and a lot about sound, especially sound as it travels through water. Peter teaches in the department of communication disorders at the University of Cincinnati's College of Allied Health Sciences, where he has been encouraged in his wide-ranging, peripatetic interests. He is an expert on neuroaudiology and the physics of hearing, and he knows a great deal about dogs and their hearing (his lab at the university is called FETCH-LAB). But the marine environment is Peter's real umwelt. He listens especially to the voices of whales and dolphins and is pursuing some difficult questions about their calls, their social lives, and their well-being. At the same time, doctoral student Dominie Writt is investigating dolphin calls as perceptual events in the dolphin innenwelt. The cognitive gap between hearing and reaction, the gap Simon

Townsend and Stephan Reber are edging close to, is Dominie's territory. Taken together, Peter's work and Dominie's have a lot to tell me about vocalizing and a complicated social life.

Peter is the reason I have come with my husband, John, to Tadoussac, Quebec, where a fjord empties into the St. Lawrence River. Peter is based at the University of Cincinnati, but his unusual mix of specialties—marine acoustic environments, marine mammals, and exotic animal training—carries him to aquariums all over the country and into projects with a number of research organizations, including the one in Tadoussac, Le Groupe de recherche et éducation sur les mammifères marins (GREMM). He has been involved in GREMM's long-term study of the belugas here, one of several wild populations he keeps tabs on. Although I have visited his beluga project at the Mystic Aquarium in Connecticut, I want to see the whales swimming free. John has come along with me because French is the language in this remote part of Quebec. English is not an option, and my French consists of snippets remembered from my high school text.

Tadoussac is a village of brightly painted houses, several restaurants, and a grand hotel from the nineteenth century that still presides over a broad sunny lawn that sweeps down to the harbor where the whale-watching boats put in. Established by the French in 1600 as their first fur-trading outpost in North America, Tadoussac is now supported by whale watching. Seeing whales near Tadoussac is a certainty, and every summer thousands of tourists fill the hotel and the many bed-and-breakfasts. They are predominantly Europeans and some Canadians—we are only the second Americans to stay at our bed-and-breakfast this year.

Whales like it here, and during the summer months they congregate in what locals like to call whale soup. They feed on a lively buffet of fish and krill that extends from the Gulf of St. Lawrence and the shores of the Gaspé Peninsula to a few miles upstream of Tadoussac. Stirring about in this soup are members of both major whale families, the baleen whales and the toothed whales. The baleen that visit here most frequently are the minke whale, the short-finned pilot whale, and the humpback whale, and the giant of the earth—the blue whale—also shows up. The toothed whales include animals ranging from the familiar bottlenose dolphin who performs so delightfully at urban aquariums to the short-finned pilot whale and the beluga, the convivial white whale that is the poster child of the Parcmarin du Saguenay-Saint Laurent. The belugas are the only whales who stay. They are year-round residents. Beginning in April and throughout the summer months, the fjord is the belugas' nursery. They leave their usual haunts out in the river and gather in the calmer waters of the fjord to give birth and raise their calves.

Just as the sun comes up, we arrive at GREMM's headquarters a few hundred feet from the edge of the village on the fjord side of the narrow peninsula that shapes the harbor. A few minutes later Michel Moison, a wildlife specialist who is GREMM's "person in charge of research operations," and his assistant, Renaud Pintiaux, pull in. We walk across the street to start out from the harbor hours ahead of the tourists. Michel finds it more productive to get out on the water before traffic in the river and the fjord gets heavy. By late morning the tourists will board either the large cruise boats or the open Zodiac skiffs with inflatable gunnels and get out to see the whales as up close and personal as you can get—just about. The tour operators are required by law to keep their boats four hundred meters away from the whales, but the whales themselves frequently violate this rule by swimming toward the boats, surfacing to show their fins and blowing. GREMM's research vessels operate without this restriction.

Waiting for us at the dock is *Le Bleuvet*, whose name is what the Quebecois call a baby beluga. It looks like a sawed-off lobster boat, with an open cockpit and a small cabin, but it's faster. It was made for police and coast guard work in Canada and Europe, and it can move quickly from point to point. The boat is not terrific in a storm swell, Michel explains from his place at the helm down in the cockpit, but it is good for maneuvering close to the whales. Michel came to Tadoussac from Dalhousie University in Nova Scotia and has been with GREMM for more than fifteen years. He is a very slight, dark-haired man in a foul-weather jacket who will not be surprised by anything the weather or the river can send his way. The younger Renaud, who is long-haired and fairly strapping, originally came to Tadoussac from France because he was interested in studying birds. But eventually he landed at GREMM, where he makes a highly coordinated team with Michel.

*Le Bleuvet* tools noisily out of the harbor, rounds the point, and comes up into the estuary where the flow from the Saguenay Fjord meets the St. Lawrence River. The noise of the *Bleuvet*'s engine makes it difficult to talk, but Michel and Renaud have done this work together for so long they don't need to talk. At some moments, we are looking straight up through the fjord. The walls of the fjord plunge straight down for more than a quarter mile to the water, vertical pleats of granite studded, sometimes heavily, sometimes sparsely, with spruce, other conifers, and spindly birch. When a glacier ripped through this rock, it scooped out a channel for a green-brown river that is often more than six hundred feet deep. Its excavation did not halt at the estuary but moved out along the shores of the St. Lawrence, carving a trench where the land meets the water. The water is brackish. A salt current from the Gulf of St. Lawrence runs in and out of the fjord with the tides and carries freshwater from several rivers that fall down the sides of the fjord and fill the lake at the fjord's north end. This is the south-ernmost fjord in the northern hemisphere, and its dramatic geology reaches from the estuary at Tadoussac, where our boat rides the water, north through the Canadian wilderness almost to the industrial out-post of Chicoutimi.

The predawn gray and mist gradually give way to a day of brilliant sunshine. Renaud stands at the bow with a pair of binoculars, a hand-held voice recorder, and a heavy-duty camera with a lens so long it looks like heavy artillery. In the cockpit Michel heads the boat purposefully across the estuary and then steers a path with equal purpose back toward Tadoussac, watching the water on the side of the boat away from Ren-aud's view. He seems to have expectations about what we will find and ignores a dark minke whale breaching close to the peninsula. After a few minutes, he calls, "Did you see the belugas?" It is a rhetorical ques-tion, but neither of us has seen anything in the water because there is so much chop in the estuary. Farther out, in the St. Lawrence itself, where the water is so wide and the shores so distant that you might as well be on the ocean, the wind is higher and the water too rough to take *Le Bleuvet* out into the river itself today. Michel is surprised we haven't spotted the belugas, and he points to the white curls of the waves and froth a hundred yards away.

"It's the teenagers," he advises, "the young males." We look out to where the estuary begins to flow into the river and yes, of course, we can see the gray shapes of the young whales rising and dipping in the short waves so that they look like waves themselves. I am surprised that the belugas, or at least the portion of their bodies that we can see, are not larger. We expect any animal called a whale to be gigantic. But while the belugas' size isn't impressive, the power of their swimming is. I have always thought that the sight of young horses galloping together is the most stirring experience to be had. Now I think that it is whales quietly breaking the surface of the estuary in quick succession, arcing and diving under.

"They can get pretty rambunctious," Michel says. He is having to tack and turn the boat often to keep the young belugas in sight. To me, though, the way these animals slice through the turbulence looks calm and powerful.

"See the color?" he calls about a pair swimming close enough for us to distinguish the outlines of two animals. "Still gray. That's how you can tell they're young. They're born a kind of café au lait color and gradually lighten up year by year." At this stage of life the young beluga is named for its color. It is a *bleuvet,* a little blue. This phase lasts until the animals are four to six years old and almost fully grown, and after that the belugas live slowly, almost as slowly as humans. They reach sexual maturity and produce offspring only about the age of seven, and the females produce a single calf only every three years. Their life span, currently estimated at seventy years, is not much different from our own.

Although the International Union for the Conservation of Nature classifies the beluga as "Near Threatened," a conservation status with a fairly low level of urgency, that worldwide generalization doesn't take into account the condition of specific populations. The population in Alaska's Cook Inlet is in crisis as a result of commercial operations, and the St. Lawrence population, which bottomed out in the 1970s from a combination of hunting and high levels of cancer caused by pollutants, has recovered to some extent. Canada banned the hunting of whales in 1979 and has maintained an effort to clean up the St. Lawrence. Michel estimates there are now about fourteen hundred belugas in the St. Lawrence, but he cautions us that the population is stagnant, neither falling nor rising to any significant extent.

One of *Le Bleuvet*'s missions in the Parc marin du Saguenay-Saint-Laurent is to pry open the mysteries of beluga society in order to preserve the animals. GREMM was founded in 1984 by Robert Michaud, a young Canadian scientist who had begun studying the whales of the whale soup and had become passionate about their conservation. His research focused on the social structure of the resident belugas, and while he manages to continue this work, he told me that a great deal of his time is devoted to fund-raising to support this and quite a number of other research projects devoted to a range of whales that visit the Saguenay. In order to see what's going on within a population of whales, in order to assess their well-being or understand their social life—which for the gregarious belugas are inextricably intertwined—you have to do more than census and get samples from dead whales. You have to be able to recognize individual whales. This is the thrust of Robert Michaud's current work. In 1994 he began using photographs and DNA samples to identify the members of the beluga pods off Tadoussac. The work has been painstaking, time-consuming, and catch-as-catch-can, because the whales are visible for only a few moments at a time. Michel, who has been involved in this study since its inception, and Renaud observe the belugas on an almost daily basis in the months when ice doesn't clog the fjord. In their work for Michaud they have gained detailed descriptions and knowledge of two hundred of the estimated fourteen hundred whales in the Saguenay herd.

After an hour or so of play in the estuary, the teenagers split into two groups and rollick off toward the rough water of the river, and *Le Bleuvet* heads up into the calm of the fjord. We are motoring with the tide running into the mouth of the fjord when Renaud spots the first female of the day. He comes back from the bow to point her out. When she rises in the current, her side and fin are a startling white. I have heard that in the productions of nature there is no example of "pure" white, but the cold shimmering white of the adult beluga, gently porpoising through dark water and waves curling with tendrils of a lesser white, has to be as close to pure white as nature gets. Like *Le Bleuvet,* she is headed from the mouth of the fjord toward the narrow place where the ferries crisscross the fjord every ten minutes. She disappears for a couple of long minutes as Renaud straps on the big camera and watches the water for her to reemerge. Just as she surfaces near the steep fjord wall, another flash of brilliant white announces another whale on the opposite side of the channel. Michel throttles down the engine expectantly, and on each side of the channel, a new whale appears. Within moments each of the whales along opposite walls of the fjord is joined by a second whale, and without turning his attention from the diving and sounding of the two pairs of whales, Michel says something he will repeat in different ways throughout the day, "All we really know about the whales is what we see when they come to the surface." In our travels that day I discover just how difficult it is to observe animals that live underwater and how essential sound is to our learning anything about them.

The two pairs fish their way to the slick path made by the ferry, and then they sound. When the whales resurface at a safe distance from the ferry crossing, the two pairs are together in a loose gathering of four. What we are seeing is part of a continual dance of linking up and breaking off. Each pair of whales arcs and dives so close to each other and so amicably that a single word keeps popping into my mind: *intimate.* This impression of closeness, attachment, is remade over and over throughout the day, every time two belugas roll up out of the water and dive back down.

Belugas are intensely social, as any number of aerial photos of the large closely packed herds off Alaska in the Beaufort Sea illustrate. From four or five hundred feet up, the backs of the whales crowd the lens like sperm cells on a microscope slide. The herd in the fjord has an organization almost as complex as that of the meerkats. It is a gathering of smaller, more closely associated pods. The pod of teenagers, the gray swimmers we saw in the estuary, is in a kind of holding pattern anticipating maturity and mating. Then there is a pod consisting of adult males who roam fairly freely in nearby areas of the St. Lawrence as well as in the fjord, and last is the pod of females that shelter and forage with their young in the fjord. It is not uncommon for a female beluga to travel with a calf who is the young-of-the-year as well as the calf born previously. Where the beluga family seems to differ from meerkat families is that there is no apparent dominance hierarchy among the males or the females that determines which males sire and which females bear young. Like many parrots, the belugas live in a fission-fusion society in which the pods and subpods split off from one another and reconverge in a fluid manner.

Here in the fjord the water is glassy, almost still, and it is not difficult to pick up the telltale signs that a whale will momentarily come up for air. This is foreshadowed by a deeper, stiller gloss of water in the shape of a torpedo. Then what looks like a faint crease in the water will appear just before the fin and then the back break the surface. The surprising thing about such powerful swimming is that a beluga creates such little disturbance in the water. In fact, the scene in the fjord as the whales make their way north to its far end is entirely peaceful. The whales do not appear to be disturbed by *Le Bleuvet*'s presence, and in fact, one female swims up curiously to have a look at the boat.

"Scarveau," Renaud introduces her. Down in the cabin there are a couple of big loose-leaf binders that hold photographs of the individual whales. The photographs show close-ups of gray and white whale sides and whale backs. They are labeled with numbers and quite often with names. Although the photographs appear at first to be remarkably similar and repetitious, they show each whale's markings—dings and dents in the fin, scars from wounds caused by wear and tear from underwater obstacles and rough play. Michel and Renaud have absorbed these identifiers so thoroughly that, without consulting their family albums, they can train binoculars on a whale a quarter mile away from the boat and recognize that whale. Scarveau is named for the jagged lightning streak scar along her spine. She was identified shortly after her birth, and her travel has been documented for the past five years. Although they have an affectionate interest in all the whales we see, Michel and Renaud seem especially fond of Scarveau. She is the first member of the herd they have followed from birth.

Scarveau inspects us, and we inspect her. We find that our first impression of a beluga's size was accurate. Although Scarveau is smaller than most adult male belugas, on average a beluga is only somewhat larger than the bottlenose dolphin you can see at almost any public aquarium. Scarveau's head is also reminiscent of a bottlenose dolphin, except that its snout is blunter and foreshortened and instead of making a smooth aerodynamic curve from the tip of this snout back over its head to her dorsal fin, her forehead is swollen by a globelike pad of fatty tissue called a melon. The opening for Scarveau's jaw turns up in a constant smile, and her small, round eyes seem cheerfully myopic. They do not blink. Farther back beyond her eyes is the blowhole, the single nostril that the belugas use for breathing.

The blowhole is a sphincter muscle, and its default, involuntary position is shut. To breathe, Scarveau must decide to open her blowhole. To do this, she faces a challenge something like a flute player, who needs to program when to take in air without interrupting the flow of the melody. Every species of whale has developed its own "breathing sequence," a pattern of where they are in the water and what they do with their bodies when they exhale and inhale. An experienced observer can identify a whale's species by its breathing sequence. For some whales, exhaling is an explosion through the blowhole as they surface, while for the beluga, which doesn't show many acrobatics in its sequence, exhaling often begins underwater, which produces a string of large bubbles. To make the enormous variety of sounds it uses to communicate with its family and to echolocate, the beluga forces air through its nasal cavities located behind the blowhole and out through its blowhole.

Scarveau has feeding to do, and she moves off toward the fjord walls. Renaud suddenly passes his binoculars to John. Michel locates her without glasses and says to John, "See her spitting?" She does it again, sending a thin stream of water to plop into the fjord a little distance ahead of her.

"She does that to scare the fish back toward her. They'll think it's a predator, and they'll turn around and swim toward her."

Another brilliant white back arcs up beside the hunting whale, a new partner evidently joining Scarveau to take advantage of some by-catch from the fish swimming back toward the spitting whale. Watching the two of them sound and come to the surface, dive and then break the surface of the water, I am suddenly impressed by a fact that should have been obvious to me before I even boarded *Le Bleuvet*: the whale, any whale or dolphin, is locked into a life of constant motion, constant physical exertion, constant coordination of breathing and swimming. If a whale stops swimming, it dies. How exhausting.

When Michel brings *Le Bleuvet* out of the main channel into a sunny cove and cuts the engine, we sit on the cockpit floor to eat sandwiches. "Do they sleep?" I ask Michel. "I mean, how can they sleep?"

"We're not sure about that," he says carefully, "because so much of their life takes place underwater. But there have been some studies that show they sleep with one side of their brain at a time. One side of their brain goes off duty, then the other one."

Other than the bare facts of sociality and quantity of vocalizing, what we know about how the belugas live we have learned mostly from catching glimpses of them swimming wild, watching them in an aquarium, or finding them stranded. It is water, the marine environment, that makes understanding the beluga or any marine mammal so difficult, and it is the animals' enormous intelligence that makes this difficulty so frustrating. It is almost impossible to visually track a whale or dolphin for more than brief intervals, and the inability to see what the whales are doing when they vocalize, combined with the fact that sound behaves in a radically different way in water than it does in air, makes it immensely problematic to sort out what exactly is going on when the belugas chirp and whistle and click.

➤ ❧ ➤

For the past eight or nine years, Peter Scheifele has been coming out into the fjord with Michel and his assistant to try to capture the sounds made by the belugas. Often called sea canaries because of their remarkable range of clicks, thunks, chirps, and twitters and their readiness to use these sounds, the belugas and their cousins in the toothed whale family, the dolphins, are the most vocal of whales. Their sounds have a frequency range of 100 Hz to 120,000 Hz, which a gifted singer like Sheila Jordan or Placido Domingo should envy. We hear sounds in the range from 20 Hz to 20,000 Hz, so we can perceive the beluga voice in only part of its vocal range. Exactly how the beluga controls the frequencies of its calls and clicks is not understood.

Water's density makes it a very efficient medium for transmitting sound waves, which travel five times as fast through a body of water as through the atmosphere over land. Sound intensity, what we think of as loudness, is also multiplied by water, so much so that underwater decibels have a different basis of measurement than the airborne decibels we hear from our stereos and limit with our zoning ordinances. The ocean is an especially effective medium for low-frequency sound and the even lower infrasound because these sounds take a long time to decay as they travel. This is the reason that a blue whale's infrasound calls can reach other blue whales five or six hundred miles away.

Peter is a big, burly man, with a dark, chin-chopper beard and an expansive manner, a Navy man. He is always a Navy man, and it is impossible to be around him and forget that. He carries the designation of rank *LCDR USN (Ret.)* as part of his formal title, he runs on military time, and he lays the blame for his cussing as well as the credit for his education at the U.S. Navy's door. The Navy set him off on the unusual path that led to his bulging research portfolio. He was a diver and a submariner, and after his tour in Vietnam the Navy sent him to college, through a master's degree in physics and physical oceanography, then to medical school, after which he entered a PhD program in audiology. "Before I started that," he claims, "I never chose a class for myself, never had an elective." While he was stationed in Hawaii and San Diego his intensive involvement with competitive dog obedience led to an assignment training dogs for the Coast Guard's counternarcotics program. It was through a Navy research project on the auditory capabilities of marine mammals at Mystic, Connecticut, that he gathered an education in marine acoustics. In order to assess the effects of marine sound on its receivers, he had to learn how to train seals and dolphins and belugas, and for a few years while he was working toward his PhD and still on assignment for the Navy, he served as the head trainer at Mystic Aquarium.

During that period, he began working with Robert Michaud and GREMM to test the waters—literally—in the fjord and the estuary. Peter was trying to assess the level of underwater background noise created by commercial and development activities and to figure out what effect this background noise had on the belugas off Tadoussac. What he was looking for specifically is the so-called Lombard response, which is also called the cocktail-party effect. This is what happens to you and me when we try to converse in the midst of din: we raise our voices in order to be understood. This change of vocal intensity, along with shifts to more emphatic pronunciation, is involuntary. It has been observed in singers working with choruses, and it is something that experienced conductors are wary about, something that soloists are trained to resist.

The Lombard response turns up just as commonly among animals, and because of all the noise humans impose on the landscape it has been studied as a conservation issue. Animals as different as monkeys, parakeets, and cats have exhibited this party-time reflex, and it's not unusual for them to express the response as a change in pitch. The great tit, the same bird that prompted John Krebs's Beau Geste experiment, has been found to sing at higher frequencies when it encounters noise pollution.[1] Because water intensifies many kinds of sound, it is not surprising that Peter found that belugas too raised their voices against din. The whales depend on sound to navigate and find food, and underwater noise can overwhelm their calls and cause confusion. Belugas often feed on the bottom, and even in the relatively shallow water where they forage, it's dark down there. In their murky environment, they use some of their calls to locate family members and draw them close. Unfortunately, humans are noisy animals, and our noise threatens the belugas' existence. This is an important motive for Peter to continue his research looking at changes in the acoustic environments in the ocean. In addition to the Navy, there are other organizations that also want this information, and GREMM and the National Science Foundation are among these.

More recently Peter has begun to focus on the vocal output side of the belugas' communications. He explained that he wanted to use sound to develop a method for keeping track of a wild population, and he wanted to begin a rudimentary classification of the whales' sounds and relate these to their behavior.

Radio tracking a whale to observe its movements is pretty difficult and not very satisfactory, Peter told me. The researchers follow the whale in a boat, and they have a gun that functions like a dart gun. "They fire off a suction cup with a radio mounted on it. But you know," Peter said as if this would have been anyone's first thought, "a whale's skin *ripples* when it moves through the water. So the suction cup doesn't stick on very long, and the radio falls off." Peter had the idea that he could parallel Michel and Renaud's visual identification work with audio identification.

He started on this by using captive whales at the Mystic Aquarium to learn how to link specific voices to individual belugas and to try to sort the types of calls by what the whales were doing at the time they were making the sound.

For help in obtaining the unique vocal signatures he teamed up with Mike Johnson, a professor of engineering at Marquette University whose research group, the Dr. Dolittle Project, brings together scientists from universities around the world to apply digital signal processing to the problem of identifying the voices of animals that range from frogs and birds to tigers and whales. In digital signal processing, any kind of signal—audio, radar, light—is represented by a sequence of numbers. In Mike Johnson's lab, the digitally recorded sounds of animal voices are analyzed by running their number sequences through various algorithms to define the signal with precision. This yields an extremely accurate picture of specific sounds from a particular animal, and these make up that animal's vocal signature.

"Ideally," Peter told me, "once we succeed with this with captive whales, we will be able to go out into the St. Lawrence and drop a hydrophone over the side to find out which animals are there and what's going on in the pod."

But first, though, the sounds he was collecting from the belugas at Mystic would undergo a more rudimentary analysis that focuses on the degree of stress—both *eu*stress, the happy, gain-seeking experience, and *dis*tress, the negative experience—the sounds reflected. The winter of 2008-9 presented a wonderful opportunity for a study of stress. When the Shedd Aquarium in Chicago began some renovations, it needed housing for seven belugas. The whales traveled to Connecticut in a remarkable airlift operation that involved more than a hundred staff members from the two aquariums and individual tanks and flight attendants for the belugas in transit.

The arrival of the Shedd visitors created an insider-outsider situation. The Chicago whales were housed separately from the Mystic whales, but the partition between their tanks was glass so that the animals could see one another and Peter could observe the reactions within the two groups. Although his goal was to relate stress to vocal sounds, detecting indications of stress of either kind would require consistent visual observation and rather subjective judgments. As usual, "having the animals swimming in water complicates things," Peter said.

"What would stress look like?" I wondered, and he suggested that if a whale was reacting to something that caused distress, it would express this by blowing bubbles out of its blowhole, shaking its head, and buzzing aggressively. If the animal was experiencing eustress, there would be no bubbles and the whale might begin making social whistles and twitters.

"We don't really know what stress looks like," agreed Mystic's behavioral scientist, Tracey Spoon, and added that the responses of individual belugas were likely to vary. "But," she decided, "swim patterns, swimming speed, and just the way the whales interact" would be indicators. "And of course we'll be getting cortisol levels." Just as for meerkats under duress, cortisol level would be the flag.

The hydrophone went down on the Mystic whales' side of the glass, and Tracey found a good perch on the landscaped island protruding into both tanks. From there she began to make the detailed notes of the whales' moment-to-moment activities that she would keep as introduction of the two groups went along.

At first there were some revelations. The Shedd visitors were a family of two females and their calves and the male who was the father of the calves. The three Mystic whales, two females without calves and a male, were unrelated. But Inuk, the Mystic male, had for a brief period in his life been housed with one of the Shedd females. "At first, Inuk would hover by the glass and buzz," Tracey reported, "then he seemed to recognize the female and made affectionate gestures against the glass—body rubs, belly rubs." This was sexual behavior, which, on account of a whale's rather demanding sex life, it didn't hurt to practice. Their sex usually ensues after a group of males chase down a female, and when one of them catches up to her, he must then negotiate underwater to align his large body against her large body so that his small—relative to his body size—penis finds her relatively small vagina. In any case, Tracey believed that Inuk's immediately friendly overtures indicated he recognized the Shedd female.

But soon things started to go wrong. The belugas began to play with the hydrophone, and eventually their fun broke it beyond repair.

A hydrophone is expensive enough that nobody owns many of them, and Peter had sent his second hydrophone to Portugal, where Dominie Writt was studying acoustic perception of dolphins. Then the Shedd Aquarium finished its remodeling, and the visitors were shipped home. Peter's group hadn't been able to make much of the opportunity the visiting whales had created, and thus far he had been able to send only some sample sounds to Mike Johnson for signal processing. Finally, before Peter could actually put together a new plan of action, Inuk, the male beluga, died. Now there were only two belugas at Mystic, both females.

Just before I left for Tadoussac, Peter decided to turn to bottlenose dolphins for his captive vocal studies and use these results to model future work with the wild belugas. The two animals are closely related, both being members of the suborder known as toothed whales, and what Peter learned about captive dolphins could likely be transferred to his understanding of the belugas. The dolphins were more accessible to science because they were smaller and aquariums could accommodate them in groups. Not only that, Peter pointed out, but "the dolphins are easier to train." Having trained several kinds of whales, including dolphins, for a number of years, Peter had a healthy respect for their cognitive capacities.

"You've done a lot of work training dogs," I said. "How smart is a dolphin compared to a dog?"

"I don't know about *smart*," he deliberated on the word. "What I would say is that a dolphin is very *perceptive*. And quick. Very, very quick. When I teach new trainers I give them a rule of thumb—'one dolphin equals two two-year-olds.' If you tell a dolphin *A*, he's probably thinking *B, C,* and *D* immediately. But yet, this same kind of animal with the same kind of brain," he said with a little exasperation, "will swim into a net, a life-threatening object!"

∾∾∾

The dolphin's brain is a puzzle, and at the same time Peter is investigating its outward manifestations, the animal in its umwelt producing and responding to vocal sounds, his student Dominie Writt is trying to peer into the dolphin's innenwelt, its interior life of sound perceptions. Although Peter has a detailed knowledge of the auditory perceptual apparatus in whales and made some forays into testing their capacities while he was at Mystic, he is now asking questions about how whales and dolphins produce, receive, and respond to sound, questions that a conservation biologist with an understanding of neurophysiology might ask. What Dominie is asking is, How does a whale or dolphin process the sounds it receives from other whales or dolphins? How does it recognize and decode these sounds?

As I write this, Dominie is working on her dissertation at the University of Kansas under the supervision of Stan Kuczaj, a professor at the University of Southern Mississippi, and Peter serves as the technical adviser to the project. A former high school science teacher who wrote a master's thesis on child language acquisition, she regards herself as very lucky indeed to have support from Peter. "He is really a pioneer," she tells me. "He is the first one I know of to use a completely noninvasive test we use for human perception with a cetacean. He was using a P300 test on the belugas at Mystic!"

She is referring to an EEG, an electroencephalograph test, that measures brain responses to specific events.[2] The P300 is routinely administered in psychological testing and increasingly in audiology for ascertaining disabilities in people who have been in car accidents or suffered strokes and for children who show signs of auditory disorders. It has also been used as a method of lie detection. Peter had also told me about putting suction cup electrodes on one of the Mystic belugas that were wired to an EEG machine to record brain wave responses to sound stimuli. Typically, a P300 brain wave is a response to an oddball signal, a stimulus that breaks an expected pattern. It can be used to evaluate expectation and understanding of language. An oddball can be a signal that breaks with context or an alteration that creates nonsense from a word.

Dominie is using a test like the P300, the P550, to find out whether a dolphin responds to a sound or an element in a pattern of sounds that violates expectation. When a human undergoes a P300 test, electrodes connected by wires to an EEG machine are placed on the outside of the person's head to record electrical activity within the brain. The electrical impulses are expressed on the EEG screen in a jagged horizontal line traveling across the screen. The ups and downs of this line, which represent brain waves, are relatively regular until the person's nervous system responds more strongly to a stimulus. Then the line on the screen jumps up.

For her dolphins Dominie has invented a kind of headpiece that she calls a Ring-Cap. This sits on the dolphin's head to hold five electrodes in place. The dolphin is trained to remain stationary in the water beside the platform with the EEG machine as it listens to a playback of dolphin sound through an underwater microphone. In effect, the dolphin must remain motionless at the surface of the water for several minutes, and the discipline to maintain this position is where the need for skilled training comes in. Dominie says she could not work with her subjects without expert help, but Peter, who has extensive experience training dolphins to do really complicated routines for aquarium shows, doesn't make much of this. "It's just operant conditioning," he says. "It's just a matter of giving the signal, making a bridge, then giving the reward." Conditioning, the link between cause and effect, is a basic concept in cognition that was revealed to Pavlov by his dog. Operant conditioning puts that concept to work by controlling the links. "But," Peter concedes, "you have got to be quick to make that bridge, very quick."

Dominie's subjects are three impeccably trained dolphins in an aquarium in the Algarve region of Portugal. Tethered by nothing more than operant conditioning to the platform holding the EEG machine, the dolphins keep their places and register their responses liberally.

"What, exactly, is the test like?"

It is a sequence of repeated sounds that present a challenge of logic or grammar. Dominie makes an analogy to the children she tested for language acquisition capacity. "With the children, I asked them to distinguish between an animate and inanimate subject—say, some construction like 'The man broke the window' compared with 'The rock broke the window.' The kids understood the first idea easily. But even though many of them correctly recognized that the second idea made sense, their brain responses indicated initial confusion.

"With the dolphins, I get amazingly clear results, much clearer, in fact, than I got working with the children."

"What is clear?" I wonder.

"The consistent *prominence* of the peak latency—latency is the time it takes between the signal and the brain's response, the processing time. That's what the '300' refers to, 300 milliseconds. In fact," she says, "the dolphins regularly tested at 550 milliseconds—that's why this test is a P550."

"Why would a longer processing time be better performance?"

"It could mean that the brain is processing more complex material. In other words," she interpolates, "with this test I can identify which components of a sound sequence have value for the dolphin, and a longer latency means there are more sound components that have value and meaning."

"So then, the sound sequences are like phrases, and in their heads the dolphins are doing something like comprehending language."

"Nope," she says firmly. "Not like language. You don't even need to go there."

If she is interested in language acquisition, I reason, why isn't she willing to make the leap to something like language?

"Because we don't need to go there." Evidently she too has read the rules about what to attribute to whom, but for her purposes, this doesn't really matter. "In this study all I'm interested in is cognitive processing of communication, sound as communication."

We're back to signals rather than words and feelings, and now I see how useful the term *signals* is.

Then she says, "Human language is one type of communications system, and we have evolved with the cognitive means to process this kind of communication." In other words, we don't need to assume that what is churning through a dolphin's brain in response to sound from other dolphins is the same as what is churning through our human brains in response to language. It is still signal processing, but the signals are relatively complex in their construction. I suddenly understand that the term *signal* is and how right it is. It is the common denominator of any impulse that flows through the brain to prompt a response.

What Dominie is measuring is signal complexity, and what she points out is that cognition evolves in order to simplify lives, our own as well as the lives of other animals. "Cognition is really a set of short-cuts that allow efficiency in all kinds of activities, including communication. In divergent species, say dolphins and humans, those shortcuts will be very different. Human language is one type of communication system with one shortcutting process. The key to understanding what communication really is will be to be able to compare the cognitive processes across species."

"Sounds like a pretty long night of homework, to me."

Dominie doesn't find it so daunting. "There are two keys to making comparisons like these. There is the complexity of the social system"—and here I realize how complex the fluid social lives of the whales and dolphins are—"and there is the variability in the animal's environment. Lots of variability in an animal's environment also makes for complex communications."

This is the situation, I realize, of many birds, especially those that migrate. Certainly the belugas in the Saguenay, and those in Cook Inlet in Alaska even more so, have had to accommodate to both their radically changing underwater sound environments and the complexities of their family lives, and of these last we have only a few desultory hints. But what is clear is that the whales' social groups are crucial to their livelihood and that vocalizing is strong stuff that helps group members find one another and stay close to one another. This is the point where the whales' and dolphins' cognition intersects with their intricately knit social arrangements and their marine environment. The perceptual and cognitive processes that underlie their calls and clicks and whistles are essential to the whales' survival.

✒ ✒

We are turning up into a long cove on the east side of the fjord, the Baie Sainte-Marguerite, where there is a sandy beach on one side of the cove. The whales like to gather here, and campers who spend the night report hearing the whales' voices clearly. In the bow of *Le Bleuvet* Renaud scans the fjord with his binoculars, and suddenly he becomes attentive. Whatever signal he uses to notify Michel is imperceptible, but Michel slows the boat and comes back to stand beside us.

"It's Piglet," he advises us, although the surface of the water is blank. In a moment a little trail of fat bubbles announces the emergence of a beluga calf. His mother breaks the surface just ahead of him. The blue-brown calf is the smallest beluga we have seen. As soon as the little whale has shown himself for positive identification, Michel hops down into the cabin and cuts the engine. "Listen to how he breathes. Can you hear him snorting? That's how he got his name."

"You're lucky to see a calf this young," Renaud advises John in French. "He's only a month old."

Piglet sounds, then surfaces only a few yards off the stern.

"I believe I have witnessed one birth out here," Michel says. A single possible birth in more than fifteen years of following belugas in this fjord. The whales are not secretive like many land mammals, particularly the carnivores. They are more like cattle or even wild herding animals such as antelope. But their births are obscured by water. Michel describes watching an unaccompanied female swim in restless circles until at some point a calf appeared near her, flopping about clumsily on the water and before long acclimating to the water with the effortless swimming of an adult. But Michel is very clear about the fact that he wasn't absolutely certain that he had witnessed the youngster's actual birth. Science must be rigorous.

Piglet swims close to his mother in tight coordination, as if he has been tethered head and tail to her. You would expect this infant attachment from any land-dwelling animal, any kitten and cat or foal and mare, but somehow taking place as it does in water–where the uncertainty of breathing, the relentless need to keep moving, and the possibility of drowning are so immediate–the beluga calf's ties to its mother seem more tender than those of land animals.

It is impossible for me to watch Piglet and his mother without thinking of the ideas of John Bowlby, a British psychologist and psychiatrist who devoted his life's work to the mother-infant tie and gained much insight from animal mothers and their infants. Led by the emotional experiences of his own childhood, he came to see that there were two forces that shape a person's psychological development, attachment and loss, the severing of attachment. These two fundamental experiences were the universal sources of well-being and of distress and grief. Attachment began with the newest infant's attachment to his or her mother and the state of utter dependence on her. As the child grew and developed, this kind of attachment was extended to other people through a process of seeking proximity.

As Bowlby himself tells it, his traditional upbringing by nannies in an upper-crust British household, where his mother saw him for only an hour or so each day, was traumatic. It was a severing of his attachment to her that formed with his birth. Although he had been trained in what was by then conventional psychoanalysis based on Freud's ideas, Bowlby brought his new insight on attachment into direct confrontation with Freudian theory. He claimed that because his theory began with a person's birth and followed that person's development, it was more apt to be an accurate description of a psychological life than was a retrospective interpretation by an analyst who, presented with a fully developed person with fully developed problems, worked backward through that person's experiences to locate the sources of psychic disturbance. Freudian theory was not scientific because it couldn't be tested, Bowlby said, pointing out that his own ideas began with biology.

Human psychology, he reasoned, was based in the biological brain, and he began to look to animal analogs of this psychology. This led him, of course, to two contemporaries whom we have met before, Konrad Lorenz and Niko Tinbergen. Bowlby visited Lorenz in postwar Austria and participated in his research on imprinting in geese. He took into account research on deer, where mother-daughter relationships bind a herd together over successive generations, and on primates and their infants. Attachment, he concluded, is something that begins in the instant of birth and continues even after an infant becomes independently mobile, until it is severed by death or absence, when it takes the form of grief or anger. Attachment is preverbal, and not only that, it forms before a young human or animal begins to communicate.

It is separation that prompts communication. Bowlby's notion anticipated John Bonner's similar proposition that separation of another kind, the division of cells, prompts communication, and in evolutionary terms, the first communication was via chemical cues. At the moment at which an infant can move physically away from its mother,

Bowlby observed, the need for mother-infant communication arises. Here the familiar term *signal* pops up in Bowlby's writing. Because Bowlby had read the ethologists, his infants and older children *signaled*. When they cried, they gestured, they babbled, they spoke–they signaled. I'm not sure that independent mobility is as significant a factor as Bowlby thought. Many animals other than primates and kangaroos are independently mobile instantly after birth, and the need for mother-infant communication is still immediate and urgent. But this is a small quibble. Bowlby's ideas changed the ways we think about our emotional development, and psychologists after him have extended his attachment theory to see the mother-infant relationship as the source not only of sympathy but of empathy.[3] One music psychologist has gone even further, and suggested that the origins of music and language can be found in mother-child attachment.[4]

At the moment, Piglet, a perfect illustration of Bowlby's theory, is very attached to his mother. There is seldom as much as a yard between them. He is only a month beyond his risky underwater delivery, and his invisible tether to her will endure for a childhood that lasts about as long as a human infant's. Belugas nurse on their mother for anywhere from a year and a half to two years; dolphins have an even longer period of close maternal attachment that sometimes stretches to four years. A number of biologists have speculated that during this long period by their mothers' sides the whales learn social habits and form attachments to other family members and eventually to whales in associated pods. A beluga or a bottlenose dolphin is attached to others of its kind by a network of tight links–and unless you are a hermit or otherwise nonsocial, you are too. With the beluga not only are these attachments strong, but the habit of attachment is almost indestructible.

Michel tells us that there were several instances reported in Nova Scotia in which a beluga who had become separated from his network came close to the shore, saw a human, and formed an attachment to that person. While this might seem rather endearing, it can prove to be a vulnerability, for it is the same gregariousness that draws belugas and dolphins close enough to boats to get battered by the propellers. But overall, the habit of seeking social attachment is a source of survival, and though it may in fact begin with the mother-calf bonds, attachments can, like friendships, form between members of the same sex.

One day, Michel's wife, Sylvie, answered the whale rescue hotline at GREMM's headquarters in Tadoussac, and a fisherman gave her information about a beluga calf he had caught in a net. Michel and Renaud raced to the site, filled a Zodiac, one of the low pontoon boats used for whale watching, with water, and transferred the calf to it. They intended to release the calf into a pod of females, but when they located a group of females in the fjord and turned the calf loose, the females paid little attention to the hapless calf. Instead, a group of males happened along, and surrounding the baby, they carried him along on their backs until he could forage on his own.

During the period when the calf lives next to its mother learning social habits, it is also learning about voice, and apparently while the calf is learning whistles and chirps and echolocation, it is engaging an ability to adopt the sounds of other whales that it will use all its life. Vocal learning has been investigated in many species but found with certainty in only a few: birds—including most famously the parrots—humans, and cetaceans, the whales. It has been studied fairly extensively in dolphins, which have the ability to both learn and mimic the sounds of their confreres. For a long while it was thought that each dolphin has a signature whistle that it uses when it is alone and seeking company and that singles it out from the rest in its family. Then in the 1990s, Diana Reiss, an influential researcher who works at the New York Aquarium, and Brenda McCowan, at the School of Veterinary Medicine at the University of California, Davis, began to reassess the whistles that dolphins used to call from isolation and found that these whistle sounds cluster into a general call type and may also contain some kind of information about the caller's identity. More significantly, the two researchers believe that the whistles are not fixed like the photo on your driver's license but can morph over time to respond to changes in the umwelt. Apparently, dolphins, like us, can learn new lingo after they reach adulthood.[5]

In considering the question of whether or not dolphins learn their contact whistles or come into the world fully equipped, Reiss and McCowan had to come to terms with mimicry. Dolphins have long been recognized as adept mimics, and this talent has been seen as evidence of their extreme sociality. Most scientists who work in this area believe, or imply, that the tendency to imitate is innate. How this inborn predilection is exploited by the animal becomes the interesting question. To trace the links between learning and the dolphin's long-recognized talent for mimicry, Reiss and McCowan devised a delightful experiment that used a simple dolphin-sized keyboard with images of toys on the keys. The dolphins activated the keys with their beaks to produce different whistles and immediately afterward were rewarded with a toy–a ball, a ring, a float–that corresponded to the image on the key or with a rub from their handler, which they really enjoy.

Reiss and McCowan were not surprised that the dolphins readily figured out the game and mimicked the computer-generated sounds enthusiastically. But what happened next was something they hadn't expected. The dolphins began to produce the sound associated with the image on the key before they poked that key to make the computer sing the sound. They already knew how the tune would go, and so they called it before they listened to the recording.[6] In her research sessions in Portugal, Dominie witnessed something quite similar. "Some of the dolphins began to spontaneously mimic some of the nonsense whistles we had created by reversing and rearranging recorded whistles. Occasionally, as we began a session, even before that particular nonsense whistle was played, we would hear a distant whistle mimicking it from a day or two before." As Peter says, if you tell a dolphin *A*, he goes directly to *B*, *C*, and *D*.

Along with Reiss and McCowan and a number of other commentators, Dominie believes that the dolphins' fluency in adapting their voice has evolved together with the fluidity in their fission-fusion lifestyle, which in itself is adaptation that accommodates the continual shifting and changing in the undersea world. Right now, fission-fusion roughly describes the limits of what we know about this lifestyle: the very deep and long mother-infant associations, the pods, gatherings of whales by sex and age that diverge only to come together again, and the close ties among them. This is about what we know about their underwater lives.

"All we know about these animals is the part of their lives we see at the surface," Michel reminds us while Renaud positions himself to shoot a baby picture of Piglet. "So much of their lives takes place at a depth where we can't see what goes on." But we can hear them, and if we come to a place where we can interpret their sounds the way Marta Manser has translated the meerkat calls, their voices might provide the best view of their lives.

Piglet's one-month picture, which Renaud took today, will go in the family album down in the cabin, and perhaps he will grow to mating age, then to fatherhood, with Michel and Renaud still following his daily comings and goings.

A pair of whales hunting in a path along the fjord walls changes course and dives in the direction of Piglet and his mother. Renaud points out a trail of big, plump bubbles streaming out along the surface of the water in the swimming wake of one of the approaching females. When the whales surface close to the boat we can hear their breathing. The air comes out of their blowholes in long, contented sighs. This is a peaceful sound, more peaceful than the purring of a cat in your lap. The fjord whispers with the exhalations of the whales.

# 7

## The Elephant and the Mirror

～

Peter Scheifele's and Dominie Writt's work on auditory processing
by the whales and dolphins suggests that, in terms of listener expectation, there may be some rough parallels with human listeners of
language and music. Their work is about what goes on in the heads of
listeners, the whales and dolphins on the receiving end of signaling.
What goes on in animal heads during two-or-more-way vocal communication, the kind that takes place in language and music?

Elephants share with whales and dolphins—along with humans—the
facts of big brains, long lives, complicated families, complex vocalization
among family members, lengthy mother-infant ties, and great intelligence. But the fact that elephants live on land has simplified research
into their communications. This is probably the main reason that, while
Peter Scheifele and Dominie Writt have only just begun to reveal important features of vocal communication and cognition in whales and
dolphins, we know a great deal about how elephants communicate

vocally, and research on elephant voices and thinking has progressed enough to consider the cognition that drives two-way, back-and-forth signaler-receiver transactions. I want to know more about the thought processes that accompany that communication. This is what takes me to Atlanta to visit the two elephants in the zoo there.

By now you won't be surprised to learn that the two things I wanted most passionately as a child were to sit on a horse and to go to the zoo. Because we lived in a small Ohio town fifty miles from the nearest city large enough to host a zoo, the first desire was easier to satisfy than the second, and sitting on the back of a horse brought a sense of completion. I had landed where I wanted to be, the back of the horse, and what I saw was what I got. Visiting the Columbus Zoo on the hotly anticipated occasions I nagged to accomplish, however, was not so immediately fulfilling. Even at the age of eight or nine, I realized that the zoo was a façade, an elaborate façade of living animals that showed nothing of their real lives, and I had the sense that behind the scenes, where the animals were kept, was where their real lives took place. I was convinced that if I could go around to the back doors of the exhibits, I could get to know the animals as they actually were, and so I tested that possibility persistently with no good results. Now, decades later, my childhood wish has been granted.

I walk into Zoo Atlanta with Josh Plotnik a couple of hours before it opens to the public. The blacktop paths that wind among the exhibits are deserted except for an occasional employee on foot or driving a tractor and wagon, and the buildings are shut. The caretakers are setting out the morning meals, and Josh takes me through two very tall rooms, in each of which is a female elephant eating a solitary breakfast. In the first room we stand less than a yard from the elephant, closer than the public will be allowed when the zoo opens and closer than I have ever been to an elephant. My reaction is perfectly trite. I am overwhelmed. Her height and bulk are way out of scale with any animal I have been around. Josh says, "About five tons," and I realize that you could pack ten good-sized horses into that baggy hide and still leave the wrinkles slack. The legs that bear this weight are the size of harvestable timber, and each of the toenails that finishes off the broad foot is the size of my fist. Kids have a word for this these days, *gi-normous.* Trite as this reaction is, I am downright intimidated. The head keeper joins us for a moment to check on the elephant.

"Kelly," he introduces her. "She's a little clueless, socially. But her mind is always going, and she's very inquisitive." This inquisitiveness will cause Josh to make a significant detour in his research plans.

When Kelly begins to explore my arm with her trunk I have to force myself not to freeze but to continue breathing and talking with Josh. If a dog or horse can smell fear, as is often said, this vast, exquisitely sensitive animal surely has my number. But as I endure Kelly's inspection I notice something that surprises me—her ear. Although I have seen a lot of photos and read a good deal about how elephants call and how well they hear, I haven't given much thought to the structure of the ear itself. The opening to her ear canal is a long, narrow, hair-covered slit immediately in front of the giant flap of the outer ear. The opening is hardly noticeable even at this close range. It isn't obvious in photographs, and this seems incongruous with what I know is the elephant's remarkable audio perception.

We go through a hall to the outside and a ladder on the wall of the building, and we climb two stories to the flat roof of the elephant house. We are looking down into a high-walled enclosure. Even though it is Atlanta, it is still February, and a strong breeze sweeps over the roof. It is pretty cold up here. Josh gets down on his side so that his shoulders project from the roof over the enclosure and the video camera in his hand is well clear of the building. Under us a heavy door rolls, and I hear the video camera start. After a slow minute, Kelly's broad head begins to emerge in the corner of the enclosure with the far end of her trunk exploring independently off to the side. As she makes a few slow, swinging strides toward a pile of hay near the far wall, her immense, wrinkled back comes into view, then the whole of her vast self. Kelly is followed in a minute by the more tentative entrance of Tara, whose slow progress toward another pile of hay carefully glances off the space occupied by the other elephant. Kelly is dominant.

I am reporting this at about the same pace and level of detail that Josh's camera is recording it. Every stroke of an ear, shift of weight or body angle, every turn of a massive head, is documented. This is the beginning of the first stage of a mirror self-recognition test. Not only are Josh and I behind the scenes at the zoo, but he is trying to go behind the scenes inside Kelly's and Tara's huge noggins. He's trying to learn something about how they think about the world around them, other elephants, and themselves.

On the opposite wall of the enclosure a big gate made of vertical rails has been rolled across a wide opening to close the enclosure. On the gate a heavy frame is mounted, and the frame is covered with sheet metal. This frame and its covering are painted the same rusty brown as the thick concrete walls. The frame is a recent introduction to the enclosure. It is a dummy for the mirror that will replace it. The scheme behind the experiment is to first introduce the dummy mirror—to eliminate the possibility that the elephants will react to a mirror just because it is a novel object—then post a mirror in place of the dummy to let the elephants become accustomed to that and to see if they will recognize themselves in the mirror and show that they do by watching themselves and moving their bodies to make their mirror images change. The final phase in this progression in front of the mirror is the so-called mark test, in which Josh will place a visible mark or ornament on each elephant's body to see if she will respond to this change in her image.

You're probably thinking *mirror*? What happened to *sound* and *call* and *song*? Although the past twenty years have seen major advances in our understanding of elephant vocalizing—a group at Cornell University has even begun to compile a lexicon of the elephant's many vocal sounds—Josh is not studying vocal communication, and he is interested in it only insofar as it provides clues about how an elephant thinks about itself in relation to other elephants. Josh's work with his "eles" [EL-eez] is a way for me to look into the question of how much the *signaler* can understand about the *receiver* and vice versa, the question of what might go on in an elephant's brain while it's calling and listening. The elephant, along with the belugas and dolphins, is highly intelligent. While you could argue that intelligence makes elephant communication a special case among the communications of animals, it also sets the elephant closer to us humans, leaving only the primates between us on the intelligence ladder. The elephant and its communications are a good link to our own.

Josh Plotnik is remarkably at home with the two elephants. At first he doesn't appear to be a person who could so easily enter an elephant's world. He has city boy, specifically New York City boy, written all over him—shirts straight out of the Ivies, trendy glasses with narrow lenses, sneakers, and a decidedly New York accent. He talks fast, and he has a New Yorker's impatience with delay, drivers' errors, and politicians' blunders. He is passionate about baseball, and he has a wide-ranging appetite for intellectual ideas and a critical snap in his responses to them. I never would have imagined him in the place where I originally contacted him, a government elephant facility in northern Thailand.

When we visit Kelly and Tara, Josh is a doctoral candidate working in Frans B. M. de Waal's Living Links Center at Emory University, and this association too might seem at first blush to be unlikely. De Waal is well known for his work with primates, especially with chimpanzees, and Josh joined de Waal's lab at the Yerkes National Primate Research Center assuming that he would also study chimps. But de Waal, who has published a good deal on consolation and reconciliation among animals and was focusing on the notion of empathy among his chimps, was interested to find out if there were animals outside the primate family and not so closely related to humans who also showed a capacity for empathy. He wondered what Josh might find if he looked closely at the ways the highly intelligent elephants interact with one another. In a world where biology and its research pursuits seem to start from a vantage of self-interest, self-perpetuation, and a reductive account of genetic influence, de Waal has been at pains to point out ways in which cooperation among animals parallels that of humans, that empathy and sympathy have their places in biology.[1] This is where his interests converge with Josh Plotnik's elephant research.

In Thailand, Josh was investigating cooperation among the Asian elephants in the government facility where he worked. Many of them were trained to work, and for two and a half years Josh lived among the families of the mahouts, the men who train and handle the elephants. When he landed in Thailand to seek out a research site, all he knew about elephants was what he had read in books and scientific articles. He could speak very little Thai. He was there for three or four months before he knew anyone, and when he did get to know people, they were the mahouts. In spite of his urban background and probably because of his interest in the animals, he was able to make a place for himself among rural Thais. As a teenager he had worked in the Central Park Zoo and then, thinking he wanted to become a veterinarian and knowing he would need hands-on experience, he apprenticed to racetrack veterinarians at Belmont and Aqueduct, where he got an eyeful of the economic pressures on the trainers, the horses, and the people who owned them. When one of his professors at Cornell met with Josh's freshman class for the first time, he pointed out how few of these undergraduates would actually ascend to veterinary school and that, really, a career as a veterinarian might not be stimulating for everyone. Josh found truth in that. By the time he was a junior at Cornell he was working summers with Frans de Waal's team.

Josh had to make himself a plausible partner to the mahouts, and he managed to do this. By the end of his first two years in Thailand, he was relatively fluent in Thai. He lived the mahouts' lives, working seven days a week (they do not observe a sabbath rest from work) and hanging out with them at night. "If I were ever going to become an alcoholic," he says, "I would have found out then." The mahouts showed him how to be with the elephants in close quarters—he did not have steel bars between him and them—and how to teach them what he wanted them to do for his experiments in cooperation. "If I wanted one to pull on a rope and she didn't seem to get it, I just wrapped the rope around her trunk. It doesn't take much."

~ ~ ~

The elephant has lived in close conjunction with humans for at least four thousand years, and its relationship with us has been fraught with brutal ambiguities. This is especially true of elephants in Asia, where an elephant culture, in which the elephant was venerated in religion and exploited for military and economic purposes, has flourished more and persisted longer than the more limited human use in Africa. In Asia elephants were used in war and also trained for work, a practice that is now limited. Ironically, by partnering with humans to deforest many areas, they helped to destroy their habitat and strand themselves in agricultural areas where they inflict considerable damage. In Africa, the elephants' situation is much less ambiguous. They have not been useful to humans for centuries, and their foraging habits menace the livelihoods of mostly impoverished native people. It's a precarious balance for both species, and elephant populations are now "managed," a tragic fate for such a sensitive, highly intelligent animal. On both continents, elephants living on the edges of human activity have been hunted, harvested, culled, or whatever you like to call it, until wild populations remain only on marginal lands left over from human uses.

Most of what popular science knows about elephants is based on a number of long-term studies of elephant populations in Africa, many of which are still under way. A brief but hardly inclusive history of these studies begins with Iain Douglas-Hamilton and Cynthia Moss, who each began separate, still ongoing, observations of the savannah

elephants in the early 1970s. They were joined in their investigations of
the elephants' family life and social interaction in the 1980s by Joyce
Poole and then in the early 1990s by Katy Payne, who made the pioneer-
ing discovery of infrasound in elephant rumbles, at three sites in Africa.
In the mid-1990s, Caitlin E. O'Connell-Rodwell in Namibia and Megan
Wyman's mentor Karen McComb in Kenya picked up this general line
of family and communication research on elephants, and in 2000 Mya
Thompson, a protégée of Katy Payne, began a project to classify the
calls and rumbles of forest elephants in the Central African Republic.

On the savannah and in the forest elephants lead social lives that
strongly resemble the fluid arrangements of the belugas and dolphins:
the males and females gather in pods that alternately converge and separate. The older female elephants are quite clearly the heads of the family,
and they travel in groups of related females and their calves of the past
few years. Instead of male pods, elephants have bull groups, and like the
male belugas and dolphins, the adult and adolescent male elephants
wander in loose coalitions on the lookout for mating opportunities. On
the savannah elephant matriarchs and their dependent families form
so-called bond groups by intermittently sweeping close together to share
grazing areas. These are analogous to what marine biologists think of
as a herd of whales. The groups and subgroups of elephants forage and
move about their expansive and overlapping matriarchal territories in
constantly shifting fission-fusion patterns. At certain times and places,
particularly evenings at watering holes, the elephant groups converge
and keep very close company. At other times, the groups can be fifteen
to twenty miles apart.

Since Katy Payne published her discovery of elephants' infrasound communications in the late 1980s, it has been clear that the elephants' wanderings are coordinated by their voices. Payne began to realize the power of their voices earlier, when she felt vibrations in the concrete floor of a zoo in Portland, Oregon, and prevailed upon the caretakers there to let her and a couple of friends camp out there and listen. She and her colleagues were in the process of discovering that some portions of the elephants' rumbles were in frequencies too low for a person to hear. This revelation led Payne to extended field work in Kenya, Namibia, and Zimbabwe and to a fuller understanding of how the elephants' voices work for them.

The females do most of the calling, and the males do most of the listening. For purposes of contacting other elephants in their immediate vicinity, elephants use their voices in the sounds that are so familiar to us, trumpeting, bellowing, and, during what elephant biologists have labeled "mating pandemonium," the excited calls of both related and unrelated elephants when a bull has managed to mount a female. For longer distances, the elephants rely on infrasound. Low-frequency sound waves travel efficiently, both through the air and seismically, through the ground, and they do not decay as rapidly as the waves in higher frequencies. The infrasound rumbles of a matriarch can be picked up and carried through the ground throughout an area as large as 300 square kilometers, or about 116 square miles, and the elephants' exquisite sensitivity to these low frequencies, Payne proposed, was the reason that a group of elephants could suddenly and inexplicably meet up with other elephants that had been miles away.[2]

Payne's ideas were furthered by playback experiments carried out by Karen McComb and her colleagues in Kenya, who used airborne sound to test whether or not it was possible that elephants could recognize family members, bond group members, and even particular individuals by their calls and how close the animals had to be to each other for this to happen. They found that the elephants did recognize individuals as individuals, as well as family members, and in searching sonograms and examining the physiology of the elephant vocal tract for aspects of the call sounds that might serve as clues to individual identity they turned up an intriguing fact about how the elephants produced these sounds: the elephant's trunk is incorporated in its vocal tract and serves to filter its outpouring of sound.[3]

This seemed to explain a lot about calls as they are carried by air, but it left quite up in that same air questions about call sounds transmitted through the ground. Observing elephants in the Namibian desert Caitlin O'Connell-Rodwell was able to provide an explanation for the elephants' reception of and reactions to this sound. Much of their acute "hearing" takes place in their feet. The elephants' infrasound calls are transposed into Rayleigh waves, the same seismic waves generated by earthquakes, that travel very efficiently through the ground. The elephants receive these seismic waves with pads of fat behind their toes and in the structure of their heels. These pads are assisted by fat tissue in the tip of the trunk. The fat tissues operate much the same way as the fat-filled jawbones of the belugas and dolphins, by transmitting sound vibrations to and up through the elephant's skeletal system to the bones of its middle ear. What initially tipped her off to the possibility of the role of the trunk and the feet was noticing that elephants that seemed to be listening to something would lean slightly forward and seemed to test the ground with their toes and then sometimes the tips of their trunks.[4]

Although elephant researchers now knew the distances over which the elephants communicated, the biological features that made the system work, and something about the information the sounds might carry, they were still left with largely the same set of questions that whale and dolphin researchers are trying to answer: What are the elephants' calls, of all types and frequencies, for? When and how do the elephants use them, and with what expectations?

To address these issues, and especially their ramifications for conservation, Payne, who had long been associated with Cornell University, founded the Elephant Listening Project there in 1998 under the auspices of the university's Bioacoustics Research Program. At the same time she shifted her focus from the savannah elephants to the forest elephants of the Congo Basin in central Africa. In 2000 doctoral candidate Mya Thompson joined Payne's acoustic survey project to begin to classify the elephants' calls and to find out whether, like the meerkats' alarm calls, these sounds referred to things in the elephant umwelt. Thompson also wanted to determine if the structures of the rumbles fell into patterns that could serve as a census of the elephants, how many of them there were, what ages and sexes they were, and what their reproductive status was. A pretty tall order for dissertation research, but in meeting most of it, Thompson pushed the understanding of the elephants' voices ahead to a place that the whale and dolphin researchers, who have to struggle in the marine environment, would certainly envy. She found that the elephant's voice grows lower over time and also grows increasingly different from the voice of the opposite sex.[5] When I spoke with her she wondered aloud whether the inclusion of the elephant's trunk in its vocal tract, which allowed it to dampen some structural features of the calls and amplify others, could allow it "to 'intentionally' encode some kind of functional references," like those used by the meerkats, into their calls. "I'm putting quotes around *intentionally*," she advised me. She was explicit about not wanting to actually use the word *intention*, but I didn't know why until Josh clued me in later.

~ ) ~

At Zoo Atlanta Josh is trying to tease out cognitive capabilities that are the underpinnings of the elephant's abilities to perform work and to cooperate.

If it is true, as the discoverer of bat ultrasound, Donald R. Griffin, points out, that an animal's vocalizing is a window on its mind, is it possible to go in through that window and have a look around? Like the belugas and the dolphins, the eles have both a many-layered family life and a highly refined system of calls that help keep those layers tightly knit. Over the past two decades, we have learned a great deal about elephant calls and hearing. We know that their vocal range is as remarkable as the anatomical features involved in receiving their calls. We know that they use these calls for quite a number of purposes and that these calls can be categorized in a species lexicon like the one Marta Manser has constructed for the meerkats.

We have seen a number of animals for whom vocalizing acts as social glue. For a family of meerkats emitting their contact calls as they sweep slowly over the thornveldt and react to alarm calls as a unit, voice enforces cohesion throughout their dangerous lives. For a beluga mother and calf or a male dolphin traveling underwater in his pod for miles without good visual contact, the whistles of their relatives draw the families together periodically and likely help them identify which animal is calling. Likewise the elephants' daily and seasonal travels are orchestrated by calls that also help them recognize particular individual elephants.

I am behind the scenes at Zoo Atlanta because I am interested in figuring out how all this works for the individual itself. I want to see how far beyond sender-and-receiver communication science could go into matters of voice—how far mathematical models could stretch to accommodate the possibilities of intellect, of different kinds of intelligences. What Josh is able to find out about the "minds" of his elephants will probably offer some clues.

*Mind,* like *consciousness* and *language,* is one of those treacherous words that get you into trouble in science, and *theory of mind* is a real booby trap. Since Lorenz and Tinbergen struggled to create an objective way of looking at animal behavior that would separate the human umwelt from the *umwelt* of the animals they studied, their successors have maintained rigorous attempts to follow along. Sometimes they have to do a lot of dancing around to express their ideas, and sometimes they just give in and use *language, consciousness,* and *mind* with the proviso that these words will now have special meanings. Donald Griffin, who was a student at Harvard at the time when Lorenz and Tinbergen began working together, was less shackled by inhibitions about anthropomorphism. Maybe Griffin had been liberated by his youthful discovery of the previously uncharted perceptual capacities of bats, but whatever the source of his approach, he was as interested in what went on in the animal's inner experience as he was in the way it functioned in the world around it. Without ever leaving his research on the navigation of bats and birds, he began to pursue broad surveys of what was known about the behavior of all kinds of animals to glean evidence of the animal's mental experiences. Although he used the terms *mind* and *consciousness* without hesitation, he pointed out that these terms, even when used about humans, can carry you out into some deep philosophical currents, and he used the notion of *awareness* as his starting point in thinking about consciousness. Establishing even this more limited version of consciousness took considerable time and persuasive powers, and Griffin spent a good part of his career passionately explicating sharply drawn arguments about various animals and their demonstrations of awareness. Once, while he was visiting biologist friends in Africa and was touring his hosts' research area by car, his hosts drove up on five lionesses in the process of a highly choreographed hunt. Griffin is said to have jumped out of the vehicle, exclaiming, "This is it! They've got to be aware of what's going on!" His hosts commanded him sharply to get back in the car.[6]

From awareness Griffin went on to consider consciousness, or what many might consider a stripped-down version of consciousness: "An animal may be considered to experience a simple level of consciousness if it subjectively thinks about objects and events. Thinking about something in this sense means attending to the animal's internal mental images or representations of objects and events"—past, present, and future. For him, consciousness was a rudimentary mental medium through which thought could travel. It was not the self-consciousness that Josh was testing in the elephants. He did not find it necessary to include *self*-awareness or the animal's awareness of its own thinking in his definition of consciousness. "The animal did not need to be able to understand it is *I* who see that predator or smell that delicious food."[7]

Awareness of *I* is the issue that Josh is addressing with the elephants and the mirror. This juncture of thought and self-identification is where the work of cognitive psychologists like Frans de Waal takes over. In his studies of chimps and other primates, he has been focusing on the interactions that require a *me* and a *you*: consolation, reconciliation, empathy, and cooperation. Empathy, for instance, is the capacity to perceive the mental and emotional state of another being the way that being perceives it: *I* feel how *you* feel. Among our species, a sociopath is a person who may perceive the state of another person and who may, in fact, use this perception to personal advantage but who altogether lacks empathy. In order for any of these *me-you* transactions to take place between two animals, at least one of them must be able to distinguish mentally between itself and the other animal, and this requires, first of all, a sense of self. While, as Diana Reiss pointed out to me, "any animal has some sense of self—otherwise it would bump into things," the kind of self-awareness that de Waal's chimps demonstrate goes a couple of steps beyond Griffin's requirements for consciousness. Can an elephant understand that "it is *I* who sees that predator"? De Waal and his colleagues would argue that the kind of consciousness that Griffin considered beyond the essential is the kind that is important if we are to understand how vocalization mediates between the individual and the group in complex animal societies. Although there are many animals whose vocal communications do not depend on self-recognition—the túngaras, the birds that coordinate their songs—the vocalizing of the animals generally credited with more highly developed intelligence and social arrangements relies on an understanding of *self* and *others*. Of course, we human primates fall into this category.

~ ~

It is a rare animal that recognizes itself in a mirror. Self-recognition was one of the things about the orangutan brought to the London Zoological Society in 1837 that fascinated Charles Darwin. He gave Jenny the orangutan a hand mirror and reported that she was "astonished beyond measure. . . . The young Ourang in Zoolog Gardens *pouts*. Partly out of displeasure (& partly out of I not know what when it looked at the glass) when pouting protrudes its lips into point. . . ."[8] She moved her lips to play with her image in the mirror. In addition to us humans, the only animals thus far that have demonstrated self-recognition to the satisfaction of scientists are the other members of the great ape family, the gorillas, chimps, bonobos, and orangutans; the magpie; and—you probably won't be surprised to learn this—the bottlenose dolphin.

The now-classic experiment used to determine self-recognition, the mark test, was introduced in 1970 by psychologist Gordon G. Gallup Jr., who has been careful to stipulate that it is just one possible test of self-awareness. The experiment involves putting a visible mark on a part of the animal's body that it can see only in a mirror and, in a parallel location, a second mark that feels like the first but is invisible. To "pass" the test, the animal, upon meeting its reflection in the mirror, will indicate by its behavior that it is aware of the visible mark but not trouble itself about the sham mark. The chimps in Gallup's original test responded to red dye marks by attending to the mirror's image of the mark on themselves but also indicated a more general mirror self-recognition by watching themselves pick their teeth or move bits of food in and out of their mouth and by grooming themselves in parts of their body visible only by mirror.[9] The European magpies, marked on their throats with a colored sticker, ducked their heads to try to peck at the sticker or scratched at it with their claws, and dolphins swam close to the mirror, positioning themselves to repeatedly reinspect the marks on them.[10] "The animals that not only show they recognize themselves in a mirror but also pass the mark test," Josh tells me, "tend to be animals that groom themselves." They pick things off their bodies and off the bodies of an animal they consort with. "You know, like birds and primates—and, in fact, humans. We're vain animals."

Diana Reiss, the same New York Aquarium researcher who analyzed the bottlenose dolphins' whistle types and estimated their capacities for mimicry and vocal learning, was the person who put the marks on the dolphins. Now out of the watery element, Reiss is putting marks on elephants, working in parallel with Josh on his study of Zoo Atlanta's Tara and Kelly. The plan is that they will replicate the experiments with the Zoo Atlanta elephants using elephants at the National Zoo in Washington, D.C. Diana and Josh have done this work before and, with Frans de Waal, published the results in the *Proceedings of the National Academy of Sciences USA*, which posted online videos showing the experiment as it played out.

The earlier study took place in 2005-6 with three female Asian elephants in the Bronx Zoo. Watching the video, I was as intrigued with the elephants' behavior around the mirror before they were marked as with their responses to the mark. A fairly typical response to the mirror among most animals is to mistake the image for another animal of its own kind and to respond to it socially. Not so the elephants. On the first experience with the mirror, each of the three elephants immediately began checking out the mirror surface as if she suspected a trick. Apparently they perceived that the reflection in the mirror was nothing more than an image, and each of them tried to find the source of the image. They searched the mirror with their trunk, dropped to their knees, and attempted to get their trunks under the mirror. Two of them reached over the wall with their trunks to explore behind the image and then stood on their hind legs and propped themselves against the mirror to explore more of the other side of the wall. It's hard to say how they changed their interpretation of what the mirror was, but after a few days of being turned out with the mirror, they left off their detective work and began to hang out around the mirror to watch themselves eat and move. Much of this behavior—ear and mouth inspections, as well as unusual, repetitive behavior—seemed to indicate the elephants recognized the mirror images as themselves.

Then came the marks on their foreheads just over their eyes. One of the Bronx elephants, Happy, became quite obviously preoccupied with the mark Josh had painted above her right eye. She stood in front of the mirror, regularly swinging up her trunk to touch the mark above her eye and briefly explore the area. The other two Bronx elephants failed their tests by not directing their attention, their trunks, to the marks on their heads.[11] This one-third positive result left a number of their colleagues skeptical and Josh and Diana unsatisfied. They wanted more go-rounds of the test with two new groups of elephants that would create a broader group of subjects.

Right now Kelly and Tara are in the spotlight. It is only a matter of time, a couple of days maybe or even several weeks, before Josh replaces the solid rust-brown frame attached to the gate across the end of the elephants' enclosure with a "mirror," a sturdy reflective surface. When they amble into the enclosure, Kelly and Tara will see their reflections. Will they know what they are looking at? Will they know the enormous images of heads and trunks in the mirror are their own? Will each ele identify with herself? Or will she think her image is something else?

"I don't know exactly what to expect," Josh says. "I've never worked with African elephants before." The three elephants in the Bronx Zoo and the elephants that Josh worked with in Thailand were Asian elephants. The two species have superficial differences in physiology—the Africans are larger, with whopping ears and less of an arched back than the Asians—and apparently they differ in temperamental aptitude for domestication. But they share the most salient features of their family life and communications.

What if these two scored positives on the test? What would this tell Josh and Diana? What could the researchers infer from the fact that the elephants recognized their bodies as the elephant bodies in the mirror? The short answer to that question is that in order for there to be a *you* and a *me,* one has to first understand *me.* This self-recognition in turn implies its corollary: recognition of other elephants as something other than themselves. And how could self-recognition influence our understanding of their vocal communication? The short answer to this second question is that understanding one's self in contrast to others like one could imply awareness of one's own voice as opposed to the voices of others and awareness of using one's voice to reach those others. These are the short answers, and Josh makes their limitations quite apparent when he points out that "mirror use isn't really relevant in nature, you know." Well, right, it isn't often that an elephant out on the savannah comes up to a mirror and gets a chance to explore its own body.

What is important in nature is self-recognition, which incorporates the ability to separate one's self from others whom you recognize. This ability is, Josh explains, what allows an elephant seeing a family member in pain to understand that it is not the one in pain. It is the basic cognitive transaction that underlies cooperation and what Josh calls *perspective taking*. This is the capacity to understand that "what *I* see is not what *he* sees," an ability to understand the roles of other animals in its social groups and to reflect on its own role in that group. To show me an example of what elephant empathy might look and sound like, Josh showed me a scene from his work at an elephant sanctuary. "I'm not sure if the people at the Elephant Listening Project have noticed a sound like this from the African elephants, but I heard it a number of times." In the Elephant Nature Park, the herd included a blind female. She was often getting separated from her friends and confused by her surroundings. Josh filmed her as she wandered off from her group and came up against a stout post. She couldn't find her way around the post and was making what sounded like distress calls. Then, off camera, came a high elephant call that shimmered with elephantine vibrato, and another elephant's head slipped into the view.

"That's it," Josh said as the elephant in the foreground gave the call again and stood close to her blind friend. The blind elephant stopped calling and seemed to relax. "If I had to guess, I think it means something like 'Don't worry, I'm here.'"

The implications of this for vocal communication are obvious, I think. It means that the signaler can now be aware of sending its vocal message to another animal and that other animal can be aware that the sound is coming from the signaler. But how do we get from an animal that recognizes itself visually and distinguishes itself from others it sees to an animal that recognizes and distinguishes itself from others vocally?

Recently Leanne Proops at the University of Sussex, working with Karen McComb and David Reby, provided a clue about how that complicated cognitive relay might work. They devised an intriguingly simple playback study of domestic horses and the connections these animals make between visual and vocal identity. It used horses that were pastured together at a commercial stable and had formed friendship bonds. A "naïve" handler led one herd member past a pasture buddy, the subject, then led that horse around a corner and out of sight. Next the researchers played two calls for the subject horse, the call of the friend that had just passed in front of him and the call of a stranger. The responses of the horse to seeing a pasture buddy and then hearing the calls of the stranger were decidedly double takes. Its expectations had been thwarted.[12]

"So, if an elephant is shown to be able to take the perspective of another elephant," I suggest to Josh, "that means that an elephant understands there is another elephant out there who hears the way she hears and can call the way she calls." This would add an important dimension to her vocalizing, potentially something she might have in common with you and me. "Would her awareness of the capabilities of other elephants mean that she can now call intentionally to reach another elephant? Would it mean that she can create a strategy for call and response, and that the other elephant can do the same?"

"Nope." He stops me right there. "Intention is difficult to assign to animals, and there are competing schools of thoughts on whether or not nonhuman animals can act intentionally." Ah, another one of those hot-button words, *intention*. Maybe this will bring the interpretation of the elephant's vocalizing a step back closer to Dawkins's "manipulator," "mind reader," and "motivational state." An animal such as a frog, which has simple vocal communications with the simplest of social purposes and evolutionary functions, does not need to be aware of itself or to recognize itself in a mirror to communicate effectively. But animals with longer, more socially complex lives and necessarily more complex communications—animals like ourselves—need these kinds of awareness. Self-awareness and self-recognition as biology defines them are a sine qua non of the ways we humans use our voices. Speech, putting language in vocal form, requires a *me*, the signaler, the speaker, and a *you*, the receiver, the listener. Likewise, song, putting music in a vocal message, requires a *me*, the singer, and a *you*, the real or imagined audience.

Self-awareness, as Diana Reiss pointed out, is a rather fogbound concept susceptible to many interpretations, and self-recognition is a specific indicator of self-awareness that nails down this brand of consciousness. The mark test is not the single, unchallenged indicator of self-recognition. Most of the objections to its validity have to do with what the procedure actually tests and the implications of mirror recognition as evidence for other aspects of selfhood. Nevertheless, it has survived as the predominant technique for understanding sense of self in animals and, in certain cases, human infants. "The main problem I see with the test," Josh says, "is that it produces a lot of false negatives." That is, unless the animal actively uses the mirror to locate and in some way gesture to direct attention to the mark, it does not "pass." If a dolphin swims past the mirror, seems to notice the mark, but then does nothing more than hang around the mirror watching itself, the animal fails the test. If Kelly and Tara, like two of the female Asian elephants in the Bronx Zoo, see themselves in the mirror, give a long look at the place above their eye, but then do nothing more than watch themselves in the mirror as they use their trunks to stuff hay into their mouths, they likewise do not pass. In order to score for purposes of scientific reporting, the animal whose reflection appears in the mirror must, like Mike Ryan's female frogs deciding between whine-chucks, do it as the rules allow. De Waal's chimps pass the mark test in kindergarten, and the capuchin monkeys studied by one of his students go well beyond that to be able to sort with amazing speed through the images of capuchin faces and pick out the faces of family members. He supports Josh in his work with the elephants because he is interested to see if his ideas about conciliation and empathy can be extended to animals that are not so closely related to us as the great apes and other primates. Happy, the female Asian at the Bronx Zoo, passed summa cum laude. She stood squarely in front of the mirror and kept swinging her trunk up to touch the white X over her eye.

When this happened there was a great round of public applause. Josh and Reiss and de Waal now had a nonhuman, nonprimate animal that appeared to know itself when it saw itself. More than three hundred newspapers in the U.S. covered the story. People loved the plot and the ending. I suspect the person-in-a-fur-coat mentality here, but that doesn't matter. For whatever reason, Happy's understanding of herself seized the imagination of many people. There was something about Happy that they held in common with her.

"The mark test isn't the be-all and end-all," Josh responds to the concerns about this kind of experiment, "but what I find most interesting about it is the correlation between the animals that recognize themselves in a mirror and the animals we usually consider to have the most complex cognition, the ones we have identified as being capable of empathy and cooperation."

Josh had already seen many demonstrations by the elephants in Thailand of what would look like empathy to any of us. But as a scientific result, one elephant out of three passing the test was not a very satisfying result for Josh and his colleagues, so now they were back at it. Josh will run a round of mirror tests with the Atlanta eles, and later in the year Diana will run the same experiment with two Asian elephants at the National Zoo in Washington, D.C. Even as Diana and Josh persist with trials of the mark test, they are well aware that in terms of intelligence, what matters for an animal, as de Waal points out, is not how it performs in the laboratory on tasks that are designed by us humans but how it uses its cognitive capabilities to succeed in the wild.

Zoo Atlanta is hardly the wild. In fact, if you compare the big territories of the African elephant matriarchs with the enclosures at Zoo Atlanta you could become depressed for them. Even though I know intellectually that zoos serve important conservation and public education purposes and that both Kelly and Tara are rescue animals taken away from places where they were not welcome, I still experience empathetic tugs when I visit animals of any kind in zoo exhibits.

Confinement in captivity changes the behavior of animals used to more space, and they often respond to cramped quarters with repetitive stereotyped behavior. In the enclosure at Zoo Atlanta, Kelly, the ele described as a little antisocial, finishes her hay, defecates, and then picks up the manure with her trunk and sprays herself with it. Then she moves away from Tara and begins to shift her weight slowly from side to side.

"Captivity," Josh says briefly about Kelly weaving from side to side. "But"—nodding to the manure strewn about the dirt yard—"I've never seen an Asian elephant do *that*." Captivity, however, should not skew the results of the mark test because the animals are already accustomed to their confinement.

The dummy mirror is something new in their surroundings. Quite possibly it is working as planned, because Kelly and Tara seem to be ignoring it. Either they are accustomed to the rusty brown frame or they are not interested in it.

"They don't seem to be paying any attention to the dummy mirror," I say.

"They don't seem to be paying any attention to us up here on the roof, either," Josh points out, "but they know we're up here. Clearly, they know we are up here." Although I pride myself on being observant about animal behavior, their awareness of us is not at all clear to me. Evidently I'm not a good reader of elephants, so I have to trust him on this.

After a half hour or so Kelly slowly takes the few steps necessary to reach the gate. Using her trunk, she inspects the right side of the frame and its sheet metal surface. Then she reaches over the top of the gate to feel around the back of it. Next she reaches through the gap between the frame and where the gate meets the wall. Her right tusk fits in that gap, and she sets her left tusk against the rusty brown sheet metal. Then she retires to the side wall of the enclosure to inspect the top of that. Evidently this gives Tara the space she needs to investigate the frame on the gate, and she moves up to it tentatively. She inspects the sheet metal surface, top and bottom, puts her trunk under the gate and, briefly, through the gap on the gate between the frame and the wall. That is it. She too retires.

The next morning it is no warmer behind the zoo exhibits. There is no sunshine, and the wind is still with us. When the door to the elephants' indoor quarters rolls open, the scene plays out in almost the same sequence as it has the morning before—except that what was mere inspection becomes real testing. When Kelly finishes her hay and stops her slow weaving back and forth to go to the gate, she centers herself in front of it. Her trunk makes a brief foray through the gap between the frame and the wall and brushes the sheet metal top to bottom. Then she sets her tusks and puts her big, elephantine forehead against the sheet metal for a moment. She begins to push. It doesn't take much, she doesn't seem to be applying much elephant force, but the sheet metal buckles. This makes a quiet crunching sound, and in the big shallow dent left by Kelly's forehead, the crumpled sheet metal shows unpainted silver edges.

Josh doesn't stop the video camera, and he doesn't even appear to sigh. This man, who is so impatient with mindless human behavior, thoughtless moves in traffic, political shilly-shallying, and any other instance of stupidity, responds to the ruination of his experiment with remarkable calm. When we are back on the ground out of the wind, he says, "Well, it's got to be rebuilt. Something heavier, maybe mounted on the wall the way it was in the Bronx."

Josh points out that although elephants do not groom themselves or each other, they do like to manipulate objects with their trunks and tusks and heads. Maybe that was all Kelly had in mind for the dummy mirror.

In thinking about the mysterious minds of Kelly and Tara, I return to a second video of Thai elephants that Josh has shown me. He had his videocam in hand at the Elephant Nature Park when an old elephant went down on her side in a swampy place, a deadly situation for any large animal. A couple of other elephants hovered nearby, and when the mahouts tried to goad the old girl back up on her feet, one of her friends became frantic. She wanted to get to her fallen friend. The mahouts backed off a bit, and as soon as they had cleared the area, she went to align herself in line with her friend's back. She got down on her knees. She didn't use her trunk but tried to get her head under the other elephant's back, under her belly, to lift her friend's front quarters and help her stand. The video cut off while she was still working to resurrect her fallen friend, who had been doomed from the moment she buckled and went down.

Josh tells me that two adult elephants often place their bodies on either side of a calf that has become mired in its bath to lift it out of the mud, and Iain Douglas-Hamilton documented a remarkable episode in which a female elephant used her head and tusks under the dying matriarch of another family to lift the matriarch to her feet.[13] No doubt the mahouts who took Josh into their lives witnessed any number of similar events in their lives with the elephants.

⁓⁓⁓

As I leave Zoo Atlanta I think about the fact that Josh has quite a ways to go to get to elephant self-awareness, and I can see that, once he takes the research out of the confines of the zoo and into the field, the scientific path to establishing the *me-you* of empathy and cooperation is going to be a very long one. In the meantime, the Cornell researchers doing playback and call categorization press ahead with what they call a lexicon, a list of elephant calls and their functions.

After I return home I phone him to ask about the mirror test. "They are drilling the holes today," he reported.

"The holes?"

"In the wall—essentially what Kelly is doing is grabbing the mirror." The dummy mirror will be moved from the metal gate to the massive concrete wall of the elephant enclosure. Josh will need something very solid to back up that mirror.

But it turns out that heavier and stronger is not the eventual solution. The first part of the solution is to separate the two elephants, removing the more dominant Kelly, who will be tested later with a mirror just out of reach, and leaving Tara alone in the enclosure with the dummy mirror and then the actual mirror.

"The first day the mirror went in," Josh reports, "Tara acted like she was scared of it. But three days later, we started seeing some really cool self-directed behavior."

Tara stood in front of the mirror and repeatedly touched her tusk with her trunk. She raised her trunk to rest it on her forehead so that she could inspect her tongue, and she peered directly next to the mirror to get a close-up of her own eye, the one that was seeing her image. When a flag was tied to her tail, however, Tara did not respond to this "mark."

"But they're not groomers," Josh reminds me about elephants. "They don't pull things off their bodies like birds or primates—so maybe I shouldn't have expected her to pass a mark test." Perhaps Happy, the elephant at the Bronx Zoo, had been unusual in her interest in the mark on her forehead.

"What we're trying to do," he says about his work on the elephants' sense of self, "is guess what is salient to the elephant"—that is, figure out what reveals *I-the-elephant*.

# 8

# Slow Boat to China

ᴥ

*Animals have voice, so has man.... Man has expression.—animals signals.*
*(rabbit stamping ground) Man signals.—animals understand the language,*
*they know the crys of pain as well as we.... Man in his arrogance thinks*
*himself a great work. worthy the interposition of a deity, more humble &*
*I believe true to consider him created from animals.*

Speculating in his *Notebook C,* Darwin made an impressionistic proposal for an inquiry that scientists wouldn't begin to take up seriously
for more than a century. In spite of many biologists and psychologists
publishing hundreds of studies, we are still far from understanding
the links that Darwin suggests.[1] It has been a slow process, made even
slower by scientific bias, academic boundaries, and the presumption
that humans, the sole proprietors of language and music, have arrived
in this situation without antecedents. But even aside from these im-
pediments, the evolutionary distances between animals and between

animals and humans are vast, and the burdens of biological detail are immense. I get some good demonstrations of these distances and burdens as I rove about visiting research projects on animals that are as disparate as parrots and meerkats, frogs and elephants. What it takes for Josh Plotnik to understand an elephant or Mike Ryan to understand a túngara can consume the career of the individual scientist.

Happily, at the time I am traveling there is renewed consideration of the theme Darwin proposed. In the last five years, there has been a growing awareness on the parts of both scientists and humanists that the "biology" of language and music are avenues open for exploration and that these two modes of communication may share certain anatomical and cognitive characteristics. Research that crosses the divide between science and the humanities is making its entrance, and studies of vocalizing, music, speech, and language are now informed and accelerated by recent imaging technologies. Brain-imaging studies of humans suggest that music and language are not entirely separate functions, as has been assumed, and they may have a great deal to say about the animal antecedents of these functions. But images of electrical activity in the brain don't entirely eliminate the problem of subjectivity that every scientist in this book encounters on a daily basis. Subjects that have the power of speech can help. One advantage for scientists studying human vocal perception and production is that humans can talk. They are aware of their thoughts, and they can tell us about them. This is why I want to circle back to where I started, the human voice, and speculate about how research on humans might shed light on the voices of the animals I've been listening to.

Until now I have bypassed a very important order in the animal kingdom: the primates. At the outset I decided to exclude the "nonhuman" primates, the great apes and the various families of monkeys, because I thought that I couldn't do justice to the enormous amount of scientific data on these animals and I didn't want the fact that so many studies of their communications rely on human teaching of captive animals to distract from my focus on the calls and songs of animals living in the wild. But now I want to swing back to the human primates, our kind, and our vocalizing in music and speech. I'd like to hear from the voice I started out with, Sheila Jordan's voice.

Sheila knows what she's doing when she sings. She is aware of how she creates and controls her voice, and she talks about it because she teaches. If I want to find out something about Sheila and her song's amazing demonstration of voice, I can just ask her.

"I love to talk about 'Slow Boat to China,'" Sheila says. "That's Loesser. Frank Loesser, you know." There are no questions about self-recognition with Sheila Jordan. She has a very clear, unpretentious idea of herself. When I listen to animal voices, I always wonder what, exactly, is going on in their heads. Not with Sheila. She is open with an audience.

"I always liked the tune—I can't tell you the first time I recorded it—but I never did it with anything in particular in mind. I started really focusing on it when I realized I wasn't a supporter of George Bush. I'm one of those lower-middle-class musicians, and I live by my art. So I've never been a Republican supporter."

She is eighty-two and irrepressible. She keeps a back-to-back gigging and teaching schedule and an e-mail list of more than a thousand. Her numerous phones ring constantly. I am intrigued that her singing voice doesn't betray her eighty-two years, and I get to hear quite a bit of this voice because she sings her part of our conversation as often as she speaks it. She modulates from singing to speech as fluidly as some people modulate between languages.

"I didn't plan on it. It just happened. I was over in Europe—Paris—when I started doing the song that way."

Frank Loesser, whose "Slow Boat to China" was only one of his many Tin Pan Alley and Broadway musical hits, claimed that when he wrote the song in 1945 he had a loser in mind, the one sitting across the table in a poker game. According to Loesser, *slow boat to China* was a term for the guy who loses steadily and handsomely at the game, and Loesser was the one who injected romance into the idea. Sheila has laced the romance with just enough sadism to create a different kind of sucker.

"Most of the audiences over there laughed. They thought it was quite funny. So I'd started doing the song the way you heard it, and I went back to Paris the next year. One night there were two servicemen, American servicemen, in the crowd. They were really into the music, over the moon with it, and, you know, blah, blah. After I got into the second set, I sang 'Slow Boat to Paris,' and these two guys stood up and walked out. In the middle of the set! Was I sorry? Did I want to apologize? Hell no. It's a free country. You're entitled to your beliefs. We can sing what we please—my god, if I did that in some countries, they'd throw me in jail forever. So will I do it that way again? I guess not—I just don't have the same feelings about things now. I'll do it just regular. I go by my emotional feeling. That's the beauty of improvised music."

I ask her about the scatting in the song. Because it happens on the fly, improvisation might provide a good window on the mental activity that accompanies music.

"What happens is I learn the tune exactly the way it's written, and I hear the chord changes. I've got the chord changes in my head. Once I learn the melody I work out little guidelines on the changes. I know that there's this *bah-dah bah-dah*—" Her voice marches over the notes that outline the harmonic motion. "Doesn't matter which guideline. It doesn't have to be the one I just sang. It could be another one as long as it corresponds to the chords. And I just take off from that."

"Just the melody? Or do you use the melody and all the notes of all the chords?"

She says she has a mental map of all those tones. I wonder if she uses the keyboard to create the images of the chords. "Do you play piano?"

"Not well enough," she laughs. "But I *hear* very well."

Sheila Jordan is a remarkable animal. She can sing, she can carry the architecture of the song in her head, and she can talk about all this. She does some very fancy signaling.

ᙏ ᙏ ᙏ

One of the things talking has in common with music is that it is transmitted in "particles," an idea first put forth in 1836 about the structure of language by the Prussian linguist Wilhelm von Humboldt. Since then it has been much developed and extended to apply to music. Particles, the basis of syntax, come together to create the next level structure the way atoms join to create a molecule, and these structures aggregate to form a substance. Extrapolating just a bit from von Humboldt, in today's scientific terms, his particles can be seen as bits of signal, tiny packets of sound energy, and these fire the brain activity that flickers across the screen during brain imaging of a listener. These particles, called phonemes, have become a basic unit of investigation in research on speech, and a number of experts in music cognition have taken up the idea of particles and applied it to the study of musical perception. Recently Aniruddh D. Patel, a cognitive scientist who has done many perceptual studies of music, has taken up the idea of particles. A musical particle is a tone of a certain frequency and duration, and a speech particle is called a phoneme, the basic unit with which speech therapy is concerned. Patel has begun testing the cognitive processing of both.[2]

Not long ago, Skott Freedman was touring the country as a singer-songwriter. Now on the faculty in Ithaca College's well-known speech and hearing program, he spends a lot of time thinking about phonemes and word acquisition.

" 'What is a *word*?' " he repeats my question. "One fairly common definition is that a *word* is an arbitrary sound representation of something we want to refer to—for my purposes, though, it's a sequence of phonemes." Phonemes are the language equivalents of musical tones. He is particularly interested in how kids get the hang of phonemes. Children learn the sounds that make up words through a process called phonotactic probability that describes how often a sound occurs in a language. High-probability sounds come up frequently, low-probability sounds not very often. This idea about learning words is analogous to the statistical learning of tones and tonal relationships.

"Children are good pattern trackers," he says. "So it's easier for them to learn words that have high-probability sounds in them." Pattern tracking is an ability children share with birds, particularly songbirds like the song sparrow, which produces quite elaborate calls. As children listen to the streams of the speech that go on around them, they map these sounds and, as Skott says, "they make rules." These rules are like the rules we create for pitches and tonality. By nine months of age, an infant can distinguish between the sounds of his or her native language and those of a foreign language.

This is about the same age at which the child's intention to speak usually becomes obvious. " 'Comprehension precedes production,' " Skott quotes a standard speech therapy adage. What usually follows is a period of babbling like the period of trial and error that nestling birds go through to learn their parents' song and the test efforts of young meerkats learning to use appropriate alarm calls. Then, usually somewhere between eighteen and twenty-four months, the child begins to combine the words he or she has learned how to form by combining sounds. The entire process is based on mimicry of sound patterns. How accurately a child learns these patterns, Skott tells me, affects his or her ability to understand written language later on.

In his research Skott tries to identify the factors that help children learn to produce words. Like birdsong, words can exist in a crowded soundscape, say, the dawn chorus, or in an uncluttered sound environment like a bedroom, and one of the factors that affect how easily a child acquires a word is how crowded the word's phonetic neighborhood is, how many words in the language sound almost like it. *Bird* and *heard* and *word* live in a high-density neighborhood, *orange* in a low-density district. He believes that children find it easier to pick up words made up of sounds that occur less frequently, in other words, oddball signals. Just as in song learning in birds and pitch identification, word learning takes place more rapidly when the person is very young. By the time we reach adulthood and have learned how to learn words, we have about twenty thousand of them to use.

As soon as I discover that Skott has been a professional singer, I ask, "Do you think speech involves different thought patterns than singing?"

"Singing relies more on memory, and it's more based in emotion. When I sing," he points out, "I'm essentially replaying something I've already learned. Speech is formed more spontaneously. You're literally thinking out loud, and this makes it more cognitively taxing."

I ask Sheila about the difference between singing and talking, and it seems she's thinking out loud at the same time she re-creates the melody. "I can do the same thing with words," she says, launching back into "Slow Boat" again. "I'm up there singing, and I see you walk in and I go, 'Hey, Holly, how ya doin'? Hey, Holly, howww yaaa doin'?' I can improvise on the lyrics because I know the melody. I know the changes, and I hear them in my head.

"But I don't," she advises me, "have perfect pitch. Just good relative pitch."

You have so-called perfect—that is, *absolute*—pitch if after being wakened in the middle of the night and asked to sing a D-flat, you can produce exactly that tone. Pitch, the frequency of sound signals, has come up often in my excursions to see the animals because it is a crucial component of the vocal communications that support their survival. When they are in rut, the red deer try to work their larynx and the pitch of their roaring down to the lowest possible point, and the meerkats use the frequency of alarm calls to determine what kind of danger is present.

Pitch is the basis of musical structure—even in music not based on our twelve-tone scale. Like most people, Sheila processes pitch by fixing an initial tone and rapidly calculating the musical space between it and the pitch just ahead. If you are among the relatively few adults who have absolute pitch, you retain a rigid concept and expectation of a particular frequency no matter what the context, and retrieving it from your memory is a straightforward, streamlined process. One study of birds shows that they have absolute pitch in the purest sense: they cannot recognize a tone if it's an octave away from the original tone they were taught to memorize. Relative pitch is much easier to come by. Almost everyone who does not have absolute pitch has some form of relative pitch, which allows you to identify pitch in relation to other pitches. Because this kind of pitch identification involves both the pitch and the context, the cognitive processing of pitches in relation to each is more sophisticated.

"While people in the music world seem to think that absolute pitch is the gift of prodigies," Elizabeth Marvin tells me, "it's actually a more primitive form of processing." Elizabeth teaches music cognition at the Eastman School of Music, where she has done quite a bit of research on absolute pitch.

The difference in processing requirements is one reason there is no agreement on how absolute pitch comes about. In some theories, it is acquired only in early childhood, and according to others, being born into a society where the language is tonal facilitates this. Other perceptual psychologists believe that absolute pitch is innate but rare because most people lose it as they mature. This last line of argument is probably the one most closely related to animals and their uses of pitch in their strategies for survival, such as mating and social cohesion, and of course, if absolute pitch is innate, that raises the question of what causes people to retain or lose the knack.

Elizabeth tells me that for humans pitch and, more generally, tonality are all tied up with memory, context, and expectation, and I realize this is also true of each of the animals I visited. David Logue's duetting wrens, which communicate in code, have very fixed patterns of pitches and rhythms that they retain, use over and over, and other patterns they expect to hear from their mate. The dolphins undergoing Dominie Writt's "oddball" test show marked responses to sounds and sequences of sounds they don't expect to hear, something that conflicts with the sounds they hold in their memories. Even the little female túngara, who is so persnickety about chucks that end the male's call, has definite ideals against which she measures the actual calls, and when she hears one she thinks is best, she has to retain its sound and location as she swims out to the male.

"What interests me most about pitch and tonality in general is the function of memory," Elizabeth says. "How accurate is our memory for pitch?" I immediately think of Mike Ryan's memory test of the female frogs: fifteen minutes and you're out—the bar closes. "How widespread is it?" she continues. "And what factors influence this kind of recall?"

To look at these questions, she joined forces with linguist Elissa L. Newport, who has carried out studies of the way children learn language that are similar to Skott's. Newport's theory is that children learn words by exposure to sound patterns. They listen to an undifferentiated stream of speech—a stream of sound signals—and after a while they begin to pick out sounds that occur in close sequence and to retain these patterns. Elizabeth wanted to know if something similar happens with pitch. Newport has designed a successful experiment in which she creates artificial languages made of artificial words that consist of three nonsense syllables. Her child subjects listen to long passages of syllables in which the three syllables, when they occur, always occur glued together in the same order. The children begin to recognize the glued-together syllables as words.[3]

Elizabeth's experiments with musical particles work essentially the same way, but she substitutes three notes of the scale for the three syllables. Her adult subjects listen to streams of these tones—streams of sound signals at certain frequencies—and soon they begin to recognize the tones glued together as "melodies." Some people are better at picking out mini-themes than others. Those with musical training, like the group of Eastman School of Music students she tested, scored higher than people who have never had a music lesson, and obviously, her subjects who have absolute pitch had no trouble at all with the test.

But then Elizabeth raised the stakes. She transposed the stream of notes and the little tunes within them into another key and tested her listeners to find out if they could tell the difference between the transposed themes and the theme in the original key. The listeners who had absolute pitch easily detected the difference, while the people who had relative pitch tended to mix up the two because the intervals, the musical spaces between the notes in the themes, were identical. Somewhere in between the people who have either absolute pitch or relative pitch are the people Elizabeth characterizes as having "enhanced pitch memory." This, I discover, is what Sheila Jordan has and, oddly enough, what a surprising number of Elizabeth's "nonmusician" subjects had. They can make the leap from one key to the next and remember the musical distances between the tones in the melody.

Along with memory, expectation—working hand-in-hand with memory—is another force in pitch recognition. In the last few years music theorists and psychologists have begun to take the role of expectation seriously and to tease apart the cognitive and emotional details of expectation.[4] On the surface, its role in frequency recognition seems obvious. If the listener hears three notes glued together in the same intervals often enough, he or she comes to expect that what has happened—say, G following D—will happen again. Sheila Jordan has memorized the melody of "Slow Boat to China." The pitches occur one after the other and are tied together by a specific rhythm, so if she hears the melody begin in a new key, she will automatically know where to find each note of the melody. Not only that, but because she has trained herself to hear and to expect the chords the melody defines, her "guidelines"—her map of the song—will reveal not only the notes in the melody but also the other notes in each chord in the song.

To demonstrate how this works, how it sounds, Sheila begins singing the famous tune as everybody knows it, "I'd like to get you—" Then in her melody she departs just slightly from the chords that carry it, "—on a— No, that's not right. What *is* right?"

Now she sings again, "On a–," and she waits. ". . . Dig?"

And I do, even though I'm not trained to be able to name the chords of the song, because the notes fit with my memory of what those chords should sound like.

What's at work in Skott's word-learning research, Sheila's melodic detour, and Elizabeth's mini-theme recognition is something called statistical learning, probability playing with our expectations. Patel has tested for statistical learning in both music and language, and I am intrigued to note that he freely swaps terminology, referring, for instance, to the "melodic contours" of speech and the "syntax" of music. His studies of the cognitive processing of speech and music find that these functions overlap in certain areas of the brain, and his oddball tests of language and music, in this case P600 tests, show that listeners have learned to expect certain patterns in both kinds of vocalizing.[5]

To give you an example of statistical learning in music, if G always follows D, the listener is 100 percent likely to hear G after D, but if G follows D only about half the time and sometimes takes a melodic leap elsewhere, the listener of D only half-expects to hear G next. The same is probably true of the larger tonality in which a theme exists. Several recent studies have demonstrated that our expectations of a twelve-tone scale, and of the most important notes in that scale, are based on statistical learning. We've heard the *do-re-mi* progressions so that we anticipate only the pitches included stepwise in the twelve-tone scale, while people in cultures where music is based on other tonal systems can distinguish between frequencies from their own tonal system better than they can distinguish between the frequencies in our tonal system.

We expect to hear what experience has taught us is likely, and at least one current study finds that what we are most likely to hear is what we like to hear most. What we are familiar with—including the transitions or alterations in the signal patterns that initially surprised us but we learn to listen for—is what gives us pleasure. That is probably why, when I discover a piece of music or a performance that I think is wonderful, I play it over and over, until I'm a little dead to it. The little surprises lose their kick. That is also why there is something soothing about the monotonous little theme that Simon and the other meerkat researchers sing to reassure the meerkats. The fifth drops to the tonic, the pitch that defines the key, which is where we've come to expect it will resolve. Beethoven made good use of this expectation in the opening of his Fifth Symphony. He sounds the tonic three times—now he's established the key, and we expect to hear either an interval of a fifth or maybe a third next. But he frustrates this expectation by dropping down to the menacing minor third. This famous opening gambit is what the critics for years called "three knocks of the hand of fate." As I think about this, I realize that among the animals there are also surprises about expectation and sound. Why would the red deer hinds, usually drawn by the very low-pitched blast of the red deer stags, be so taken with the high, nervous little whinny of the sika stag? Clearly we don't understand what kinds of associations and expectations the hinds have of sounds like the sika's tremulous call.

Music plays with the fact of our own statistical learning. Sometimes it's thrilling, sometimes it makes us grit our teeth. But I suspect that statistical learning has quite different purposes in nature. Dominie Writt's dolphins have learned to expect certain sounds in the streams of dolphin voice, and when she thwarts their expectations with a sound that's unusual for them, their brains register this, and she gets a blip on the EEG screen. In the wild, dolphins and whales spend much of their time in the dark, and when the signal is what they expect to hear, it can draw them closer to their families. When they hear an oddball sound, their brain response can alert them to danger, send them swimming off in another direction. A wrong answer in a parrot duet could send the pair into a bout of clawing, biting, and feather ripping.

Pitch is not the only element of music we anticipate. Rhythm and tempo are the other important features for which it's easy to point out analogs in animal vocal communications. The female túngara certainly has very strong expectations about the rhythmic presentation of the male's whine-chuck, and for songbirds with large repertoires, rhythm is one of the traits that helps distinguish the songs from one another.

The part of the vertebrate brain that coordinates movement is the same one that processes temporal events like rhythm and tempos, as well as language. In music, rhythm is intimately tied with our perceptions of pitch.

"The context in which you hear a pitch makes all the difference in how you perceive it and how accurately you remember it," Elizabeth points out. "Try singing 'Yankee Doodle' in a different rhythm or sing it in the usual rhythm but with a different melody." I try but find I am hopelessly locked into the tune with its rhythm. I'm not able to substitute a new rhythm or a new melody, but that's what Sheila does when she takes off scatting. Except for the activities of just getting by in life day by day, animals apparently don't improvise. They produce only one kind of scat.

At the same time Elizabeth pursues her ideas about pitch, expectation, rhythm, and tempo, animals and their expectations and the ways they process these elements of music have been much on her mind. "Of course, it all comes down to evolution and precursors. Is enhanced pitch memory innate, like absolute pitch?"

"And if it is innate," I ask, "what would that mean?"

"It may show that pitch evolved for purposes other than music"– I am surprised to find out this hasn't already been established–"and it may show that absolute pitch is not a function of genius or artistry but a function of biology."

~ ~ ~

How did the biological bases for these two beautiful and instantaneous particulate signaling systems come about? In spite of the many tantalizing leads Darwin offered, the biological origins of music and language have endured scientific indifference until quite recently. For some reason, in spite of the facts that research on animal vocalizing has been ramping up for decades and brain-imaging technology has emerged and developed a good deal of sophistication, we have clung to the ideas that we are the only species with full capacities for music and language and that there is no need to account for the origins of these abilities. This has especially been the case with language evolution, which is quite surprising, because language has a long history of analysis and theorizing and because when we consider language, we can use language to communicate about the medium itself. I can talk to you about features of our language and what you are thinking about as we speak. Then I can consider your answer. Nevertheless, the question of how this wonderful communication medium arose in our species was met with a decided lack of curiosity. In fact, until about twenty years ago there was a rather doctrinaire conviction that language did not evolve. There were various squalls of debate over what *language* is but very little academic discussion of how it came about. Language was something that had developed only in humans. This precept was put forth and defended with a fair amount of force by Noam Chomsky, often in the same breath in which he described Universal Grammar, a uniquely human ability to formulate rules to put together sounds as words and to generate new combinations of words. As he saw it, this ability was controlled by a structure in the brain called the language module, which was present and evolved only in human brains.

Then in the early 1990s Steven Pinker and Paul Bloom, collaborating at MIT, began to rock the boat. While still in accord with Chomsky's theory that syntactic capabilities were unique to humans, they argued that language was like many other complex capabilities that resulted from evolution and that to deny that was to block opportunities for understanding the intricacies of language. This was an essentially theoretical debate, but during the same period a challenge to Chomsky was launched from the field of neurophysiology. Psychologist Philip Lieberman at Brown University had begun mapping the distribution of language functions in the brain. Concerned not so much about definitions of language or about who has language, he was interested in the neurobiology of how we carry out language. As his research began to home in on the ways in which the brain coordinates movement and speech, Lieberman found himself in head-on opposition to Chomsky and a number of Chomsky's colleagues. "Current research identifying the brain's center of . . . language," Lieberman wrote, "disregards hundreds of studies that show that most complex behaviors are regulated by neural circuits linking activities in many parts of the brain," and in a savvy comment, he pointed out that we tend to off-load our ignorance of the function of any human organ to an analogy to our latest and most complicated technological innovation, in Chomsky's case the computer and its processing modules. Lieberman concluded that "solid biologic evidence rules out any version of innate Universal Grammar." It is clear the human brain evolved, Lieberman argues, and in the process probably left tracks in the form of brain structures and functions. He had done a good deal of work with Joseph Friedman, a physician who studied the difficulties his patients suffering from Parkinson's disease had in coordinating motion, especially walking, and speech, which were accompanied by abnormalities in widely distributed activities in the brain. These abnormalities were eventually revealed through brain images and led Lieberman to pinpoint the portion of the brain called the basal ganglia as the centers for coordinating both speech and movement.[6]

While we used to have to rely on human subjects with injured brains, and before that on brain specimens, for evidence of brain structure and function, we are now virtually able to watch the brain in action. Recently developed techniques using fMRI (functional Magnetic Resonance Imaging) show us electrical activity as it takes place in the brain in real time. This can provide direct evidence in stimulus-response, signal-to-receiver experiments, and if used comparatively across species, these techniques not only could go a long way toward revealing how and where humans respond to music and speech but should help identify where the precursors to these abilities lie.

Lieberman believes that the route to tracing the evolution of language is through comparisons of neural activity in the communications of the human species with those of other species. This, he notes, was one of Darwin's favorite methods, and "Darwin was not a fool."[7]

Now, perhaps spurred on by Lieberman, some adventuresome biologists, such as W. Tecumseh Fitch and Marc D. Hauser, and authorities on music cognition and language, including Josh McDermott and, in an apparent reversal, Noam Chomsky, have begun joint explorations of how our music and language have developed biologically.[8] As yet, only a few of these efforts have ripened into publication, and these studies don't go very far in providing examples from the animals' actual lives, except for the primates, which are discussed at some length. The fact that primates roost so close to us on Darwin's tree of life, however, may draw our attention away from the earlier, more rudimentary precursors of our musical and linguistic abilities.

~ ~ ~

It has been generally accepted that music emerged before language and that the mental processing of the two occurred in different hemispheres of the brain, music being channeled in the more fluid, emotive right brain and language being controlled by the more hierarchical processes of the left brain. Pianist Garrick Ohlsson, having just played a Chopin nocturne on Chopin's own piano, remarked, "There is an uninhibited emotionality about Chopin. He evokes on the piano the feeling of human song, and I think more than song even is the idea of an emotional state of consciousness which is alive and flickering. . . ." This comment looks back to those long-established ideas about lateral brain function but also ahead to the images on an fMRI screen. The advent of noninvasive brain-imaging technology has made it clear that the division of cognitive function between music and language is not rigid and that the execution of some aspects of both music and language processing is distributed through both sides of the brain. These very recent findings do not address the question of evolutionary origin. But if I had to lay money on a reliable route to tracing these origins, I would bet on real-time imaging of how we "get"–how we perceive–language and music and on comparisons of those with images of brain functions of listening animals. This is not so far-fetched as it might seem. Dominie Writt has already begun this kind of research with her dolphins.

Darwin proposed that "music and impassioned speech become

intelligible if we may assume that musical tones and rhythm were used by our half-human ancestors, during the season of courtship. . . ." But at the same time he saw no utilitarian functions that might have allowed music to have "descended" with man: "As neither the enjoyment nor the capacity of producing musical notes are faculties of the least use to man in reference to his daily habits of life, they must be ranked amongst the most mysterious with which he is endowed."

Music's lack of an evident survival function makes its origins difficult to explain in biological terms, and another confounding factor is the pleasure music gives. Pleasure, like music itself, is a biological experience that has no obvious survival benefits. Only recently have we begun research into the biological origins and bases of music—I suspect that part of this delay is due to the fairly rigid separation of science from the humanities in our university system—and in the absence of actual data, numerous speculative theories about its origins sprang up. Many of these speculations center on the survival benefits that the social bonding and family attachments promoted by music confer. Stephen J. Mithen, an archeologist whose work along these lines is probably the best known, proposes that music arose among early hominids as a communal *Hmmmmm*. (Mithen uses Hmmmm as an acronym for *Holistic, Manipulative, Multi-Modal, Musical,* but I don't think turning this sound representation into an acronym is necessary to convey how this community vocalizing worked.) The Hmmmmm functioned like the meerkats' contact calls or the dolphins' identification whistles if they were voiced in unison. It was a coming together of signals that connected individuals. It helped them locate themselves in relation to their family members. It soothed and reassured. In this idea of the reassurance of the group giving voice together, Mithen's theory overlaps with the ideas of primatologist Robin Dunbar on the origins of language.[9] Dunbar thinks that language emerged in an early musical phase as a kind of vocal grooming when social groups became too large for manual grooming. This vocalizing stimulated group cohesion and pleasure. Neurobiologist Walter J. Freeman has suggested that this pleasure might result from the release of the chemical oxytocin—the same chemical released by the drug Ecstasy—during positive social interaction. After solitary foraging during the day, group vocalizing and the pleasant reward of the gathering helped the early hominid relocate himself or herself securely within the group. Like the parrots' raucous call matching, the hominids' calling was an aid to a fission-fusion lifestyle.[10]

Other thinkers, like Steven Pinker, lean on the notion that musical capacities, like language, arose as a happy by-product of evolutionary selection for another trait linked to music. He neatly avoids the pleasure obstacle by hypothesizing that music sets into motion a number of different cognitive functions that are in fact useful to survival, and the fact that this activation is pleasurable rewards the human listening to or making these sounds. Music, he says, is "a cocktail of recreational drugs that we ingest through the ear to stimulate a mass of pleasure circuits at once."[11]

Somewhere in the space between these theories lies the proposal of two specialists in musical cognition, S. R. Livingstone and William Forde Thompson, who argue that music emerged as just one of the evolutionary outcomes of selection for *affective engagement*. This refers again to pleasure but also to animal and human abilities to monitor and manipulate the emotions and moods of others. The anthropologist Ellen Dissanayake offers a more specialized version of the affective engagement theory. She locates the beginnings of music in the attachment of mother and child and the communications between parents and their offspring. As John Bowlby pointed out, the period of mother-child attachment is a pleasurable reassurance for many animals other than humans.[12]

Every animal I have visited uses voice to engage others of its kind, from the frogs with their cold-blooded sex-only instant social life, where the *engagement* is limited to one night's embrace, to duetting birds and their offense-defense family-making strategies, to the elephants with their passionate relationships with all the members of their extended families. Vocal sound is a force in building these relationships and in locating and drawing together families. It is an instrument of engagement.

Sheila Jordan is an expert on pleasure in social engagement and on how to manipulate this with music. When I ask her about how much attention she pays to her audience while she's singing, she instinctively conjures up Mithen's Hmmmmm. "I'm sort of like in a trance, and the audience is in a trance with me," she says. "Not everybody. But some of them are."

She locates herself in the music and with the audience. When the bass and piano drop out and she is the only source of music, she can continue the Hmmmmm, carry the music alone.

"Sheila, do you ever sing yourself into a corner, a musical place you can't get out of?"

"No, if I find myself in a corner, I just immediately listen to the melody in my head and go back to what was originally written."

"What about the musicians playing with you? They don't rehearse with you. So when you take off scatting, how do they know when to come back in?"

"They're always surprised by what I'm singing because they don't know what I might do next. But what they *do* know is that I'll never go away from the original chords." She warbles over three or four chords with increasing elaboration, taking longer with each chord. "They always know 'hey, yeah, she's doing the changes.' So they just keep playing the tune because they know that I know where I'm at. It's all about connecting in the music."

It's all about getting the signals to line up. This is something the animals know how to do. The elephants know where they're at. They know where the rest of the family is at, and they know how to connect. And—looking back to where we started—so do the dolphins and whales, the meerkats, the duetting birds, the red deer and sika, the túngaras.

Likewise, when the signals line up, so do we.

# NOTES

## Chapter 1. Sheila Jordan and the Mockingbird

1. Donald R. Griffin, *Listening in the Dark: The Acoustic Orientation of Bats and Men.* (New Haven, CT: Yale University Press, 1958), 57-81.

2. Cornell University Laboratory of Ornithology, http://macaulaylibrary.org/inside/about/history/index.do.

3. Marquette University, http://speechlab.eece.mu.edu/dolittle/.

4. Charles Darwin, *The Expression of the Emotions in Man and Animals.* Barnes and Noble ed. (1872; repr., London and New York: HarperCollins, 1998), xxv.

5. Donald H. Owings and Eugene S. Morton, *Animal Vocal Communication: A New Approach.* (Cambridge: Cambridge University Press, 1998).

## Chapter 2. Don't the Girls Get Prettier at Closing Time?

1. James W. Pennebaker et al., "Don't the Girls Get Prettier at Closing Time: A Country and Western Application to Psychology," *Personality and Social Psychology Bulletin* 5, no. 1 (January 1979), 122-25.

2. Charles Darwin, *The Descent of Man, and Selection in Relation to Sex.* Original publication 1871. Republished in *From So Simple a Beginning: The Four Great Books of Charles Darwin,* ed. Edward O. Wilson (New York: W. W. Norton, 2006), 926.

3. Clive D. L. Wynne, *Animal Cognition: The Mental Lives of Animals.* (Basingstoke, Hampshire, and New York: Palgrave, 2001), 55.

4. Richard W. Burkhardt, Jr., *Patterns of Behavior: Konrad Lorenz, Niko Tinbergen, and the Founding of Ethology.* (Chicago: University of Chicago Press, 2005), 127-325.

5. Drew Rendall, Michael J. Owren, and M. J. Ryan, "What Do Animal Signals Mean?" *Animal Behaviour* 78 (2009), 240-44.

Chapter 3. Liars, Dupes, and Honesty

1. Drew Rendall, Michael J. Owren, and M. J. Ryan, "What Do Animal Signals Mean?" *Animal Behaviour* 78 (2009), 240-44.

2. J. B. S. Haldane, *A Mathematical Theory of Natural and Artificial Selection* (Cambridge: Cambridge Philosophical Society, 1924-34); Ronald Fisher, *The Genetical Theory of Natural Selection,* rev. ed. (Oxford: Oxford University Press, 1930); W. D. Hamilton, "The Genetical Evolution of Social Behaviour, 1 and 2," *Journal of Theoretical Biology* 7 (1964), 1-52.

3. R. L. Trivers, "The Evolution of Reciprocal Altruism," *Quarterly Review of Biology* 46 (1971): 35-57, and "Parental Investment and Sexual Selection," in *Sexual Selection and the Descent of Man, 1871-1971,* ed. B. Campbell, (Chicago: Aldine, 1972), 136-79.

4. This theme resonates throughout Janet Browne, *Charles Darwin: The Power of Place.* (New York: Alfred A. Knopf, 2002).

5. R. Dawkins and J. R. Krebs, "Animal Signals: Information or Manipulation?" in *Behavioral Ecology,* ed. J. R. Krebs and N. B. Davies (Oxford: Blackwell Scientific Publishing, 1978), 282-309.

6. John Maynard Smith and D. Harper, *Animal Signals* (Oxford and New York: Oxford University Press, 2003).

7. Thomas Nagel, "What Is It Like to Be a Bat?" *The Philosophical Review* 83 (1974), 435-450.

8. Christopher S. Evans and Linda Evans, "Chicken Food Calls Are Functionally Referential," *Animal Behaviour* 58 (1999).

9. Donald H. Owings, Matthew P. Rowe, and Aaron S. Rundus, "The Rattling Sound of Rattlesnakes (*Crotalus viridis*) as a Communication Resource for Ground Squirrels (*Spermophilus Beecheyi*) and Burrowing Owls (*Athene cunicularia*)," *Journal of Comparative Psychology* 116, no. 2 (2002), 197.

10. J. R. Krebs, "The Significance of Song Repertoires: The Beau Geste Hypothesis," *Animal Behaviour* 25, part 2 (1977).

11. Amotz Zahavi and Avishag Zahavi, *The Handicap Principle: A Missing Piece of Darwin's Puzzle* (New York: Oxford University Press, 1997).

12. Benjamin D. Charlton, David Reby, and Karen McComb, "Female Red Deer Prefer the Roars of Larger Males," *Biology Letters* 3 (2007), "Female Perception of Size-related Formant Shifts in Red Deer (*Cervus Elaphus*)," *Animal Behaviour* 74 (2007), and "Effect of Combined Source (*Fo*) and Filter (Formant) Variation on Red Deer Hind Responses to Male Roars," *Journal of the Acoustical Society of America* 123 (2008).

## Chapter 4. Rules to Sing By

1. Richard Mabey, *Gilbert White: A Biography of the Author of the Natural History of Selborne,* paperback ed. (Charlottesville: University of Virginia Press, 2007), x.

2. Among the recent works of Karten and his colleagues is Anton Reiner, Kel Yamamoto, and Harvey J. Karten, "Organization and Evolution of the Avian Forebrain," *The Anatomical Record*, 278A, 1: 1080-1102.

3. N. A. Cobb, "The Sheep-Fluke," *Agricultural Gazette of New South Wales.* (1897); Michelle L. Hall, "A Review of Vocal Duetting in Birds," *Advances in the Study of Behavior* 40 (2009).

4. John Tyler Bonner, *The Evolution of Culture in Animals.* (Princeton, N.J.: Princeton University Press, 1980), *The First Signals: The Evolution of Multicellular Development* (Princeton, NJ: Princeton University Press, 2000).

5. Richard Dawkins, *The Selfish Gene,* rev. 1989 ed. (Oxford: Oxford University Press, 1976).

6. Jack W. Bradbury, "Vocal Communication in Wild Parrots," in *Animal Social Complexity: Intelligence, Culture, and Individualized Societies*, ed. Frans B. M. de Waal and Peter L. Tyack (Cambridge, MA: Harvard University Press, 2003).

## Chapter 5. A Verb, Perhaps

1. In one of his earlier works exploring the idea of generative grammar, Chomsky declared that there was "no substance" to any assertion that evolution had contributed to the mental structures through which language was carried out: Noam Chomsky, *Language and Mind* (New York: Harcourt Brace Jovanovich, 1972), 97-98.

2. Charles F. Hockett, "The Origin of Speech," *Scientific American* 203 (1960).

3. Richard Sorabji, *Animal Minds and Human Morals: The Origins of the Western Debate,* (Ithaca, NY: Cornell University Press, 1993), 2, 8-16, 80; John Cottingham, " 'A Brute to the Brutes?': Descartes' Treatment of Animals," *Philosophy* 53 (1978).

4. W. D. Hamilton, "The Genetical Evolution of Social Behaviour, 1 and 2," *Journal of Theoretical Biology* 7 (1964): 1-52.

5. For instance, P. Marler, "Vocalizations of East African Monkeys II: Black and White Colobus," *Behaviour* 42, no. 3-4 (1972).

6. David Premack, "On the Origins of Language," in *Handbook of Psychobiology,* ed. M. S. Gazzaniga and C. B. Blakemore (Burlington, MA: Academic Press, 1975).

7. R. M. Seyfarth, D. L. Cheney, and P. Marler, "Monkey Responses to Three Different Alarm Calls: Evidence of Predator Classification and Semantic Communication," *Science* 210, no. 4471 (1980).

8. Philip Lieberman, *Toward an Evolutionary Biology of Language,* (Cambridge, MA: Harvard University Press, 2006), 9.

9. Christophe A. H. Bousquet, David J. T. Sumpter, and Marta B. Manser, "Moving Calls: A Vocal Mechanism Underlying Quorum Decisions in Cohesive Groups, *Proceedings of the Royal Society B,* 278, 1711: 1482-88.

10. Robin Dunbar, *Grooming, Gossip, and the Evolution of Language.* (Cambridge, MA: Harvard University Press, 1997).

11. Helmut Prior, Ariane Schwarz, and Onur Güntürkün, "Mirror-induced Behavior in the Magpie (*Pica pica*): Evidence of Self-Recognition," *PLoS Biology* 6, no. 8 (2008).

## Chapter 6. A Phrase by Any Other Name

1. H. Slabbekoorn and M. Peet, "Ecology: Birds Sing at a Higher Pitch in Urban Noise," *Nature (London)* 424 (2003), 267.

2. A much earlier attempt to capture brain waves in dolphins had to rely on physical invasion: David L. Woods et al., "Middle- and Long-Latency Auditory Event-related Potentials in Dolphins" in Schusterman et al., *Dolphin Cognition and Behavior*, 61-77. (1986).

3. John Bowlby, *Attachment and Loss*, vol. 1, *Attachment* (New York: Basic Books, 1969).

4. E. Dissanayake, "Antecedents of the Temporal Arts in Early Mother-Infant Relations," in *The Origins of Music*, ed. Nils L. Wallin, Björn Merker, and Steven Brown (Cambridge, MA: MIT Press, 2000).

5. Brenda McCowan and Diana Reiss, "The Fallacy of 'Signature Whistles' in Bottlenose Dolphins: A Comparative Perspective of 'Signature Information' in Animal Vocalizations," *Animal Behaviour* 62 (2001).

6. Diana Reiss, Brenda McCowan, and Lori Marino, "Communicative and Other Cognitive Characteristics of Bottlenose Dolphins," *Trends in Cognitive Sciences* 1, no. 4 (1997).

## Chapter 7. The Elephant and the Mirror

1. Frans B. M. de Waal, *The Age of Empathy: Nature's Lessons for a Kinder Society* (New York: Harmony Books, 2009).

2. Katy Payne, *Silent Thunder: In the Presence of Elephants.* (New York: Simon & Schuster, 1998).

3. Karen McComb et al., "Long-Distance Communication of Acoustic Cues to Social Identity in African Elephants," *Animal Behaviour* 65 (2003).

4. Caitlin E. O'Connell-Rodwell, "Keeping an 'Ear' to the Ground: Seismic Communication in Elephants," *Physiology* 22 (2007).

5. Mya Thompson, "African Forest Elephant (*Loxodonta Africana Cyclotis*) Vocal Behavior and Its Use in Conservation" (Ithaca, NY: Cornell University, 2009).

6. Carolyn A. Ristau, "Reminiscences," in *Cognitive Ethology: The Minds of Other Animals,* ed. Carolyn A. Ristau (Hillsdale, NJ: Lawrence Erlbaum Associates, 1991).

7. Donald R. Griffin, "Progress Toward a Cognitive Ethology," in Ristau, *Cognitive Ethology,* 5.

8. Paul H. Barrett et al., eds., *Charles Darwin's Notebooks: 1836–1844.* (Ithaca, NY: Cornell University Press and British Museum, 1987), 551.

9. G. G. Gallup, Jr., "Chimpanzees: Self-Recognition," *Science* 167, no. 3914 (1970).

10. Helmut Prior, Ariane Schwarz, and Onur Güntürkün, "Mirror-induced Behavior in the Magpie (*Pica pica*): Evidence of Self-Recognition," *PloS Biology* 6, no. 8 (2008): e202.

11. Joshua M. Plotnik, Frans B. M. de Waal, and Diana Reiss, "Self-Recognition in an Asian Elephant," *PNAS* 103, no. 45 (2006).

12. Leanne Proops, Karen McComb, and David Reby, "Cross-Modal Individual Recognition in Domestic Horses (*Equus Caballus*)," *PNAS* 106, no. 3 (209).

13. Iain Douglas-Hamilton, "Behavioral Reactions of Elephants Towards a Dying and Deceased Matriarch," *Applied Animal Behaviour Science* 100 (2006).

## Chapter 8. Slow Boat to China

1. Paul H. Barrett et al., eds., *Charles Darwin's Notebooks: 1836–1844.* (Ithaca, NY: Cornell University Press and British Museum, 1987), 286.

2. Aniruddh D. Patel, *Music, Language and the Brain.* (New York: Oxford University Press, 2008).

3. See, for instance, Patricia A. Reeder, Elissa L. Newport, and Richard N. Aslin, "Novel Words in Novel Contexts: The Role of Distributional Information in Form-Class Category Learning," in *Proceedings of the 32nd Annual Meeting of the*

*Cognitive Science Society*, ed. S. Ohlsson and R. Catrambone (Austin, TX: Cognitive Science Society, 2010), 2063-68.

4. David Huron, *Sweet Anticipation: Music and the Psychology of Expectation*. (Cambridge, MA: MIT Press, 2006).

5. Patel, Aniruddh. *Music, Language and the Brain*. (NY: Oxford University Press, 2010), 271-77.

6. Christine Kenneally, *The First Word: The Search for the Origins of Languages* (New York: Viking, 2007), 75-78.

7. Philip Lieberman, *Toward an Evolutionary Biology of Language* (Cambridge, MA: Harvard University Press, 2006).

8. See, for example, W. Tecumseh Fitch, "The Biology and Evolution of Music: A Comparative Perspective," *Cognition* 100 (2006); Marc D. Hauser, Noam Chomsky, and W. Tecumseh Fitch, "The Faculty of Language: What Is It, Who Has It, and How Did It Evolve?" *Science* 298 (2002); and Marc D. Hauser and Josh McDermott, "The Evolution of the Music Faculty: A Comparative Perspective," *Nature Neuroscience* 6 (2003).

9. Steven J. Mithen, *Singing Neanderthals: The Origins of Music, Language, Mind and Body* (Cambridge, MA: Harvard University Press, 2006).

10. W. J. Freeman, "A Neurobiological Role of Music in Social Bonding," in *The Origins of Music*, ed. B. Merkur and S. P. Brown (Cambridge, MA: MIT Press, 2000).

11. Steven Pinker, *How the Mind Works* (New York: W. W. Norton, 1997), 528.

12. S. R. Livingstone and William Forde Thompson, "Multi-Modal Affective Interaction: A Comment on Musical Origins," *Music Perception* 24, no. 1 (2006); William Forde Thompson, *Music, Thought and Feeling* (New York: Oxford University Press, 2009); E. Dissanayake, "Antecedents of the Temporal Arts in Early Mother-Infant Relations," in *The Origins of Music*, ed. Nils L. Waring, Bjorn Merker, and Steven Brown (Cambridge, MA: MIT Press, 2000), 389-405.

# BIBLIOGRAPHY

Alcock, John. *Animal Behavior.* 4th ed. Sunderland, MA: Sinauer Associates, 1989.

Anderson, Stephen R. *Dr. Dolittle's Delusion.* New Haven, CT, and London: Yale University Press, 2004.

Barrett, Paul H., Peter J. Gautrey, Sandra Herbert, David Kohn, and Sydney Smith, eds. *Charles Darwin's Notebooks: 1836–1844.* Ithaca, NY: Cornell University Press and British Museum, 1987.

Bernal, Ximena, A. Stanley Rand, and Michael J. Ryan. "Sexual Differences in the Behavioral Response of Túngara Frogs, *Physalaemus Pustulosus,* to Cues Associated with Increased Predation Risk." *Ethology* 113, no. 8 (2007): 755–63.

Bonner, John Tyler. *The Evolution of Culture in Animals.* Princeton, NJ: Princeton University Press, 1980.

———. *The First Signals: The Evolution of Multicellular Development.* Princeton, NJ: Princeton University Press, 2000.

Bouley, D. M., C. N. Alarcón, T. Hildebrandt, and Caitlin E. O'Connell-Rodwell. "The Distribution, Density, and Three-Dimensional Histomorphology of Pacinian Corpuscles in the Foot of the Asian Elephant (*Elephas maximus*) and Their Potential Role in Seismic Communication." *Journal of Anatomy* 211 (2007): 428–35.

Bowlby, John. *Attachment and Loss.* Vol. 1, *Attachment.* New York: Basic Books, 1969.

Bradbury, Jack W. "Vocal Communication in Wild Parrots." In *Animal Social Complexity: Intelligence, Culture, and Individualized Societies,* edited by Frans B. M. de Waal and Peter L. Tyack. Cambridge, MA: Harvard University Press, 2003.

Browne, Janet. *Charles Darwin: The Power of Place.* New York: Alfred A. Knopf, 2002.

Burkhardt, Richard W., Jr. *Patterns of Behavior: Konrad Lorenz, Niko Tinbergen, and the Founding of Ethology.* Chicago: University of Chicago Press, 2005.

Catchpole, Clive. *Vocal Communication in Birds.* London: E. Arnold, 1979.

Catchpole, C. K., and P. J. B. Slater. *Bird Song: Biological Themes and Variations,* 1st ed. Cambridge: Cambridge University Press, 1995.

Charlton, Benjamin D., Karen McComb, and David Reby. "Free-Ranging Red Deer Hinds Show Greater Attentiveness to Roars with Formant Frequencies Typical of Young Males." *Ethology* 114 (2008): 1023-31.

Charlton, Benjamin D., David Reby, and Karen McComb. "Effect of Combined Source ($F$o) and Filter (Formant) Variation on Red Deer Hind Responses to Male Roars." *Journal of the Acoustical Society of America* 123 (2008): 2936-43.

——. "Female Perception of Size-related Formant Shifts in Red Deer (*Cervus Elaphus*)." *Animal Behaviour* 74 (2007): 707-14.

——. "Female Red Deer Prefer the Roars of Larger Males." *Biology Letters* 3 (2007): 382-85.

Cheney, D. L., and R. M. Seyfarth. *How Monkeys See the World.* Chicago: University of Chicago Press, 1990.

Chomsky, Noam. *Aspects of the Theory of Syntax.* Cambridge, MA: MIT Press, 1965.

——. *Language and Mind.* New York: Harcourt Brace Jovanovich, 1972.

——. *Syntactic Structures.* Gravenhage, the Netherlands: Mouton, 1957.

Clutton-Brock, T. H., P. N. M. Brotherton, M. J. O'Riain, A. S. Griffin, D. Gaynor, L. L. Sharpe, R. Kansky, Marta B. Manser, and G. M. McIlrath. "Individual Contributions to Babysitting in a Cooperative Mongoose, *Suricata Suricatta.*" *Proceedings of the Royal Society Biological Sciences Series B* 267 (2000): 301-5.

Clutton-Brock, T. H., P. N. M. Brotheerton, R. Smith, G. M. McIlrath, R. Kansky, D. Gaynor, M. J. O'Riain, and J. D. Skinner. "Infanticide and Expulsion of

Females in a Cooperative Mammal." *Proceedings of the Royal Society Biological Sciences Series B* 265 (1998): 2291-95.

Clutton-Brock, T. H., F. E. Guinness, and S. D. Albon. *Red Deer: Behavior and Ecology of Two Sexes.* Chicago: University of Chicago Press, 1982.

Clutton-Brock, T. H., S. J. Hodge, G. Spong, A. F. Russell, N. R. Jordan, N. C. Bennett, L. L. Sharpe, and M. B. Manser. "Intrasexual Competition and Sexual Selection in Cooperative Mammals." *Nature (London)* 444, no. 7122 (2006): 1065-68.

Clutton-Brock, T. H., and G. A. Parker. "Punishment in Animal Societies." *Nature (London)* 373 (1995): 209-15.

Cobb, N. A. "The Sheep-Fluke." *Agricultural Gazette of New South Wales* (1897).

Cottingham, John. " 'A Brute to the Brutes?': Descartes' Treatment of Animals." *Philosophy* 53 (1978): 551-59.

Darwin, Charles. "The Descent of Man, and Selection in Relation to Sex." In *From So Simple a Beginning: The Four Great Books of Charles Darwin*, edited by Edward O. Wilson. New York: W. W. Norton, 2006.

———. *The Expression of the Emotions in Man and Animals,* 1872. Reprint, Barnes and Noble ed., London and New York: HarperCollins, 1998.

Dawkins, M. S. *Through Our Eyes Only?: The Search for Animal Consciousness.* Oxford: Oxford University Press, 1998.

Dawkins, Richard. *The Selfish Gene,* rev. ed. Oxford: Oxford University Press, 1989.

Dawkins, R., and J. R. Krebs. "Animal Signals: Information or Manipulation?" In *Behavioral Ecology,* edited by J. R. Krebs and N. B. Davies, Oxford: Blackwell Scientific Publishing, 1978.

de Waal, Frans B. M. *The Age of Empathy: Nature's Lessons for a Kinder Society.* New York: Harmony Books, 2009.

———. "The Thief in the Mirror." *PLoS Biology* 6, no. 8 (2008): 1621-22.

de Waal, Frans B. M., and Peter L. Tyack, eds. *Animal Social Complexity: Intelligence, Culture, and Individualized Societies.* Cambridge, MA: Harvard University Press, 2003.

Dissayanke, E. "Antecedents of the Temporal Arts in Early Mother-Infant Relations. In *The Origins of Music,* edited by Nils Wallin, Björn Merker, and Steven Brown. Cambridge, MA: MIT Press, 2000.

Douglas-Hamilton, Iain. "Behavioral Reactions of Elephants Towards a Dying and Deceased Matriarch." *Applied Animal Behaviour Science* 100 (2006): 87-102.

Dunbar, Robin. *Grooming, Gossip, and the Evolution of Language.* Cambridge, MA: Harvard University Press, 1997.

Evans, Christopher S., and Linda Evans. "Chicken Food Calls Are Functionally Referential." *Animal Behaviour* 58 (1999): 307-19.

Evans, Christopher S., and P. Marler. "Food Calling and Audience Effects in Male Chickens, *Gallus Gallus*: Their Relationships to Food Availability, Courtship, and Social Facilitation." *Animal Behaviour* 47 (1994): 1159-70.

Fisher, Ronald. *The Genetical Theory of Natural Selection,* rev. ed. Oxford: Oxford University Press, 1930.

Fitch, W. Tecumseh. "The Biology and Evolution of Music: A Comparative Perspective." *Cognition* 100 (2006): 175-215.

Fitch, W. Tecumseh, and David Reby. "The Descended Larynx Is Not Uniquely Human." *Proceedings of the Royal Society Biological Sciences Series B* 268 (2001): 1669-75.

Fontaine, Pierre-Henry. *Whales and Seals: Biology and Ecology.* 2d ed. Translated by Gillian Sales. Atglen, PA: Schiffer Publishing, 2007.

Freeman, W. J. "A Neurobiological Role of Music in Social Bonding." In *The Origins of Music,* edited by B. Merkur and S. P. Brown, 411-24. Cambridge, MA: MIT Press, 2000.

Furrer, Roman D., and Marta B. Manser. "The Evolution of Urgency-based and Functionally Referential Alarm Calls in Ground-dwelling Species." *The American Naturalist* 173, no. 3 (2009): 400-410.

Gallup, G. G., Jr. "Chimpanzees: Self-Recognition." *Science* 167, no. 3914 (1970): 86-87.

——. "Self-Recognition in Primates: A Comparative Approach to the Bidirectional Properties of Consciousness." *American Psychology* 32 (1977): 329-38.

Gould, Stephen Jay, and Richard C. Lewontin. "The Spandrels of San Marco and the Panglossian Paradigm: A Critique of the Adaptationist Programme." *Proceedings of the Royal Society Biological Sciences Series B* 205, no. 1161 (1979): 581-98.

Graw, Beke, and Marta B. Manser. "The Function of Mobbing in Cooperative Meerkats." *Animal Behaviour* 74 (2007): 507-17.

Gridi-Papp, M., A. Stanley Rand, and Michael J. Ryan. "Complex Call Production in Túngara Frogs." *Nature (London)* 441 (2006): 38.

Griffin, Donald R. *Animal Minds.* Chicago and London: University of Chicago Press, 1992.

——. *Listening in the Dark: The Acoustic Orientation of Bats and Men.* New Haven, CT: Yale University Press, 1958.

——. *The Question of Animal Awareness.* New York: Rockefeller University Press, 1981.

Grubbins, Cara, Brenda McCowan, Spencer K. Lynn, Stacie Hooper, and Diana Reiss. "Mother-Infant Spatial Relations in Captive Bottlenose Dolphins, Tursiops Truncatus." *Marine Mammal Science* 15, no. 3 (1999): 751-65.

Haldane, J. B. S. *A Mathematical Theory of Natural and Artificial Selection.* Cambridge: Cambridge Philosophical Society, 1924-34.

Hall, Michelle L. "A Review of Vocal Duetting in Birds." *Advances in the Study of Behavior* 40 (2009): 67-121.

Hamilton, W. D. "The Genetical Evolution of Social Behaviour, 1 and 2." *Journal of Theoretical Biology* 7 (1964): 1-16, 17-52.

Hauser, Marc D. *The Evolution of Communication.* Cambridge, MA: MIT Press, 1996.

Hauser, Marc D., Noam Chomsky, and W. Tecumseh Fitch. "The Faculty of Language: What Is It, Who Has It, and How Did It Evolve?" *Science* 298 (2002): 1569-79.

Hauser, Marc D., and Josh McDermott. "The Evolution of the Music Faculty: A Comparative Perspective." *Nature Neuroscience* 6 (2003): 663-68.

Herman, L. M. *Cetacean Behavior: Mechanisms and Functions.* New York: John Wiley, 1980.

Hockett, Charles F. "The Origin of Speech." *Scientific American* 203 (1960): 89-97.

Hollén, Linda I., T. H. Clutton-Brock, and Marta B. Manser. "Ontogenetic Changes in Alarm-Call Production and Usage in Meerkats (*Suricata Suricatta*): Adaptations or Constraints?" *Behavioral Ecology and Sociobiology* 62 (2008): 821-29.

Hooper, Stacie, Diana Reiss, and Brenda McCowan. "Importance of Contextual Saliency on Vocal Imitation by Bottlenose Dolphins." *International Journal of Comparative Psychology* 19, no. 1 (2006): 116-28.

Hopp, Steven L., Michael J. Owren, and Christopher S. Evans, eds. *Animal Acoustic Communication*. Heidelberg and Berlin: Springer, 1998.

Huron, David. *Sweet Anticipation: Music and the Psychology of Expectation*. Cambridge, MA: MIT Press, 2006.

Irie-Sugimoto, Tessei Kobayashi, Takao Sato, and Toshikazu Hasegawa. "Evidence of Means-End Behavior in Asian Elephants (*Elephas Maximus*)." *Animal Cognition* 11 (2008): 359-65.

Kenneally, Christine. *The First Word: The Search for the Origins of Languages*. New York: Viking, 2007.

Krebs, J. R. "The Significance of Song Repertoires: The Beau Geste Hypothesis." *Animal Behaviour* 25, part 2 (1977): 475-78.

Kroodsma, Donald E., and Edward H. Miller, eds. *Ecology and Evolution of Acoustic Communications in Birds*. Ithaca, NY: Cornell University Press, 1996.

Lieberman, Philip. *Toward an Evolutionary Biology of Language*. Cambridge, MA: Harvard University Press, 2006.

Livingstone, S. R., and William Forde Thompson. "Multi-Modal Affective Interaction: A Comment on Musical Origins." *Music Perception* 24, no. 1 (2006): 89-94.

Loesser, Susan. *A Most Remarkable Fella*. New York: D. I. Fine, 1993.

Logue, David M. "Cooperative Defence in Duet Singing Birds." *Cognition, Brain, Behavior* 9, no. 497-510 (2005): 497-510.

——. "The Duet Code of the Female Black-Bellied Wren." *The Condor* 108 (2006): 327-36.

——. "How Do They Duet? Sexually Dimorphic Behavioural Mechanisms Structure Duet Songs in the Black-Bellied Wren." *Animal Behaviour* 73 (2007): 105-13.

Logue, David M., C. Chalmers, and A. H. D. Gowland. "The Behavioural Mechanisms Underlying Temporal Coordination in Black-Bellied Wren Duets." *Animal Behaviour* 75 (2008): 1803-8.

Logue, David M., E. Droessler, D. Roscoe, J. Vokey, D. Rendall, and R. Kunimoto. "Sexually Antithetical Song Structure in a Duet Singing Wren." *Behaviour* 144 (2007): 331-50.

Lorenz, Konrad. *The Foundations of Ethology*. New York: Springer Verlag, 1911.

Mabey, Richard. *Gilbert White: A Biography of the Author of the Natural History of Selborne*. Paperback ed. Charlottesville: University of Virginia Press, 2007.

Manser, Marta B. "The Acoustic Structure of Suricates' Alarm Call Varies with Predatory Type and the Level of Response Urgency." *Proceedings of the Royal Society Biological Sciences Series B* 268 (2001): 2315-24.

——. "Response of Foraging Group Members to Sentinel Calls in Suricates, *Suricata Suricatta*." *Proceedings of the Royal Society Biological Sciences Series B* 66 (1999): 1013-19.

Manser, Marta B., and Greg Avey. "The Effect of Pup Vocalisations on Food Allocation in a Cooperative Mammal, the Meerkat (*Suricata Suricatta*)." *Behavioral Ecology and Sociobiology* 48 (2000): 429-37.

Manser, Marta B., Matthew B. Bell, and Lindsay B. Fletcher. "The Information That Receivers Extract from Alarm Calls in Suricates." *Proceedings of the Royal Society Biological Sciences Series B* 268 (2001): 2485-91.

Manser, Marta B., Robert M. Seyfarth, and Dorothy L. Cheney. "Suricate Alarm Calls Signal Predator Class and Urgency." *Trends in Cognitive Sciences* 6, no. 2 (2002): 55-57.

Marler, P. "Vocalizations of East African Monkeys II: Black and White Colobus." *Behaviour* 42, no. 3-4 (1972): 175-97.

Marquette University. http://speechlab.eece.mu.edu/dolittle/.

Maynard Smith, John, and D. Harper. *Animal Signals*. Oxford and New York: Oxford University Press, 2003.

McComb, Karen, David Reby, Lucy Baker, Cynthia Moss, and Soila Sayialel. "Long-Distance Communication of Acoustic Cues to Social Identity in African Elephants." *Animal Behaviour* 65 (2003): 317-29.

McCowan, Brenda, and Diana Reiss. "The Fallacy of 'Signature Whistles' in Bottlenose Dolphins: A Comparative Perspective of 'Signature Information' in Animal Vocalizations." *Animal Behaviour* 62 (2001): 1151-62.

——. "Whistle Contour Development in Captive-Born Infant Bottlenose Dolphins (Tursiops Truncatus): Role of Learning." *Journal of Comparative Psychology* 109, no. 3 (1995): 242-60.

——. "Quantitative Comparison of Whistle Repertoires from Captive Adult Bottlenose Dolphins (Delphinidae, *Tursiops truncatus*): a Re-Evaluation of the Signature Whistle Hypothesis." *Ethology* 100 (1995): 194-209.

——. "Vocal Learning in Captive Bottlenose Dolphins: A Comparison with Humans and Nonhuman Animals." In *Social Influences on Vocal Learning,* edited by Charles Snowdon and Martine Hausberger. Cambridge: Cambridge University Press, 1997.

Mithen, Steven J. *Singing Neanderthals: The Origins of Music, Language, Mind and Body.* Cambridge, MA: Harvard University Press, 2006.

Nagel, Thomas. "What Is It Like to Be a Bat?" *The Philosophical Review* 83 (1974): 435-50.

O'Connell-Rodwell, Caitlin E. "Keeping an 'Ear' to the Ground: Seismic Communication in Elephants." *Physiology* 22 (2007): 287-94.

O'Connell-Rodwell, Caitlin E., Jason D. Wood, Colleen Kinzley, Timothy Rodwell, Joyce H. Poole, and Sunil Puria. "Wild African Elephants (*Loxodonta Africana*) Discriminate between Familiar and Unfamiliar Seismic Alarm Calls." *Journal of the Acoustical Society of America* 122, no. 2 (2007): 823-30.

Ornithology, Cornell University Laboratory of. http://macaulaylibrary.org/inside/about/history/index.do.

Owings, Donald H., and Eugene S. Morton. *Animal Vocal Communication: A New Approach.* Cambridge: Cambridge University Press, 1998.

Owings, Donald H., Matthew P. Rowe, and Aaron S. Rundus. "The Rattling Sound of Rattlesnakes (*Crotalus Viridis*) as a Communication Resource for Ground Squirrels (*Spermophilus Beecheyi*) and Burrowing Owls (*Athene Cunicularia*)." *Journal of Comparative Psychology* 116, no. 2 (2002): 197-205.

Patel, Aniruddh D. *Music, Language and the Brain.* New York: Oxford University Press, 2008.

Pauly, B., Ximena Bernal, A. Stanley Rand, and Michael J. Ryan. "The Vocal Sac Increases Call Rate in the Túngara Frog *Physalaemus Pustulosus*." *Physiological and Biochemical Zoology* 79, no. 4 (2006): 708-19.

Payne, Katherine B., Mya Thompson, and Laura Kramer. "Elephant Calling Patterns as Indicators of Group Size and Composition: The Basis for an Acoustic Monitoring System." *Journal of African Ecology* 41 (2003): 99-107.

Payne, Katy. *Silent Thunder: In the Presence of Elephants.* New York: Simon & Schuster, 1998.

——. "Sources of Social Complexity in Three Elephant Species." In *Animal Social Complexity: Intelligence, Culture and Individualized Societies,* edited by Frans B. M. de Waal and Peter L. Tyack. Cambridge, MA: Harvard University Press, 2003.

Pennebaker, James W., Mary Anne Dyer, R. Scott Caulkins, Debra Lynn Litowitz, Phillip L. Ackreman, Douglas B. Anderson, and Kevin M. McGraw. "Don't the Girls Get Prettier at Closing Time: A Country and Western Application to Psychology." *Personality and Social Psychology Bulletin* 5, no. 1 (January 1979): 122-25.

Pepperberg, Irene M. *The Alex Studies: Cognitive and Communicative Abilities of Gray Parrots.* Cambridge, MA: Harvard University Press, 1999.

Phelps, Steven M., A. Stanley Rand, and Michael J. Ryan. "A Cognitive Framework for Mate Choice and Species Recognition." *The American Naturalist* 167, no. 1 (2006): 28-42.

——. "The Mixed-Species Chorus as Public Information: Túngara Frogs Eavesdrop on a Heterospecific." *Behavioral Ecology* 18 (2007): 108-14.

Pinker, Steven. *How the Mind Works.* New York: W. W. Norton, 1997.

——. *The Language Instinct.* New York: William Morrow and Company, 1994.

Plotnik, Joshua M., Frans B. M. de Waal, and Diana Reiss. "Self-Recognition in an Asian Elephant." *PNAS* 103, no. 45 (2006): 17053-57.

Premack, David. "On the Origins of Language." In *Handbook of Psychobiology,* edited by M. S. Gazzaniga and C. B. Blakemore. Burlington, MA: Academic Press, 1975.

Prior, Helmut, Ariane Schwarz, and Onur Güntürkün. "Mirror-induced Behavior in the Magpie (*Pica pica*): Evidence of Self-Recognition." *PLoS Biology* 6, no. 8 (2008): 1642-50.

Proops, Leanne, Karen McComb, and David Reby. "Cross-Modal Individual Recognition in Domestic Horses (*Equus Caballus*)." *PNAS* 106, no. 3 (209): 947-51.

Reby, David, Régine André-Obrecht, Arnaud Galinier, Jerome Farinas, and Bruno Cargnelutti. "Cepstral Coefficients and Hidden Markov Models Reveal Idiosyncratic Voice Characteristics in Red Deer (*Cervus Elaphus*) Stags." *Journal of the Acoustical Society of America* 120, no. 6 (2006): 4080-89.

Reby, David, and Karen McComb. "Anatomical Constraints Generate Honesty: Acoustic Cues to Age and Weight in the Roars of Red Deer Stags." *Animal Behaviour* 65 (2003): 519-30.

Reby, David, Karen McComb, Bruno Cargnelutti, Christopher Darwin, W. Tecumseh Fitch, and T. H. Clutton-Brock. "Red Deer Stags Use Formants as Assessment Cues During Intrasexual Agonistic Interactions." *Proceedings of the Royal Society Biological Sciences Series B* 272, no. 941-947 (2005).

Reeder, Patricia A., Elissa L. Newport, and Richard N. Aslin. "Novel Words in Novel Contexts: The Role of Distributional Information in Form-Class Category Learning." In *Proceedings of the 32nd Annual Meeting of the Cognitive Science Society*, edited by S. Ohlsson and R. Catrambone. Austin, TX: Cognitive Science Society, 2010: 2063-68.

Reiner, Anton, Kel Yamamoto, and Harvey J. Karten. "Organization and Evolution of the Avian Forebrain. *The Anatomical Record*, 2784, 1: 1080-1102.

Reiss, Diana, and Lori Marino. "Mirror Self-Recognition in the Bottlenose Dolphin: A Case of Cognitive Convergence." *PNAS* 68, no. 10 (2001): 5937-42.

Reiss, Diana, Brenda McCowan, and Lori Marino. "Communicative and Other Cognitive Characteristics of Bottlenose Dolphins." *Trends in Cognitive Sciences* 1, no. 4 (1997): 140-45.

Rendall, Drew, Michael J. Owren, and M. J. Ryan. "What Do Animal Signals Mean?" *Animal Behaviour* 78 (2009): 233-40.

Ristau, Carolyn A., ed. *Cognitive Ethology: The Minds of Other Animals*. Hillsdale, NJ: Lawrence Erlbaum Associates, 1991.

Ryan, M. J., ed. *Anuran Communication*. Washington, DC: Smithsonian Institution Press, 2001.

Ryan, M. J. "Female Mate Choice in a Neotropical Frog." *Science*, no. 209 (1980): 523-25.

———. "Sexual Selection and Communication in a Neotropical Frog." *Evolution* 37, 2 (1983): 261-272.

———. *The Túngara Frog: A Study in Sexual Selection*. Chicago: University of Chicago Press, 1985.

Ryan, M. J., J. H. Fox, W. Wilczynski, and A. Stanley Rand. "Sexual Selection for Sensory Exploitation in the Frog *Physalaemus Pustulosus*." *Nature (London)* 343 (1990): 66-67.

Ryan, M. J., and A. Stanley Rand. "Mate Recognition in Túngara Frogs: A Review of Some Studies of Brain, Behavior, and Evolution." *Acta Zoologica Sinca* 49 (2003): 713-16.

——. "Sexual Selection in Female Perceptual Space: How Female Túngara Frogs Perceive and Respond to Complex Population Variation in Mating Signals." *Evolution* 57, no. 11 (2003): 2608-18.

Ryan, M. J., W. Rand, P. L. Hurd, Steven M. Phelps, and A. Stanley Rand. "Generalization in Response to Mate Recognition Signals." *The American Naturalist* 161 (2003): 380-94.

Scheifele, Peter M., Andrew S. Cooper, R. A. Cooper, M. Darre, and F. Musiek. "Indication of a Lombard Vocal Response in the St. Lawrence Beluga Using a Vocal Classification Identifier." *Journal of the Acoustical Society of America* 117, no. 3 (2005): 1486-91.

Schibler, Fabian, and Marta B. Manser. "The Irrelevance of Individual Discrimination in Meerkat Alarm Calls." *Animal Behaviour* 74 (2007): 1259-68.

Searcy, William A., and Ken Yasukawa. "Song and Female Choice." In *Ecology and Evolution of Acoustic Communication in Birds,* edited by Donald E. Kroodsma and Edward H. Miller. Ithaca, NY: Cornell University Press, 1996.

Searcy, William A., and Stephen Nowicki. *The Evolution of Animal Communication: Reliability and Deception in Signaling Systems.* Princeton, NJ, and Oxford: Princeton University Press, 2005.

Sebeok, Thomas A., ed. *How Animals Communicate.* Bloomington: Indiana University Press, 1977.

Seyfarth, R. M., D. L. Cheney, and P. Marler. "Monkey Responses to Three Different Alarm Calls: Evidence of Predator Classification and Semantic Communication." *Science,* 210, 4471 (1980): 801-03.

Shuster, Stephen M., and Michael J. Wade. *Mating Systems and Strategies.* Edited by John R. Krebs and T. H. Clutton-Brock. *Monographs in Behavior and Ecology.* Princeton, NJ: Princeton University Press, 2003.

Slabbekoorn, H., and M. Peet. "Ecology: Birds Sing at a Higher Pitch in Urban Noise." *Nature (London)* 424 (2003): 267.

Sorabji, Richard. *Animal Minds and Human Morals.* Ithaca, NY: Cornell University Press, 1993.

Suarez, S. D., and G. G. Gallup. "Self-Recognition in Chimpansees and Orang-utans But Not Gorillas." *Journal of Human Evolution* 10 (1981): 175-88.

Sukumar, R. *The Asian Elephant: Ecology and Management.* Cambridge and New York: Cambridge University Press, 1989.

Taylor, A. M., and David Reby. "The Contribution of Source-Filter Theory to Mammal Vocal Communication Research." *Journal of Zoology* 280 (2010): 221-36.

Thompson, Mya. "African Forest Elephant (*Loxodonta Africana Cyclotis*) Vocal Behavior and Its Use in Conservation." Cornell University, 2009.

Thompson, William Forde. *Music, Thought, and Feeling.* New York: Oxford University Press, 2009.

Thorpe, W. H. *Duetting and Antiphonal Song in Birds: Its Extent and Significance.* Leiden: E. J. Brill, 1972.

Tinbergen, Niko. *The Animal in Its World.* 2 vols. Cambridge, MA: Harvard University Press, 1972.

——. *The Study of Instinct.* New York: Oxford University Press, 1989.

Trivers, R. L. "The Evolution of Reciprocal Altruism." *Quarterly Review of Biology* 46 (1971): 35-57.

——. "Parental Investment and Sexual Selection." In *Sexual Selection and the Descent of Man, 1871-1971,* edited by B. Campbell. Chicago: Aldine, 1972, 136-79.

Tuttle, M. D., and M. J. Ryan. "Bat Predation and the Evolution of Frog Vocalizations in the Neotropics." *Science* 214 (1981): 677-78.

Tyack, Peter L. "Dolphins Communicate About Individual-Specific Social Relationships." In *Animal Social Complexity: Intelligence, Culture and Individualized Societies,* edited by Frans B. M. de Waal and Peter L. Tyack. Cambridge, MA: Harvard University Press, 2003.

Tyack, Peter L., and Laela S. Sayigh. "Vocal Learning in Cetaceans." In *Social Influences on Vocal Development,* edited by Charles Snowden and Martine Hausberger. Cambridge: Cambridge University Press, 1997.

Woods, David L., Sam H. Ridgway, Donald A. Carter, and Theodore H. Bullock. "Middle- and Long-Latency Auditory Event-related Potentials in Dolphins." In *Dolphin: Cognition and Behavior: A Comparative Approach,* edited by R. J. Schusterman, J. A. Thomas, and F. G. Wood. (Hillsdale, NJ: Lawrence J. Erlbauman, 1986).

Wynne, Clive D. L. *Animal Cognition: The Mental Lives of Animals.* Basingstoke, Hampshire, and New York: Palgrave, 2001.

Zahavi, Amotz, and Avishag Zahavi. *The Handicap Principle: A Missing Piece of Darwin's Puzzle.* New York: Oxford University Press, 1997.

# ACKNOWLEDGMENTS

The sound worlds of the animals in this book would have been closed to me without the generous help and advice of the scientists who led me into them. I want to offer my thanks.

For starters, there were Eugene S. Morton and David Logue, each of whom provided essential assistance as I launched the project. Later, as I began to react to some of the dominant ideas in behavioral ecology, Gene, his wife, biologist Bridget Stutchbury, and David provided important perspective on the questions with which I was struggling.

I also followed David's work to Puerto Rico where, always intellectually leapfrogging my slowly expanding understanding of birdsong, he led a merry chase up the mountain, down to the rain forest, and through the thickets of behavioral ecology.

It was my great luck that Mike Ryan made himself available and welcomed me in his labs at the University of Texas, Austin, and at the Smithsonian Tropical Research Institute. In addition to being a genial host, he introduced me to his colleagues Karin Akre, Alexander Baugh, Amanda Lea, and Ryan Taylor. Each of these researchers shared their particular projects with me in great detail.

I was equally fortunate that Marta Manser was willing for me to arrange a visit to the extraordinary Kalahari Meerkat Project in her absence and to trust me to work there with Simon Townsend and Stephan Reber and to travel the meerkat family territories with Luci Kirkpatrick. Rus en Vrede is a remarkable place, and I treasured my time there.

Before I ever contacted Peter Scheifele, I was told he was "the real thing." How true. Peter's energetic research agenda in hearing and acoustics has an octopuslike reach into a number of watery as well as terrestrial realms, and his tutoring on acoustics was enormously helpful. Dominie Writt, having studied child language comprehension and just now finishing her dissertation on dolphins' sound perception, introduced me to ideas about perception that were startlingly new to me.

My luck held. Megan Wyman, patiently reporting on the matings of red deer and sikas from two alternating hemispheres, is using her inquiries into vocalization to address more global questions of speciation. Josh Plotnik, enduring his elephants' demolition of his mirror experiment, is beginning to address some enormous questions about animal minds. One working in behavioral ecology, one in psychology, Megan and Josh have their work cut out for them and for scientists to come. Both cheerfully allowed me to witness some of their early efforts.

I come now to Sheila Jordan, who lives song, to Elizabeth Marvin, an accomplished singer and organist who studies how music churns through our brains, to Skott Freedman, a singer who is learning how we learn language. They were a little puzzled to be interviewed by someone writing about animals, but in spite of this, each gave me new insight. Their gifts were invaluable.

For help in shaping my experiences and the ideas that emerged from them into this book, I owe some pretty big debts to my agent Ethan Bassoff at Ink-Well Management and to George Witte, my editor at St. Martin's. I have come to think an agent should be compensated according to how much patience a book and its author require and an editor according to how much risk they present. But how do I measure my luck in having these two colleagues?

To all of you, so many thanks.